A Shared Morality

A Shared Morality

A Narrative Defense of Natural Law Ethics

Craig A. Boyd

Brazos Press
Grand Rapids, Michigan

Published by Brazos Press
a division of Baker Publishing Group
P.O. Box 6287, Grand Rapids, MI 49516–6287
www.brazospress.com

Printed in the United States of America

Library of Congress Cataloging-in-Publication Data
Boyd, Craig, A.
    A shared morality : a narrative defense of natural law ethics / Craig A. Boyd.
        p.   cm.
    Includes bibliographical references and index.
    ISBN 10: 1-58743-162-9 (pbk.)
    ISBN 978-1-58743-162-3 (pbk.)
    1. Ethics. 2. Natural law. I. Title.
BJ1012.B6135 2007
171'.2—dc22   2007016911

To my mother Gloria Boyd
and
the memory of my father, Harold Boyd

Contents

Acknowledgments

The idea for this book has developed from a number of disparate themes and ideas that I have been working on over the past decade. My doctoral research focused on the relationship between the divinely revealed precepts of the Decalogue and the natural law in the work of St. Thomas Aquinas. Initially, my interests focused upon natural law morality and the challenges to it made by divine command theorists. However, as I read various narrative theologians and virtue ethicists I became convinced that natural law theory could not stand alone as a complete theory of ethics.

During the summer of 1997 I participated in a seminar at Houghton College on Postmodernism and Christian ethics directed by Arthur Holmes. Holmes's balanced and thoughtful reflection on the challenges raised by postmodern thought provoked my own interest in natural law apologetics without simply rejecting the challenges as having no merit. This approach combined with the narrative approach advocated by Alasdair MacIntyre enabled me to see how one could incorporate insights of one's critics into one's own theory without either abandoning the original theory or rejecting the critics *in toto*.

Following my experience at Houghton College I participated in two summer seminars at Calvin College. During the course of these two seminars, the first directed by Jeffrey Schloss and Philip Clayton in 2001, and then again in another directed by Stephen Post in 2004, I explored how evolutionary biology provided an unexpected ally for a theory of natural law and specifically Christian theories of ethics.

Because very few natural lawyers had appealed significantly to biology as a resource for their understanding of nature since the time of Aquinas, I found that a serious consideration of evolutionary thought could contribute to a theory of nature that would not depend on a biology that had been discredited for more than 300 years.

Many people, in addition to those noted above, have contributed to my research by supporting me with financial resources, library access, and time release. My thanks to Fr. Theodore Vitali, Dr. John P. Doyle, and the Philosophy Department at St. Louis University for their gracious hospitality and support for the 2003–04 academic year I spent as a visiting scholar there working on the first draft of this book. I am also especially grateful to the John Templeton Foundation and Dr. Paul Wason for their generous financial support for this work, without which it is highly unlikely that the book would have been completed in a timely fashion.

I also wish to thank Aaron Cobb, Scott Crothers, Lisa Cagle, and especially my editors Rodney Clapp and Rebecca Cooper for their helpful comments and insights that have made this a better book than it would have been otherwise. John Hare, Stanley Hauerwas, Arthur Holmes, Dan Speak, and Stephen Pope offered insights that have improved the manuscript greatly. However, any mistakes or shortcomings in the text are ultimately my responsibility.

Finally, I wish to thank the three most important women in my life: my wife, Janine and my two beautiful daughters, Joanna and Eliza, for all their gracious forbearance during this time.

1 | Introduction

Natural law morality boasts one of the longest genealogies in the history of ethics. From the ancient Greeks down through the Middle Ages to today, professional philosophers, Christian theologians, and many lay people subscribe to some version of natural law morality which maintains that there are some basic truths about human nature which require the prohibitions of some values and the practice of others. Natural law theorists believe that they can discern in human nature—and its various inclinations and desires—a basic orientation to the goods that all people pursue. These inclinations, when rightly understood and ordered, direct us to some activities and away from others. There is, on the natural law perspective, a basic desire to seek peaceful coexistence with others since peaceful communal life is a necessary condition for pursuing other goods. Prohibitions on murder, lying, and adultery are all seen as violations of the ideal for "human nature" since they thwart the peaceful coexistence of humans in community. Moreover, natural law theorists also contend that all human societies know these precepts to be true regardless of particular cultural contexts since they all require peace as a basic good for communal life. These specific principles which ground various prescriptions and prohibitions can be discovered by all people without regard to cultural or religious diversity.

In an increasingly global society where religious and cultural differences are often accentuated and form the basis for conflict between peoples and among nations, it would seem that natural law morality, if it can be coherently defended, may provide a plausible common ground for people of diverse backgrounds. The issue of moral diversity has created problems for defenders of the natural law; if there is such diversity with regard to moral practices throughout the world, how can we say that there is some underlying notion of human nature that could serve as the basis for normative ethics?

The theory has frequently been attacked and its obituary has often been prematurely written by its critics.[1] Yet, as Yves Simon observes, "The theory of natural law, attacked and rejected many times, always comes back with fresh energy."[2] The present work is an attempt to defend natural law despite the many challenges it currently faces.

Although the arguments here appeal to the classic articulation of natural law morality formulated by St. Thomas Aquinas (1225–1274), the book is not merely an apologetic for eight centuries of Thomism. Rather, I attempt to salvage what still has value in his work while simultaneously rejecting those aspects of the theory that are hopelessly beyond rehabilitation. For example, I find his appeal to nature as a necessary condition for morality an important corrective to much of analytic philosophy's preoccupation with linguistic analysis. His emphasis on transcultural moral norms serves an important role in refuting various kinds of relativism; and his articulation of virtue as a necessary development of the precepts of natural law enables us to see the two elements in a complementary relationship.

Although these valuable insights in Aquinas's work offer the contemporary ethicist much to ponder, unfortunately there are those elements that simply need to be abandoned or stand in need of serious rehabilitation. Contemporary natural law moralists should resist the temptation to follow Aquinas down the path of Aristotelian ontology and archaic medieval patterns of human nature. A genuine theory of the natural law must move beyond the sexism of the medieval church as well as the confusion of identifying cultural norms with transcendent moral principles.

1. One well-known critic of natural law in Protestant circles is Carl F. H. Henry, who unfortunately often misrepresents the theory and sees it as inconsistent with "biblical" Christianity. "Natural Law and a Nihilistic Culture," *First Things* 49 (January 1995): 55–60.
2. Yves Simon, *The Tradition of Natural Law: A Philosopher's Reflections*, ed. Vukan Kuic (New York: Fordham University Press, 1992), 3.

A contemporary approach to natural law requires a serious consideration of human nature in light of recent developments in the sciences. Any moral theory that appeals to human nature as normative while failing to consult the important developments in psychology and biology can hardly expect to be taken seriously by an educated audience.

Even though scientific discoveries have radically altered our understanding of what it means to be human, we should do what we can to sift through the accumulated wisdom of the last twenty-five centuries. It may be possible to draw upon the rich insights of the long tradition of natural law theorists without being unnecessarily bound to the philosophical anthropology of the thirteenth century. My approach exploits the scientific tradition of sociobiology and evolutionary psychology in a similar way to how Aquinas used Aristotle. Undoubtedly Aristotle would not have welcomed Aquinas's transformation of his own views, but that does not mean the transformation did not have value in itself. Likewise, my use of research in the fields of sociobiology and evolutionary psychology may not please scientists in either discipline. But it must be pointed out that these thinkers conduct their proper research in the sciences; the role of the philosopher and the theologian is to reflect on the significance of the sciences for questions concerning human meaning and purpose. Hopefully, this book will appeal not only to professional philosophers but also to biologists, theologians, and cultural critics who see their own work as having implications for other disciplines.

In this introductory chapter, I begin with the problems of contemporary moral discourse. I then briefly trace the history of ethics in the twentieth century and then point to how one might plausibly respond to the challenges confronting a theory of natural law.[3]

1.1 The Contemporary Scene

Alasdair MacIntyre has documented the failures of the Enlightenment tradition of ethics through the end of the twentieth century. He

3. The history I offer below focuses primarily on philosophical traditions in ethics. However, I think that the contemporary scene in theological ethics is at least as, if not a good deal more, contentious than the situation in philosophy. Competing theories of theological ethics include liberation theories, feminist ethics, divine command morality, biblical ethics, narrative ethics, and neo-orthodox ethics. I consider theological issues in ethics throughout the book, especially in chapters 4 and 7.

begins his *After Virtue* with a troubling thought experiment intended to shed light on the contemporary scene in ethics. He asks his readers to

> imagine that the natural sciences were to suffer the effects of a catastrophe. A series of environmental disasters are blamed by the general public on the scientists. Widespread riots occur, laboratories are burnt down, physicists are lynched, books and instruments destroyed. Finally a Know-Nothing political movement takes power and successfully abolishes science teaching in schools and universities, imprisoning and executing the remaining scientists. Later still, there is a reaction against this destructive movement and enlightened people seek to revive science, although they have largely forgotten what it was. But all they possess are fragments: a knowledge of experiments detached from any knowledge of the theoretical context which gave them significance.[4]

This fictional world is a world in which scientific terms have been radically severed from their original context; and although they may appear to be employed in scientific fashion, there is no coherent context that is sufficient to the task. People may think that they are engaged in the practices of the sciences, but with no guidance or coherent method to form their behaviors what they are doing is more closely akin to alchemy rather than genuine science. MacIntyre concludes by noting that "in the actual world which we inhabit the language of morality is in the same state of grave disorder as the language of natural science in the imaginary world which I described."[5] The contemporary world of moral discourse is a cacophony of competing voices with no common language or contextual framework.

MacIntyre extends the critique by examining a number of arguments employed in current discussions on the ethics of war, abortion, and economic justice.[6] He demonstrates that arguments that are formally valid can generate contradictory conclusions. He observes that although each argument has its own formal validity, there must be some further problem with the current state of moral discourse. Each argument arises out of its own unique historical background and is incommensurable with the other arguments. MacIntyre contends that we must first start

4. Alasdair MacIntyre, *After Virtue* (Notre Dame, IN: University of Notre Dame Press, 1981), 3.
5. Ibid., 5.
6. Ibid., 7–10.

with an account of how we come to understand how moral language works within various communities and what practices contribute to that understanding. This approach to moral language distinguishes MacIntyre from most analytic philosophers who, following G. E. Moore, have simply ignored the context of moral language and the ways in which we find it embedded in communities of character.

Beginning with the publication of Moore's *Principia Ethica* in 1903, analytic philosophers have focused their attention on the meaning of moral terms, or on meta-ethical issues concerning the nature of moral language.[7] Moore's key question is, "How do we define 'the good?'" The answer to this question determines how we think about ethics, since "the main object of Ethics, as a systematic science, is to give correct *reasons* for thinking that this or that is good; and unless this question be answered, such reasons cannot be given."[8]

But the answer Moore gives to the question, "What is the good and how is it to be defined?" is quite surprising. He says that it cannot be defined, since it is a simple, non-natural property. If we are to argue that the good is the pleasurable, Moore says this will not work because we can always ask of *any* pleasurable activity, "Yes, but is it good?" Moreover, if we define the good with any proposed definition, we can continue to ask, "Yes, but is it good?" This procedure became known as the "open question" argument, since one could always ask of a proposed definition of the good, "Yes, but is x good?" The point of the question is to draw a conceptual distinction between any proposed definition of the good and the idea of the good. If there is a difference between the two concepts—and Moore thought that there always was—then the good cannot be defined in that particular manner.

In this way, Moore rejects any account of ethical naturalism that appears to confuse a natural property of things with a moral property. This attempt to identify the good with a natural property—such as pleasure or happiness—Moore calls the "naturalistic fallacy." He therefore concludes that terms like "the good" and "the right" are simple, non-natural properties intuited by moral agents.

Among the many difficulties for Moore is the issue of how it is possible to agree on our moral intuitions. One could easily argue that the intuitionist is having moral hallucinations, or maybe it is the

7. G. E. Moore, *Principia Ethica* (Cambridge: Cambridge University Press, 1903).
8. Ibid., 58.

case that the objector is simply morally blind? The faculty by which we intuit good and evil seems to be one that is committed to an unavoidable subjectivism. This problem, among others, has proven to be intractable for the intuitionists.

A further problem concerns the naturalistic fallacy. Many have argued that it simply isn't a fallacy at all—a point I shall argue in chapter 6. If the naturalist fallacy, which has been leveled against all kinds of ethical naturalism, fails to make good on its claims, then the intuitionist's agenda has suffered a devastating blow.

Picking up where Moore left off, the emotivists, or non-cognitivists, held that moral language was indeed unique.[9] However, moral language's uniqueness lies in its meaninglessness: moral terms do not refer to any object of empirical observation but instead merely express the emotions of the speaker. Being thoroughly imbibed with logical positivism, these thinkers believe that for a statement to have meaning it must conform to the "verificationist principle": in order to have meaning a statement must be either analytically true or empirically verifiable. Since moral judgments do not have the status of *a priori* analytically true statements such as 7+5=12, they cannot be known merely by the meaning of the terms. Yet neither can they be understood as empirically verifiable, since appeals to empirical methods fail to yield the results that science can. It is impossible, they argue, to give any empirical evidence that "Lying is wrong." Therefore, the emotivists conclude that moral language is merely the expression of approval or disapproval. "Lying is wrong" can be redescribed as "Lying, boo!" Since expressions of disapproval do not have truth value, the emotivist concludes that these expressions have no cognitive meaning.

An embarrassing weakness in the emotivist account is that the verificationist principle itself is unverifiable—it is neither analytically true nor empirically verifiable! Another significant problem is that although moral language certainly has an emotive element to it, most people understand their moral claims to be doing considerably more than simply expressing their emotions; they are appealing to some kind of moral truth beyond their own preferences.

In the wake of the failures of emotivism, a more sophisticated and substantial meta-ethical approach was developed by R. M. Hare,

9. C. L. Stevenson, *Ethics and Language* (London: Methuen, 1945); A. J. Ayer, *Language, Truth and Logic* (New York: Dover, 1954).

called "prescriptivism."[10] According to Hare, moral language has a descriptive task in explaining a particular state of affairs, but its more important task is to recommend behavior to others. "Lying is wrong" amounts to a description of a lie as "a verbal or written statement by an agent, A, to mislead or deceive agent B," combined with the further recommendation that "you ought to avoid such an activity." Thus, prescriptivism consists in a locution in the indicative mood combined with one in the imperative mood.

Hare says that his theory of moral language centers around three critical ideas, that a moral judgment is (1) prescriptive, (2) universalizable, and (3) overriding.[11] Prescriptive language is such that an act in question can be recommended to other agents in morally relevant similar situations. Hare says that something is prescriptive "if and only if, for some act A, some situation S and some person P, if P were to assent (orally) to what we say, and not in S, do A, he must logically be assenting insincerely."[12]

The criterion of universalizability echoes Kant's categorical imperative and Hare intends to salvage this remnant from the wreckage of Kant's moral theory. In order for us to be logically, and morally, consistent, Hare believes that "if we make different moral judgments about situations which we admit are identical in their universal descriptive properties, we contradict ourselves."[13]

Finally, "overridingness" is the property of moral judgments wherein we let a moral principle "override other principles when they conflict with it and, in the same way, let it override all other prescriptions, including non-universalizable ones."[14] Moral judgments override aesthetic judgments and those moral judgments that are not universalizable.

Critics have accused Hare of developing a conceptual account of rationality that fails to preclude the judgments of moral fanatics. It may be possible for a Nazi to claim that her judgments concerning

10. R. M. Hare, *The Language of Morals* (Oxford: Clarendon Press, 1952); also his *Moral Language: Its Methods, Levels and Point* (Oxford: Clarendon Press, 1981). Continuing in the analytic tradition Hare states, "My hope then is that by investigating the meanings of the moral words we shall manage to generate the logical canons which will govern our moral thinking." *Moral Language,* 20.

11. Ibid., 55.

12. Ibid., 21.

13. Ibid., 21.

14. Ibid., 56.

the extermination of the Jews are universalizable, prescriptive, and overriding. If so, then Hare's theory has little more to recommend it than Kant's earlier failed attempts at employing the "universalizability" criterion. Although Hare attempted to respond to the problem of the fanatic, a greater danger loomed for prescriptivism.

Hare's creative synthesis of Kantian and utilitarian morality relies upon rules developed by the agent that in some cases will override the aesthetic preferences of the agent. In other cases, the agent uses the rules to justify one moral preference over another. But in any case, the agent always employs the rule to justify a preference. If we ask what justifies the initial preference we simply come to the end of our justification sequence. MacIntyre points out that "each individual implicitly or explicitly has to adopt his or her own first principles on the basis of such a choice. The utterance of any universal principle is in the end an expression of the preferences of an individual will and for that will its principles have and can have only such authority as it chooses to confer upon them by adopting them. Thus emotivism has not been left very far behind."[15] What had started out as an attempt at universal justification in the end turns out to be nothing more than personal preferences dressed up as absolute moral norms.

As an alternative to the emphasis upon clarity and precision in moral language, John Rawls argues that morality is simply a private matter of individual interests and tastes.[16] However, the idea of justice—as a political concept—could be rehabilitated as the "first virtue of institutions." On Rawls' view, the analytic tradition in ethics was a failure because it focused upon the meaning of moral terms, to the exclusion of the practical problems of political life—primarily the problems of moral agreement and political fairness.

Rawls argues that we can only get moral agreement by getting members of political communities to set aside the circumstances of their particularity and adopt an objective point of view—the view of any rational agent. The means by which he attempts to generate this view is by asking his readers to imagine that they must choose moral principles from behind a "veil of ignorance," where no one knows his position or place in society. Rawls contends that this procedure guarantees what he calls "pure procedural justice" by ensuring that no one

15. MacIntyre, *After Virtue*, 20–21.
16. John Rawls, *A Theory of Justice* (Cambridge, MA: Harvard University Press, 1971).

will be able to "stack the deck" in her own favor. He says that rational agents will agree to two principles of justice. These are: "Each person is to have an equal right to the most extensive total system of equal basic liberties compatible with a similar system of liberty for all. . . . Social and economic inequalities are to be arranged so that they are both (a) to the greatest benefit of the least advantaged, consistent with the joint savings principle and (b) attached to offices and positions open to all under condition of fair equality of opportunity."[17]

Rawls's approach, like Hare's, is an attempt to combine the important insights of Kantian and utilitarian ethics. However, he expresses no concern for specifying the particular goods or duties incumbent upon individuals *qua* moral agents. On the contrary, he intends to establish the parameters of morality (in terms of political justice) and then let individuals discern for themselves what constitutes "the good."

Unfortunately, Rawls begs the question of what it means to be a rational agent. His theory of justice and the description of the rationality of its agents is plausible only when we already have a prior commitment to his characterization of reason. And once we have subscribed to his economic notion of rationality we will undoubtedly choose his principles of justice. Again Rawls, like Hare, has attempted to justify universal norms on the basis of personal preferences. But how we come to those preferences is never justified. We have an elaboration and limitation of our preferences but no coherent account of how we came to possess them in the first place. What seems to be lacking in all of these analytic theories is a sustained theory of human nature that gives rise to moral norms.

In a radical departure from the prior six decades of analytic philosophy, Elizabeth Anscombe made the startling proposal that "the concepts of obligation, and duty—*moral* obligation and *moral* duty, that is to say . . . ought to be jettisoned."[18] The justification for this claim is that the context for terms like "moral duty" and "moral obligation" is one that assumes a divine lawgiver.[19] Since there is no longer a generally held

17. Ibid., 302.

18. G. E. M. Anscombe, "Modern Moral Philosophy," *Philosophy* 33 (1958): 1.

19. Anscombe says, "To have a *law* conception of ethics is to hold that what is needed for conformity with the virtues failure in which is the mark of being bad *qua* man (and not merely, say, *qua* craftsman or logician)—that what is needed for *this*, is required by divine law." Ibid., 6.

belief in a divine legislator, these terms have ceased to function. They are an example of "the survival of a concept outside the framework of thought that made it a really intelligible one."[20] Since modern moral philosophy for over two hundred years had made no use of such a concept, the ideas of duty and obligation have no meaning. In light of these realities, Anscombe argues that what is needed is a theory of virtue.

The virtues Anscombe advocates takes us to an Aristotelian model, one that predates the Christian notion of the divine lawgiver. "Moral obligation" and "moral duty" are terms that must be replaced by terms like "human flourishing" and "excellence." But in order to develop a coherent account of the virtues we need to attend to other ideas first; namely, "action," "intention," "pleasure," "wanting."[21] These are descriptions, not of the nature of moral language, but descriptions of moral activities.

Thus, Anscombe calls for a developed moral psychology and "an account of human nature, human action, the type of characteristic a virtue is, and above all of human 'flourishing.'"[22]

Anscombe's insistence on engaging moral psychology served as the catalyst for the rediscovery of "virtue" ethics. This renewed approach to ethics that sees virtue as a central element in human flourishing provides a helpful corrective to the blind alleys of analytic ethics.

However, Anscombe's analysis falls short on at least two counts. Although she argues that one cannot have a coherent understanding of moral obligation apart from the concept of "law" and "lawgiver," it seems that she gives up too easily. She assumes that the Enlightenment project doomed all analysis of moral obligation when it departed from a theocentric understanding of morality as divinely ordained. It may be possible to reconstruct the idea of "law" in ways that Anscombe did not imagine. If nature itself provides an understanding of law (as natural law contends), then it may be possible to argue that there are demands upon us that nature prescribes.

Second, an understanding of "human flourishing" still requires a philosophical anthropology and any attempt at this without consulting the sciences is at best naïve. What Anscombe needs is an account of human nature that can account not only for what terms such as "wants" and "desires" mean, but also for what it means to be

20. Ibid., 6.
21. Ibid., 15.
22. Ibid., 18.

human. Not only do we need what is classically known as a "moral psychology"; we also need a "moral biology." In what ways can the sciences of biology and psychology illuminate what it means to be human and act in moral ways? Anscombe's work, while furthering the conversation, fails to account for these important factors.

1.2 Natural Law and Its Rivals

Twenty years after the publication of *After Virtue*, the scene may be even worse than MacIntyre's thought experiment illustrates. Although he considers the challenges to intelligible moral discourse from the perspectives of analytic and continental philosophy, these are merely two of the voices clamoring for attention. In addition to these we find scientific naturalism and divine command theories demanding their place at the table. The advocates of scientific naturalism contrast the failures of philosophical ethics with the great progress and successes of the natural sciences. They then make the further claim that ethics should be reassigned to a discipline that seems to be much more competent. The divine command theorists likewise see the poverty of philosophy and hope to rehabilitate the idea of the divine legislator as providing a coherent account of moral discourse.

My own view is one of yet another competitor; which sees human nature as a necessary condition for morality. An ethical theory, if it is not doomed from the start, *must* consider human nature as playing a significant part in a normative theory. Our analysis of competing theories starts with the scientific challenge to natural law and how sociobiology and evolutionary psychology contribute to an intelligible understanding of human nature and the ongoing narrative of the natural law. From the approach of sociobiology and evolutionary psychology, human nature is seen evolving in specific ways with the consequence that human persons *must* behave in specific ways.

1.3 The Scientific Challenge: Sociobiology

Since the time of Newton, practitioners in the natural sciences have gained academic and cultural dominance and have seen no reason to subject themselves to any authority other than the empirical method.

Although Galileo and Newton's views have been revised repeatedly, natural scientists generally see their own methods as self-correcting and making progress in the discovery of truth that is simply out of reach for scholars in the humanities. Empiricism is an approach, in Kant's language, that attempts to "save the appearances" of natural phenomena; and the consensual results of empirical data serve the purpose of falsifying theories and corroborating other theories. As a result, dominant paradigms play the role of judge and jury in what counts as genuine research.[23] This approach to research creates a chasm between how scientists conduct scholarship and how scholars in the humanities proceed.

Some, like E. O. Wilson and Richard Dawkins, believe that the humanities can ultimately be explained by our evolutionary heritage. Wilson has made the bold claim that "scientists and humanists should consider the possibility that the time has come for ethics to be removed . . . from the hands of the philosophers and biologicized."[24] That is, biology (especially sociobiology), as the newly crowned queen of the sciences, should play the role of sovereign judge in all matters academic. Dawkins has attempted to show that sociobiology provides a grand meta-narrative that can, in principle, explain—or will be able to explain—all human values and practices.[25]

The primary challenge sociobiology presents is a modified version of traditional materialist metaphysics. The sociobiologist contends that all human behavior can be explained by reference to how our genes have evolved for the purpose of adaptation. Conventional morality, therefore, can be explained entirely by evolutionary theory. On Wilson's view, "Ethics is an illusion fobbed off on us by our genes."[26] The illusion is not that we don't need ethics in order to cooperate—we do. Indeed, we have evolved principles of cooperation. However, the illusion Wilson refers to is that there is a "transcendent moral order" that exists independently of our social constructions and conventions.

Sociobiology, therefore, contends that morality is simply an evolved adaptation that needs no further explanation than natural causes.

23. Thomas Kuhn, *The Structures of Scientific Revolutions* (Chicago: University of Chicago Press, 1996).

24. E. O. Wilson, *Sociobiology: The New Synthesis* (Cambridge, MA: Harvard University Press, 1975), 262.

25. Richard Dawkins, *The Selfish Gene* (Oxford: Oxford University Press, 1989).

26. E. O. Wilson and Michael Ruse, "The Evolution of Ethics," *The New Scientist* 108, no. 1478 (1985): 50.

There is no need to invoke a creator since materialism does not, and cannot, appeal to transcendent principles. The universal nature of morality has been salvaged by these thinkers, but its transcendent source has been jettisoned.

But using human nature as somehow foundational, this raises a critical question. That question is: in what sense can human nature be normative? It is either too corrupt, too much of a myth, or philosophically too naïve to play such an important role.

1.4 The Religious Challenge: Divine Command Theory

Divine Command Theory contends that human nature, among other things, is entirely too corrupt to function in a normative role. Humans are thoroughly sinful and their attempts at constructing a moral theory based upon the quicksand of a corrupt and perverse human nature is an exercise in futility. Humans are noetically corrupted by sin and, as a result, morally incapable of *knowing* the good—to say nothing of *doing* the good. Only a divine command can play this important role; any other attempts are sheer *hubris*. Furthermore, natural law morality, by starting with human nature and its normativity, seems to be committed to a position that must preclude the importance of God in moral theory. Surely this cannot be an acceptable position for the serious Christian.

In contrast to sociobiology and evolutionary psychology, divine command theory holds that the sole source of obligation can only be found in the will of God. Janine Marie Idziak writes, "Generally speaking, a 'divine command moralist' is one who maintains that the content of morality (i.e., what is right and wrong, good and evil, just and unjust, and the like) is directly and solely dependent upon the commands and prohibitions of God."[27]

Defenders of divine command theory have a variety of reasons for preferring their own moral theory to others. These reasons invariably appeal to specific religious and theological claims.[28] William Ockham

27. Janine Marie Idziak, *Divine Command Morality: Historical and Contemporary Readings* (New York: Edwin Mellon Press, 1979), 1.

28. Idziak catalogues these nicely in the introduction to her *Divine Command Morality*, 9–10. She lists seven reasons why the religious believer would think the DCM is plausible: "Divine Command Morality is a correlate of the Divine Omnipotence . . . Divine Command Ethics is Involved in the Divine Liberty . . . Divine Command Ethics

argued for one version of divine command theory on the basis of divine freedom. If God was bound by some principle other than God's own being, then omnipotence was threatened.[29]

Others have maintained that it is hubris for the human mind to determine what God can and cannot command; while still others maintain that if we agree to any other theory (theological in tone or not), it represents a kind of sinful departure from our supreme loyalty to, and love for, God our Creator. Here human nature, especially human biology, is simply irrelevant to morality. Since morality is based upon the commands of God, nothing else has any relevance.

Idziak has recently attacked natural law morality as suspect for two reasons. First, it asks the believer to adopt "methodological atheism," wherein God apparently becomes irrelevant to the tasks of ethics. That is, one can do ethics without ever appealing to God as creator and supreme object of our loyalties.

Her second criticism is one that appeals to a post-Darwinian construal of human nature that natural law simply cannot defend itself against. She asks,

> Is it really so clear what constitutes "human nature" on which moral precepts are based? The post-Darwinian view of human beings is not the same as the traditional Judeo-Christian view. . . . The plausibility of a natural law approach to ethics can be challenged from a scientific point of view. Human beings no longer appear to be directly designed by God. . . . Since this is so, the question is seriously raised: "Why should 'human nature' be taken as morally normative?"[30]

Recognizes the Importance of the Divine Will . . . Divine Command Morality Must be Espoused in the Realm of Ethics Because There Cannot be Anything Independent of God . . . Divine Command Ethics is Related to Man's Dependency on God as Creator . . . Divine Command Ethics Satisfies the Religious Requirement that God be the Supreme Focus of One's Loyalties . . . Divine Command Ethics is Grounded in God's Graciousness to Man in Jesus Christ."

29. In Ockham's view, God was in no way morally bound by the natures God Himself had created. In contrast to all the moral thinkers before him who claimed that God, as the supreme object of love, had to command creatures to love Him, Ockham goes so far as to say that God could even command humans to hate God. William Ockham *Opera Philosophica et Theologica: in. IV sent.*, q.16 (Editionis Instituti Franciscani Universita S. Bonaventurae, 1963–90).

30. Idziak, "Response to Boyd and van Arragon," *Contemporary Debates in Philosophy of Religion*, ed. Michael L. Peterson and Raymond J. van Arragon (Malden, MA: Blackwell Publishers, 2004), 312.

The approach of natural law, she contends, is impossible to maintain in an evolutionary world. I will argue that this is not so.

Divine command theorists rightly point out that there is a problem with human nature serving as a normative basis for ethics. Indeed, any theory of ethics that didn't see a problem here would certainly not have much value. However, this objection is hardly insurmountable since natural law morality recognizes that there is more than one sense in which we can understand the term "nature." Divine command theorists also rightly insist that God must play an important role in any moral theory that aspires to being called "Christian," as many natural law theories do. Once again, natural law theory not only accommodates God, but sees God as critical to the development of the theory.

1.5 The Cultural Challenge: Postmodern Relativism

In radical contrast to the advocates of divine command theory, postmodernists most emphatically reject any meta-narrative that appeals to the divine. Oddly enough, defenders of postmodernism and divine command theorists agree that human nature simply cannot function as a normative basis for ethics. The postmodern approach is to reject any and all meta-narratives including the so-called myths of human nature and of God as simply masks for power—leftovers from a bygone era of human civilization.

Postmodernists contend that any attempt to provide a meta-narrative for morality is an exercise in self-deception. Religious and Enlightenment versions of ethics are both simply an attempt to project onto the world what is really only a cultural, or linguistic, model. If models can be constructed, they can certainly be deconstructed.

The postmodern ethos began with Friedrich Nietzsche and his *Genealogy of Morals*.[31] On this view, moral language initially developed as a self-descriptive exercise: groups of individuals describe themselves as good and those who depart from those self-descriptions are evil. If this is the case, then the foundations for moral principles can be dismantled and we can see the raw desire for control over others as the root of moral systems. Genealogy is the primary weapon in the deconstruction of Western moral theory.

31. Friedrich Nietzsche, *Genealogy of Morals* (New York: Vintage Books, 1967).

Closely tied to the linguistic deconstruction of moral language is postmodernism's attack on essentialism. The idea that there are transcendent essences that comprise the world is merely a fiction we have developed because of our misuse of language. There are no essences because we can never know whether our language truly corresponds to some extra-mental reality. The reason for this is that we are never capable of getting beyond our own language games. Richard Rorty argues that "there is no way to step outside the various vocabularies we have employed and find a meta-vocabulary which somehow takes account of all possible vocabularies."[32] If this is so, then any talk of essences is literal "non-sense."

The rejection of essences entails a rejection of meta-narratives; but according to the postmodernists, a meta-narrative is a grand scheme or explanatory archetype that attempts to give coherence and continuity to our lives and values. A meta-narrative of any kind is an illusory ideal created by Western philosophy. Morality, essences, God, the soul, human nature, and the progress of knowledge all represent failed meta-narratives in the West. Instead, what is called for is the rejection of the meta-narrative *in toto*.

Postmodernists insist that these "myths" have been harmful and have served as exploitive ideologies to subjugate entire classes of people (e.g., women, minorities, and citizens of developing nations). Yet it does not follow that simply because a theory has been misused the theory itself is at fault. It may be that, as in the case of the natural sciences, a theory must be altered, refined, and recontextualized.

1.6 The Philosophical Challenge: Analytic Ethics

Analytic philosophers, as we have seen, contend that one cannot move from the descriptive to the prescriptive.[33] That is, statements about facts can never result in moral imperatives. Since natural law morality makes the claim that human nature is somehow the starting point for ethical reflection, it would seem *prima facie* that it is

32. Richard Rorty, *Contingency, Irony, and Solidarity* (New York: Cambridge University Press, 1989), xvi.
33. It is clear that not all in the analytic tradition accept the idea that it is impossible to move from the descriptive to the normative. However, in the interests of simplicity I call this the "challenge from analytic philosophy," since the objection arose historically from within this tradition.

subject to the "Is-Ought" objection. The concern here, as in the case of divine command theory, is that one could easily take the case of some human aberration and use it for a normative ethic. One could imagine a sociopath or pedophile making the claim that I have reflected on my nature as a human being and found a particular desire. This desire needs to be satisfied. Therefore, I am justified in acting on my desires.

Rejecting any kind of ethical "definism," many analytical philosophers launched a two-pronged attack on all kinds of ethical naturalism: the "is-ought" problem and the "naturalistic fallacy." Following David Hume, they believed that one cannot make a logical move from an understanding of what human nature *is* to how humans *ought* to behave. Premises containing descriptions can't result in conclusions containing prescriptions. Hume's argument was taken as analytic orthodoxy and what follows is the "sacred text":

> In every system of morality, which I have hitherto met with, I have always remark'd that the author proceeds for some time in the ordinary way of reasoning, and establishing the being of a God, or makes observations concerning human affairs; when of a sudden I am surpriz'd to find, that instead of the usual copulations, *is, is not*, I meet with no proposition that is not connected with an *ought*, or *ought not*. This change is imperceptible; but it is, however, of the last consequence. For as this *ought*, or *ought not*, expresses some new relation or affirmation, 'tis necessary that it should be observ'd and explain'd; and at the same time that a reason should be given, for what seems altogether inconceivable, how this new relation can be a deduction from others, which are entirely different from it.[34]

This argument has been dubbed "Hume's Guillotine," since it apparently cuts off any attempt at ethical naturalism. The other attack, launched by Moore against the ethical naturalists of the late 19th century (viz., the utilitarians), further stipulates that any identification with natural goodness is to be avoided.

As we have seen, Moore employed the naturalistic fallacy against a wide variety of ethical naturalisms, but a noteworthy example of this was early versions of so-called "evolutionary ethics." The idea here was that since evolution seemed to point in a particular direction, it

34. David Hume, *A Treatise of Human Nature*, ed. L. A. Selby-Bigge (Oxford: Clarendon Press, 1888), 468.

seemed to follow that we must follow the direction of evolution in our moral thinking. As Mary Midgley points out, Moore was right to criticize this naïve form of ethical naturalism:

> The trouble with these theories is not so much that (as Moore said) they are using natural facts as a guide to values. It is that they have picked out quite unsuitable natural facts. Not only do they confine themselves to facts about evolution, but among the vast range of evolutionary facts they select a single strand, arbitrarily, in response to standards they have already accepted for other reasons and do not criticize.[35]

The reluctance to use evolution, or any other natural facts about human nature, turned philosophers away from biology and human nature for decades. However, our study may prove that not all versions of ethical naturalism are susceptible to Moore's critique. The perspective of the analytic tradition is helpful in refuting this kind of argument, but it does not follow, I argue, that all instances of moving from descriptive judgments to prescriptive ones are always fallacious.

1.7. The Ethics of Virtue

Different versions of narrative or virtue ethics contend that attempts to start with universally applicable rules for human morality are subject to the postmodernist critique of Enlightenment ethics. However, unlike postmodernism one can provide an epistemological basis for morality through the development of the virtues. According to Stanley Hauerwas, the Enlightenment version of natural law morality is guilty of a number of transgressions. "It confuses the claim that Christian ethics is an ethic that we should and can commend to anyone with the claim that we can know the content of that ethic by looking at the human. . . . (and) It fails to appreciate that there is no actual universal morality."[36] Hauerwas seems to object to the idea that natural law morality can provide a universal ethic; or rather he seems to think that since it is a product of the Enlightenment it is doomed to postmodernism's deconstruction of it.

35. Mary Midgley, *Beast and Man: The Roots of Human Nature* (New York: Routledge, 1998), 156.
36. Stanley Hauerwas, *The Peaceable Kingdom: A Primer in Christian Ethics* (Notre Dame, IN: University of Notre Dame Press, 1983), 63.

Instead of focusing on either the nature of moral language—as the analytic philosophers did in the 20th century—or considering the nature of the moral act itself—as Kant and the utilitarians did—virtue theorists have concentrated their efforts on specific character traits. Moral language is merely the reflection of morally mature persons, and moral acts originate from persons with relatively enduring character. Thus, the question of moral psychology and character formation lie at the heart of virtue ethics. And yet it may be the case that morally mature persons must be guided by the consideration that specific kinds of acts will never lead to the kind of happiness that all people desire. This is precisely the point that defenders of natural law morality make; it is not in competition with virtue ethics but rather provides a necessary basis for human character.

I intend to examine the traditions of analytic ethics, postmodernist relativism, scientific naturalism, and divine command theories from the perspective of a natural law morality that is compatible with the virtue ethics of Anscombe and MacIntyre. On my view, natural law morality meets Anscombe's demand for an account of human nature while simultaneously providing the basis for an ethic of virtue. I develop my arguments for natural law morality against the backdrop of its competitors by considering the relative merits and weaknesses of each approach to morality and contrasting them with my own version of natural law. Further, I attempt to incorporate the criticisms of each competitor into my own theory, thereby making my account of natural law stronger than it would otherwise be.

1.8 Natural Law Morality: A Provisional Definition

As an alternative to these competing theories of human nature and morality, I conclude this chapter with a preliminary account of natural law that will be fleshed out throughout the remainder of the book. That theory will include the following elements: (1) all human beings have a specific nature in common, (2) moral precepts are grounded in that human nature, (3) the basic moral precepts cannot change unless human nature changes, (4) these precepts are teleological in character—they direct human beings to their end, but this end also requires a theory of the virtues, and (5) all properly functioning human beings know what the basic moral precepts are.

What do we mean by saying that humans share a "nature in common"? Initially, at least, it means that there is an identifiable essence or species—biologically speaking—that each member shares with every other member of that species. Furthermore, the human species has evolved in such a way that there are clearly activities that promote survival and propagation (e.g., cooperation in groups). It also means that this nature in common is transcultural. Regardless of the culture or geographic location, certain kinds of activities will always necessarily be required for human cooperation. Although the manifestations of these principles may vary from culture to culture, the principle remains the same. Finally, a common human nature applies to both members of the sexes equally. Even though men and women differ in important ways regarding their biological nature, they are both equally human and whatever moral obligations are owed to, and expected from, them apply with equanimity. This nature also serves as the basis for our moral obligations.

The second element concerns what we might call philosophical anthropology. It serves as a necessary condition for ethics because in order to know the human good one must first know *what* a human is. In this respect, biology is a necessary but insufficient condition for ethics. Rational evaluation and discernment among our various impulses are required. Moreover, it may be the case that reason provides goods of its own that transcend the merely biological.

Our third element of natural law is that moral precepts don't change unless human nature changes. Certainly, if human nature does change—and this is an issue we must allow for if we admit that evolutionary theory is true—then there is the possibility that, in some respect, the most basic precepts of natural law morality may change as well. However, it seems that it would always be the case that we are required to "practice justice" and "seek truth," since these principles would act as necessary formal constraints on human behaviors given our social nature. Yet the idea that the precepts of natural law morality may be open to change seems to confer an advantage on the theory, because its perceived rigidity has been a constant source of criticism throughout the ages. In any case, the precepts are always directed toward the human good.

Our fourth element of natural law morality concerns its teleological dimension. Since the Enlightenment, and even more so since Darwin, teleology has come into disrepute. When we say that moral precepts are teleological we need to ask what kind of statement we are making. It may be that biological organisms are not teleologically oriented toward pre-ordained goals, or ends; however, that does not mean that human activity is not teleological.[37] I believe that the teleological orientation of the natural law is fulfilled by an account of the virtues.

The natural law does not delineate every detail of the moral life; rather, it lays down those commonly understood truths that provide the bare minimum for human coexistence. Traditionally understood, this means that natural law morality is not a complete moral system but requires the development and practice of the virtues as perfecting the agent. Thomas Aquinas, the "father of natural law morality," says, "All the acts of the virtues are prescribed by natural law, since each person's reason naturally dictates that he is to act according to virtue."[38] The key point here is that all the acts of the virtues fall under the sphere of the natural law since they are prescribed by reason. [39] However, the natural law does not dictate precisely how one is to act according to reason. For Aquinas, the natural law simply indicates what specific kinds of actions are *per se* good, and those that are evil. But he does not specify in his theory of the natural law just how one goes about determining what kind of behavior is required. Natural law morality does not simply provide *prima facie* obligations; it also requires the development of virtue, which enables a person to act consistently for the right reasons and in the right circumstances.

My fifth and final point, concerning the nature of natural law, is that its basic precepts are available to all humans whose reason is functioning in a normal fashion. Although this claim has been challenged

37. Biologists have historically avoided discussions concerning teleology as this would imply that evolution somehow has a "direction." However, recently biologists have begun to use the term "teleonomy" to refer to the idea that some particular adaptations seem to be for the "purpose" of facilitating survival.

38. Thomas Aquinas, *Summa Theologiae* IaIIae.94,3. He says that the virtues are good habits that perfect the various powers of the soul. Thus there are intellectual virtues that perfect the rational powers of the soul. Included in these virtues are understanding, wisdom, science, prudence, and art (IaIIae.57). The moral virtues perfect the appetitive powers of the soul and must be shaped by human reason and its grasp of the peculiarly human goods (IaIIae.60). In the case of both types of virtue, reason, not instinct, understands what the good is and guides the agent to its proper end.

39. Aquinas, Ibid., IaIIae.94.3. For further discussion on the relationship between virtue and natural law see Vernon Bourke, "Is Thomas Aquinas a Natural Law Ethician?" *The Monist* 58 (1974): 52–66.

by sociobiologists, divine command theorists, and postmodernists, I will argue that there is enough of the divine spark in all humans that enables them to apprehend the basic precepts of natural law morality. Thinkers from St. John the Apostle to C. S. Lewis have affirmed the ability of humans to know what the natural law requires. For St. Paul it consisted in natural revelation; for Augustine it was "divine illumination"; and for Aquinas it was the "natural light of reason." There is a normative capacity in all human cultures to understand these moral principles. Moreover, these principles have their ontological and teleological basis in a relatively stable human nature that is accessible to anyone who will but consult it.

1.9 The Narrative Trajectory

If MacIntyre is right, living traditions must be able to incorporate the insights of their critics into their own theories. This, in turn, makes the theory that much stronger. It would seem that natural law has had such resilience due to its ability to adapt to changing contexts and situations. I see this book as a continuation of that project. Some will undoubtedly take issue with my approach as abandoning traditional natural law morality in favor of appeasing its postmodern critiques or of adopting a naturalism inconsistent with Thomistic metaphysics. My response is that, if the theory is to continue to flourish, it must not be bound by its purely cultural manifestations but must acknowledge its own historic limitations, and not avoid these challenges as inimical to the development of the theory. Rather, defenders of natural law morality should embrace the progress made in these various disciplines as friends who help make the theory that much more viable.

With this in mind, I believe that there is too little dialogue among the disciplines, and that the academic divisions of labor have seriously damaged the prospect for ethical discourse. There is clearly a need for interdisciplinary work in the development of any moral theory. One can easily point out that the defenders of divine command theory have failed to take nature seriously, but this charge can also be leveled against the most prominent voices in the natural law tradition. One can ask, In what sense can we meaningfully talk about a "natural" law when we continue to ignore the valuable insights of biology and the other sciences? If natural law morality does not begin to consider precisely how nature functions in the theory, I suggest that these thinkers simply drop the term "natural" from their own self-descriptions.

Another important point regarding interdisciplinary research is the idea that being in dialogue with other disciplines enables us to transcend our academic provincialism. The ghettoization of the academy impoverishes us all. In the spirit of mutual learning from among the disciplines, I hope that this work will engage and further moral discussion, not only within the domain of natural law ethics, but also across the artificial boundaries that separate the academic disciplines.

2 | A Narrative of Natural Law Morality

Introduction

Natural law possesses one of the longest narratives in the history of ideas, but it seems to be one of the most ambiguous concepts as well. As A. P. D'Entreves observed, "There is really not one tradition of natural law but many."[1] There have been secular Greek manifestations of it as well as distinctly Christian developments. Some have employed it as a basis for political theories, and others see it primarily as normative moral theory. In this chapter I will briefly sketch the

1. A helpful historical approach to natural law is chapter 2 from Yves Simon's *The Tradition of Natural Law: A Philosopher's Reflections* (New York: Fordham University Press, 1992); also see A. P. D'Entreves, *Natural Law: An Historical Survey* (New York: Harper Torchbooks, 1965), 11. This book also provides one of the more popular histories of natural law in its various manifestations. Unfortunately, D'Entreves focuses primarily on natural law as a political idea rather than on its value as a moral theory. John Finnis has also criticized D'Entreves for failing to make a distinction between the historical developments of theories about natural law and the idea of natural law itself. According to Finnis, the natural law does not change, but there have been many doctrines and theories proposed about the theory. Accordingly he says, "Anyone who considers that there are principles of natural law . . . ought to see the importance of maintaining a distinction between discourse about natural law and discourse about a doctrine or doctrines of natural law. Unhappily, people often fail to make the distinction." *Natural Law and Natural Rights* (Oxford: Clarendon Press, 1980), 25. In my view, Finnis fails to see that natural law may provide various interpretations, or narratives, and this may account for the diverse understandings of the term.

important historical developments of the theory as a backdrop for my own appropriation and use of the term.

A first distinction we can make is between natural law as political idea and its use as a moral theory. Even though there is continuity between the two ideas, an important distinction should be made. As a political theory, natural law vies with contractarianism, natural rights, and communism, and in this context it focuses upon the concerns of commutative, legal, and distributive justice.[2] Justice, as the first virtue of political and social organization, addresses questions of what we owe to others in society. What do we owe the government? What does the government owe us? And what do we owe one another as citizens who all contribute to the common good? Considered in this way, natural law functions as a regulative principle that keeps the peace.[3]

In contrast to the political understanding of natural law, an ethical understanding of natural law is wider in scope—and in many respects serves as a foundation for political appropriation of the theory. It concerns not only the question of what is owed to whom, but also what constitutes the human good—how is it known and how should it be pursued? But maybe more importantly, it addresses the issue of human nature and in what sense it can function as normative for ethics.

A second important distinction concerns natural law's relationship to God. Some contemporary defenders of natural law see its traditional formulation as an edict issuing forth from a divine legislator as an outdated anachronism.[4] They lay claim to the idea that "nature" can instruct us and that God is an unnecessary complication in defense of the theory. On the more traditional account of natural law, God is included not only as the legislator of natural law but also its final

2. See Josef Pieper, *The Four Cardinal Virtues* (Notre Dame, IN: University of Notre Dame Press, 1966), 70–113.

3. According to Aquinas, this is simply one of the functions of natural law. In his well-known discussion of the natural law, Aquinas says that the human goods people desire include knowing the truth about God and living in society. Yet the natural law also prescribes how we should order our private lives with respect to the pursuit of virtue and the regulation of our appetites.

4. Cf. Alan Donagan, *The Theory of Morality* (Chicago: University of Chicago Press, 1977); Anthony Lisska, *Aquinas's Theory of Natural Law: An Analytic Reconstruction* (New York: Clarendon Press, 1997); also D. J. O'Connor, *Aquinas and Natural Law* (London: Macmillan, 1967).

telos. Furthermore, the traditionalist sees the exclusion of God from moral and political discourse as an accommodation to modernity. Why should all views except religious ones be permitted in the public square? Both the question of religion's relationship to natural law as well as the political appropriation of natural law have been recurring themes throughout the historical development of the theory and these issues will play an important part in the remainder of this chapter.

I begin with a preliminary treatment of competing views on nature and how the various thinkers we consider employ the term. I discuss how natural law traces its origins to the ancient Greeks and biblical authors, through the Middle Ages and into the modern era. In my discussion of the various elements of natural law morality I consider how one thinker builds upon or rejects his predecessors' views on key elements of the natural law. In particular, I focus upon the modernist move from natural law as an ethical theory to its development as a political theory, as well as on how nature and reason play either increasing or diminished roles in the historical development of the theory.

2.1 Nature or Natures?

A term as problematic and open to debate as "natural law" is "nature." But our understanding of the former term depends primarily on an adequate definition of the latter if we want to avoid needless equivocation and ambiguity. A preliminary understanding of nature, at the very least, must guide our discussion from the start so that we can think about how the word has, can, and should be employed.

Those who wish to defend natural law morality must distinguish among the competing accounts of nature, yet these competing accounts of nature are embedded in particular contexts with particular narratives that shape the use of the term. The term has often been invoked to defend local or cultural customs; for example, the cultural belief that women were inferior to men was seen as part of the ancient and medieval understanding of nature, and clearly represents the institutionalization of sexism. At other times, theologians have chosen to avoid the term because we may unwittingly base a moral theory on a sinful and corrupt nature which would lead only to a sinful and corrupt moral theory. These two different construals of nature demonstrate that "nature" is not an unmediated category directly accessible to the senses. Alister McGrath says,

> "Nature" is thus not a neutral entity, having the status of an "observation statement;" it involves seeing the world in a particular way—and the way in which it is seen shapes the resulting concept of "nature." Far from being a "given," the idea of "nature" is shaped by the prior assumptions of the observer. One does not "observe" nature; one constructs it. And once the importance of socially mediated ideas, theories and values is conceded, it is impossible to avoid the conclusion that the concept of nature is, at least in part, a social construction. If the concept of nature is socially mediated—to whatever extent—it cannot serve as an allegedly neutral, objective or uninterpreted foundation of a theory or theology. *Nature is an already interpreted category.*[5]

Two points need emphasis here. First, the observer, or rather the interpreter, of nature always brings prior commitments to her experience of "nature," and it is for this reason that McGrath says that the perceiver necessarily "constructs" nature. This construction on the part of the observer, however, does not necessarily lead to a naïve epistemological relativism or a postmodernist rejection of meta-narratives. Instead, McGrath tempers his statement by saying that nature is "in part" constructed, thereby allowing a critical realist position—that is, a view that acknowledges the reality of the external world as mediated by conceptual frameworks—to guide his views on how to think about which constructs work better than others.

For our purposes I want to consider at least three different meanings of the term "nature" and how they reflect different ways to mediate the category of natural law. These three different meanings reflect (1) an "empirical" understanding of nature that emphasizes the characteristics of organic and inorganic life, (2) a particular theological understanding of nature that appeals to the radical distinction between the categories of corrupt nature and redeeming grace, and (3) a metaphysical understanding of the term that captures the important elements of the empirical but also considers an important teleological dimension that certain animals, especially humans, may have.

---

5. Alister McGrath, *A Scientific Theology, vol. 1: Nature* (Edinburgh: T & T Clark, 2001), 113 (emphasis original).

nature[1]: the object of various scientific inquiries that focuses upon explanations of how natural objects and living beings act and are acted upon.

nature[2]: a principle of corruption resulting from a primeval fall of humanity wherein the active power of nature is contrasted with the restorative powers of grace.

nature[3]: as the fulfillment of the natural *telos* embedded in humans in creation; it includes but is not reducible to nature[1].

Nature[1] has its roots in modernist conceptions of the sciences. Scientists in various disciplines ranging from biology to physics posit an intelligible "nature" that can be objectivized, studied, and manipulated in order to understand the mechanisms of various operations. This view of nature focuses more on the mechanisms of how natural organisms function in their appropriate environments and less on the teleological questions of why they developed in this or that particular way.

Nature[2] has been primarily associated with the Reformed thinkers who saw in the Bible a contrast between nature and grace. These thinkers see nature as a principle of corruption that has resulted from Adam's fall. On this view nature is a dubious category, one we must avoid at all costs in the construction of an ethical system. Since nature is fallen, especially human nature, any moral theory constructed on its crumbling foundations dooms itself.[6]

Nature[3] is the view of those Christian metaphysicians (and others) who see nature neither as the fallen creation of a good God nor as a merely empirical construct, but as an ontological category that reveals to us what a being's essential *telos* is. Thinkers who appeal to nature[3] include Aristotle, Cicero, St. Paul, Augustine, and Aquinas. All held that to understand a thing required more than merely knowing its material operations.[7] Rather, nature included an

6. Most theories of natural law avoid the naïve assumption occasionally attributed to the theory that one cannot base a theory of morality on nature since the fall corrupted human nature. Few thinkers in the natural law tradition would be so foolish as to support this view, yet some critics of the theory attribute precisely this perspective to natural law. Cf. Helmut Thielicke, *Theological Ethics: Foundations* vol. 1 (Philadelphia: Fortress Press, 1966).

7. According to James Barr, *Biblical Faith and Natural Theology* (New York: Clarendon Press, 1993), St. Paul appeals to nature as normative in Romans 1, since he clearly condemns "acts against" nature. In the Middle Ages, Aquinas makes a clear distinction

ontological theory that could not, in principle, be reduced to mere mechanism but always appealed to some final causality operating within the agent. The narrative of natural law I develop in this chapter focuses primarily on those thinkers who employ nature in this last sense—avoiding the more reductionistic account favored by the materialist ontologies as well as the more pessimistic theologies of the Reformed tradition.

2.2 The Ancient Greeks

In a very broad sense the origin of natural law in ancient Greece can be traced to Sophocles' *Antigone*. When King Creon proclaims that Antigone is permitted to bury only one of her two dead brothers, she protests that the king's command violates all known laws of what is right and good. She claims,

> Zeus never promulgated such a law.
> Nor will you find that justice publishes
> such laws to man below. I never thought
> your edicts had such force they nullified
> the laws of heaven which, unwritten,
> not proclaimed, can boast
> a currency that everlastingly is valid;
> An origin beyond the birth of man.[8]

---

between what he calls "material" and what is "natural" (IaIIae.10.1). A material nature concerns the physical constitution and powers of any being in the natural world. Rocks, trees, and squirrels all have a material nature. Rocks possess only a material form, while trees an organic form, and squirrels also possess an animal form, which provides them with a principle of locomotion. For a human, her nature consists of her material form, which includes her matter as well as the various principles of locomotion. Yet humans are more than mere matter in motion; humans are also rational beings. The term "nature" has a more inclusive meaning that refers to the specific nature of any being. Although the first sense of the term emphasizes the physical aspects of a being, the second sense emphasizes the essential characteristics of a being, physical or immaterial. In the same place Aquinas makes a careful distinction between these two uses. "The term nature is used in a manifold sense. For sometimes it stands for the intrinsic principle in movable things. In this sense, nature stands for any substance, or even for any being. And in this sense, that is, said to be natural to a thing which befits it according to its substance; and this is what is in a thing essentially."

8. Sophocles *Antigone*, 2nd episode, from *The Oedipus Plays of Sophocles*, trans. Paul Roche (Mentor, 1958), 179.

Antigone appeals to an "unwritten law" which transcends mere human promulgation and applies not only to particular times and places but is "eternally valid." Even though Sophocles offers no "theory" of natural law, it seems that he appeals to an intuitive basis for morality that stands over and above human convention. As such, human conventions must conform to these unchanging principles of justice, or risk the wrath of the gods. The two key ideas in Sophocles' work are (1) there is an unwritten law that all people seem to be responsible for knowing, and (2) it is eternally valid.

More well-known for his opposition to the poets than for his endorsement of them, Plato also seems to corroborate Sophocles' appeal to an eternally valid principle as the basis for moral judgments. In Plato's work we see two elements that contribute considerably to the development of natural law, even though he never employs the term himself. The first of these ideas is the famous theory of the forms. For Plato, every particular being in the physical world "participates" to some extent in the universal form that is its intelligibility. Every particular human being participates in the universal "human nature," and it is this universal element in all human beings that enables us to distinguish humans from other sorts of things like dogs, oak trees, and skyscrapers.

The universal form is eternal and changeless. It provides the intelligibility for all particular beings. In this way, we see the first rendering of a "human nature" that applies to all members of the species regardless of their temporal existence or their geographic location. The universal nature of the form insures the constancy, and continuing identity, of the particular. Thus, the form provides an ontological grounding for epistemological certainty. That is, we can be certain that even though particular humans may vary in shape, size, color, and appearance, the universal form of humanity will not vary from place to place or from time to time, since it is the eternal changeless form in which all the particulars participate. The forms not only account for the essentialism of Plato's understanding of human nature and its universality, they also provide an understanding of particular moral acts.

Given the fact that there is a transcendent human nature, it follows that some actions will inevitably lead to the flourishing of that nature and others to its corruption. For Plato the human good consisted in a life of virtue where justice orders the soul in such a way that each element of the tri-partite soul does its appropriate work. Wisdom, the virtue of the intellect, commands the other elements and enables its possessor to make sound judgments and decisions. Courage, the virtue of the "spirited element," obeys the intellect and faces fear with resolve. And self-control enables its possessor to resist the temptations of the appetites and obey the intellect. Each element of the soul has its appropriate work, or *ergon*, thereby contributing to the good of the whole person; or, as Julia Annas calls it, "psychic harmony."[9] For example, an act of courage results from thoughtful deliberation and enables the agent to act for the true good and not merely what may be convenient. As such, this act not only preserves the integrity of the soul but also participates in the form of courage.

A second element of Plato's thought relevant to our discussion is his notion of the good. In the *Republic*, the idea of the good appears and reappears at critical points throughout the dialogue.[10] He devotes all of Book VII to an explication of how the good functions in the moral life by his famous allegorical arguments; the most famous is the Cave Allegory in which Plato argues that the form of the good is that which serves as the source of all reality and goodness. Terence Irwin claims, "The Good is the formal and final cause of the Forms' being what they are; they are rightly defined when they are shown to contribute to the Good which is superior to them."[11] In the Cave Allegory, the philosopher is the hero who ventures out from the world of shadows (read the world of particulars) into the sunlight (read the intelligible world of the forms), and discovers that the true nature of all reality owes its existence to the sun—the form of the good. The form of the good illuminates the other forms and provides the "light" by which they can be perceived. Plato thus sees the good as self-same everywhere and that in which all good particular acts participate, given the changeless form of human nature.

9. Julia Annas, *An Introduction to Plato's Republic* (New York: Oxford University Press, 1987), 132. Annas says, "A person is just, then, if each part is acting virtuously and as it should: if reason is ruling, spirit is ensuring that reason has adequate motivational backing and desire is acquiescing in control by the other two rather than pressing its own particular claims. Justice in the individual is the appropriate and harmoniously flourishing of all aspects of him or her."

10. Plato *The Republic*, in *The Collected Dialogues of Plato*, ed. Edith Hamilton and Huntington Cairns, trans. Paul Shorey (Princeton, NJ: Princeton University Press, 1965).

11. Terence Irwin, *Plato's Moral Theory* (New York: Oxford University Press, 1987), 225.

Like Plato, Aristotle offers no theory of natural law but recognizes a transcendent order in nature and in human morality.[12] According to Yves Simon, "Aristotle is one of the founders of the theory of natural law, although he did not carry its explicit development very far."[13] Aristotle's discussion of the virtues clearly reflects an understanding of human nature that is grounded in biology but guided by reason. Aristotle appeals to (1) nature, (2) the universal quality of human nature immanent in each person, (3) the primacy of first principles, and (4) right reason.

The normative role of nature is central to Aristotle's ethics, since a being's nature always reveals itself in its teleology. We may always ask, "For what purpose does this thing exist?" The ends always tell us what the being's nature is, and this becomes particularly instructive when the being in question is human. Aristotle defines humans as "rational animals." For Aristotle this means the end for human nature is to act "according to reason." But this vague definition must yield more specific determinations if it is to avoid being a meaningless tautology.

The teleological nature of human rationality manifests itself in the universal desire for happiness. Aristotle's teleological understanding of the cosmos permeates not only his account of human nature and all the objects of sensation, but of the human sciences as well. He says, "Every art and every inquiry, every action and choice, seems to aim at some good; whence the good has rightly been defined as that at which all things aim."[14] Happiness functions as the natural *telos* for all human beings and we can only attain happiness by living a life in accordance with reason.

As Aristotle considers the human person, he argues that humans share three kinds of "soul" with other living creatures.[15] On this account, "soul" does not refer to some discreet ontological essence but

12. It is true, however, that Aristotle uses language that seems to anticipate natural law parlance in his *Rhetoric* when he says, "Universal law is the law of Nature. For there really is, as every one to some extent divines, a natural justice and injustice that is binding on all men, even on those who have no association or covenant with each other," in *Basic Works of Aristotle*, ed. Richard McKeon, trans. W. Rhys Roberts (New York: Random House, 1941), 1373b6–7.

13. Yves Simon, *The Tradition of Natural Law*, 27.

14. Aristotle *Nicomachean Ethics*, trans. Richard McKeon, *The Basic Works of Aristotle*, 1094a1–3.

15. Aristotle *Nicomachean Ethics* 1102a5–1103a10; also *On the Generation of Animals*, trans. Richard McKeon, *The Basic Works of Aristotle*, 736a35–b5.

rather to certain kinds of abilities or powers. All life has the power to preserve itself and this he calls the "vegetative," or organic, soul. All animals have the abilities to fight, flee, reproduce sexually, and to eat; this soul he calls the "sensitive," or animal, soul. But humans also have the capacities to do geometry, consider the nature of God, tell jokes, plan holidays, and evaluate behavior. These abilities clearly transcend the merely organic and animal, and so Aristotle sees these as all belonging to the rational soul.

The rational soul has the capacity to apprehend basic principles, make judgments, and deliberate concerning both operables and non-operables. Nature has endowed humanity with the ability to apprehend basic principles, such as the principle of non-contradiction, that the sum is greater than its parts, and that the good is that at which all things aim. These basic principles guide our judgments and deliberations in both speculative and practical affairs.

In any kind of deliberation, we reason from first indemonstrable principles to particular conclusions. First principles are grasped immediately by the intellect, such as the law of noncontradiction, the principle of identity, and the basic precepts of the natural law. All "sciences" proceed from their own first principles, but we can distinguish between those that are speculative—which concern matters of truth—and those that are practical—which concern matters of action.

Given the nature of the discipline, Aristotle held, we can expect varying degrees of certainty from our conclusions. In geometry we can be reasonably certain that in a right triangle $a^2 + b^2 = c^2$. We can know this since geometry, as a mathematical discipline, has for its subject matter formal properties that do not admit of variability due to empirical conditions. However, when we consider politics or ethics we cannot always be certain that our judgments will yield the same predictability we expect from geometry. If a ruler contemplates going to war with another sovereign nation, a number of variables may affect the outcome of the decision (e.g., the number of troops, the number of helpful allies, the preparedness of the troops, the perception among other nations regarding the justice of the cause). This capacity to reason correctly and the ability to come to sound judgments Aristotle calls "right reason."

For Aristotle, *orthos logos*, or right reason, enabled its possessor to perceive real relationships that exist among various persons or objects. The person of practical wisdom, Aristotle's ideal moral judge, could negotiate difficult moral problems not by simply applying the first principles of practical reason indiscriminately to various particular cases, but by being able to see the real relationships that existed. Consider Plato's famous example of a neighbor who wants a weapon returned for the purpose of an unwarranted insurgency against the government. We do not reason by applying the principle that "Borrowed items ought to be returned." Rather, we see that the situation calls for a more thoughtful decision that results in the conclusion that "I ought not to facilitate my neighbor's poorly conceived plan as it may harm both my neighbor and others in my community."

Aristotle's understanding of ethics is such that he attends to the fact that ethics is simultaneously an imprecise "science" that must be contextualized by the development of right reasoning, but also that it utilizes first principles that do not vary. He also believes that biology must play an important role in any theory of human nature and the ethical theory that follows from it. As a result, Aristotle seems to understand ethics not merely as the "participation" in eternal changeless forms of morality, but also as a uniquely human endeavor that may vary much more than Plato anticipated.

2.3 Roman Law

Three great thinkers in the tradition of Roman law contribute to the ongoing narrative of natural law: Cicero, Justinian, and Ulpian. Cicero sees human nature as fundamentally rational and capable of discovering the immutable moral laws of nature. Throughout his writings, we find the phrase *naturam et ratio* used liberally with reference to humanity's basic moral capacities within a basically Aristotelian framework. Aristotle's three powers of the soul reappear in Cicero's account of human nature, without much modification:

> Nature has endowed every species of living creature with the instinct of self-preservation . . . and of procuring and providing everything needful for life. . . . A common feature of all creatures is also their reproductive instinct . . . and also a certain amount of concern for their off-spring.[16]

16. Cicero *De Officiis* I, iv (Cambridge, MA: Loeb Classical Library, 1913).

Like Aristotle, Cicero sees the powers of self-preservation, sexual reproduction, and care for the young as part of nature's way of guiding
and directing all life. Yet humanity also possesses a rational power.
Cicero says that the human, "because he participates in reason, by
which he comprehends the chain of consequences, perceives the
causes of things . . . draws analogies . . . easily surveys the course of
his whole life and makes the necessary preparations for its conduct."[17]
Reason is a power that enables the human to transcend merely biological existence. In fact, its distinctive characteristic is its desire for
the truth. Accordingly, "primarily, the search for truth and its eager
pursuit are uniquely proper to humans."[18]

More than any thinker before him, Cicero binds together human
rationality and law. On his view, law becomes the embodiment of
practical reason. Again, following the lead of Aristotle, he says that
law is right reason; that is, law is a practical articulation of the real
relationships that exist among people. "For those creatures who have
received the gift of reason from Nature have also received the gift
of Law, which is right reason applied to command and prohibition.
And if they have received law, they have received Justice also. Now
all people have received reason; therefore all people have received
justice."[19] Reason is clearly nature's way of revealing to all humanity
what kinds of activities are appropriate to it—that is, what kinds of
action are just, and those that aren't—and this is the role of law.

Building upon Aristotle's appeal to right reason and the eternal
and immutable nature of the eternal law, Cicero says,

> True law is right reason in agreement with nature; it is of universal
> application, unchanging and everlasting; it summons to duty by its
> commands, and averts from wrong-doing by its prohibitions. And it
> does not lay its commands or prohibitions upon good men in vain,
> though neither have any effect on the wicked. It is a sin to try to alter
> this law, nor is it permissible to attempt to repeal any part of it, and
> it is impossible to abolish it entirely. We cannot be freed from its ob-
> ligations by Senate or People, and we need not look outside ourselves
> for an expounder or interpreter of it. And there will not be different
> laws at Rome and at Athens, or different laws now and in the future,

17. Ibid.
18. Ibid.
19. Cicero *De Legibus* I, x, 29; xii, 33 (Cambridge, MA: Loeb Classical Library,
1928).

but one eternal and unchangeable law will be valid for all nations and for all times, and there will be one master and one ruler, that is, God, over us all, for He is the author of this law, its promulgator and its enforcing judge.[20]

Cicero's comments provide the first detailed description of the natural law. Drawing upon a variety of sources and descriptions, he contends that the natural law has the following characteristics:

1. God has established it in nature.
2. It is eternally valid and invariant from culture to culture.
3. All people recognize it.
4. It cannot be abolished.
5. It directs us to the good and away from evil.

Although Cicero has no "doctrine of creation," he does claim that God is the "author" of our nature who has established the laws of right and wrong.

Law does not vary from culture to culture because it addresses a universal human nature. At various places he says, "We should understand that we are endowed by nature with two qualities, as it were: one of these being universal, arising from the fact that we are all alike endowed with reason. . . . We must do nothing contrary to the universal laws of human nature."[21] Cicero assumes, rather than argues for, this essentialist understanding of human nature. Given to a practical orientation in his work, he is less interested in metaphysical arguments for the basis of law as he is in its practical application.

Finally, law directs us to the good and away from evil and sets the basic parameters for good action and helps us avoid the more harmful evils. Those activities that promote the welfare of the state, peaceful family life, and equity among citizens all come under the heading of law. We naturally see that murder, theft, and dishonesty thwart communal life while their opposites contribute to it. The life lived in accordance with "nature and reason" is one that leads to happiness and well-being.

The great Roman encyclopedia of law, Justinian's *Corpus Iuris Civilis*, played an important role in the narrative of natural law by

20. Cicero *De Republica* III,xxii,33.
21. Cicero *De Officiis* I, xxx, xxxi.

gathering quotations from various sources and compiling them in one place. Of central importance to the editors was the issue of the varieties of law. Some laws hold universally and without exception: the natural law. Other laws express merely the convention of that particular state, and these are positive laws; still others express the means by which states relate one to another, and these are the laws of nations. This taxonomical approach did not always yield consistent and clear results, but it did provide a resource and a narrative for the classical lawyers to appeal to for various kinds of judgments.

Consistent with the Ciceronic tradition, the editors of Justinian's *Corpus* saw natural law as applying universally and with equity to all humanity, for the purpose of teaching about justice. The natural law is *both* a universal standard of justice as well as firmly rooted in nature. As Ulpian says, "Natural law is that which nature has taught all animals; this law indeed is not peculiar to the human race, but belongs to all animals. From this law springs the union of male and female, which we call matrimony, the procreation of children and their education."[22] Ulpian's understanding of nature is one that seems to conflate nature[1] with nature,[3] since the instincts by which animals reproduce and care for their young are simplistically applied to humans. However, we should not overlook the fact that what Ulpian is trying to do is to provide an account of natural law that has its origins in the metaphysical principles nature provides. His confused discussion of nature's role in natural law would later be clarified by Thomas Aquinas.

2.4 The Bible: Natural Theology in Genesis and the New Testament

Like most of the other ancient literature of its time, the Bible does not delineate sophisticated theories or philosophies. Its purpose is to narrate God's activities in the world and to encourage appropriate human responses. However, there are sources in the Bible that natural law moralists have employed for their own purposes.[23]

22. Justinian, *The Digest of Justinian*, trans. C. H. Munro (Cambridge: Cambridge University Press, 1904), I,i,1.
23. My concern here is not to read natural law theory into the biblical texts but to show how the Bible served as an important resource for the development of natural law theory.

In the book of Genesis, we read that God creates each animal "after its own kind."[24] This could suggest a proto-essentialism. There are clearly natural kinds of things in the world that are readily identifiable. Moreover, these beings have stable, identifiable natures that are not subject to radical change. Their inherent natures are constituted by their various properties and powers, as well as by their typical ways of operating. In other words, the very structure of creation makes these beings the kinds of things they are and thus the laws that govern them cannot change without bringing about different kinds of beings.

For Christians, the Genesis narrative of creation provides an account of the goodness of creation, the importance of human beings in the cosmos, and most importantly the idea that the entire created order is the contingent creation of a loving and wise God. The creation narrative also demonstrates that God has established an order to the creation. While Genesis affirms the goodness and orderliness of creation, we find in the Epistle to the Romans not only a reiteration of the Genesis account of created natures, but also an epistemological affirmation concerning the universal accessibility of the natural law.

According to St. Paul, there are "natural" activities (e.g., worship of the creator, monogamy, and benevolence) as well as "unnatural" behaviors (e.g., idolatry, promiscuity, and malice), given human nature as God created it. It is their distinct nature that determines how human beings should act and be treated, and in this regard St. Paul assumes a notion of nature[1] as a normative guide to our behavior. When humans act in accordance with their created natures, it is fitting and good; when they deviate from their created nature, the results are morally evil. Moreover, St. Paul declares that God has made known to all humanity the truth about God and about the moral order. Accordingly, he declares, "For what can be known about God is plain to them, because God has shown it to them. Ever since the creation of the world his invisible nature, namely, his eternal power and deity, has been clearly perceived in the things that have been made."[25] God

24. Gen. 1:25.
25. Rom. 1:20. Yet many biblical scholars do not see the passages from Romans 1 and 2 as a reflection of natural law theory in the text. Joseph A. Fitzmyer says, "the upshot is that 2:14–16 is not clearly a passage in which Paul teaches the so-called 'natural law,' an idea more at home in Greek philosophy and in patristic theology, even though one might have to admit that Paul's teaching about the Gentiles and their knowledge and conscience eventually led to the patristic formulation and understanding of natural

reveals to humans, without the aid of supernatural revelation, both theological and ethical truths.[26] However, we must also acknowledge that God does in fact give moral direction to humans through special revelation; the most notable of these instances are found in the Decalogue[27] and the Beatitudes.[28]

These precepts reveal in greater detail the fact that humans not only have a physical nature, but a spiritual and social nature as well. The first table of the Decalogue (i.e., the first four commandments) directs humans in their relationship to God (e.g., that God alone is to be worshipped). This indicates that humans have a spiritual nature, one that is capable of relationship with God.

The second table of the Decalogue (i.e., the last six commandments) guide us in our relationships with other humans (e.g., not to murder, steal from, or lie to, others). The precepts of the second table assume our nature as social beings and indicate a minimal kind of moral behavior we should exercise toward, and expect from, our neighbor. The Decalogue assumes a human nature that exists in relationship to God—a spiritual nature—and to our neighbor, a social nature. However, a striking feature of these precepts is their primarily prohibitive character, with the exceptions of keeping the Sabbath and honoring one's parents. Terence Fretheim says, "That eight commandments are negatively formulated is pertinent at this point. As such, they open up life rather than close it down; that is, they focus on the outer limits of conduct rather than specific behaviors."[29]

---

law." Joseph A. Fitzmyer, S. J., *Romans: A New Translation with Introduction and Commentary* (New York: Doubleday, 1993),129; James D. G. Dunn, *Romans: Word Biblical Commentary* (Waco: Word Books, 1988), 64, notes that the Greek *physis*, "nature," is not a Hebrew word but a Greek word, possibly borrowed from the Stoics.

26. Josef Fuchs observes that in the first chapter of Romans, St. Paul is not explicating a fully developed theory of natural law. Rather, St. Paul is concerned with the pagan world's need for redemption in light of their rejection of, what seem to him, the obvious theological and moral truths available to all humans. *Natural Law: A Theological Investigation* (New York: Sheed and Ward, 1965), 15.

27. The Decalogue is listed twice in the Scriptures. The first is found in Exod. 20:1–17 and the other in Deut. 5:6–21.

28. Matt. 5:1–12.

29. Terence Fretheim, *Exodus: Interpretation Series* (Louisville: John Knox Press, 1989), 221. Fretheim agrees with the idea that the precepts are for the good of the community when he says, "The negative formulation indicates that the primary concern is not to create the human community but *to protect* it from behaviors that have the potential of destroying it" (emphasis in the original).

The Beatitudes consist of Jesus's interpretation and development of themes found in the Decalogue. The very name "beatitude" indicates that these precepts are ways of being and acting that lead to happiness. The disciples are taught that purity of heart, peacemaking, and mercy (among other character traits) are essential to the life of happiness. The happy, or "blessed," life is one that includes both the spiritual and social dimensions of human nature.

Like the precepts of the Decalogue, the Beatitudes assume a human nature that is designed for relationship with God and other humans. Yet there are at least two important differences: (1) the Decalogue seems to focus primarily on prohibitions as minimal requirements of morality while the Beatitudes focus upon a more complete account of what kinds of people we should strive to be, and (2) the Decalogue seems to speak of specific kinds of *actions* while the Beatitudes seem to indicate what kinds of *persons* we should become. These differences should be seen as complementary accounts of the moral life rather than competing agendas.

On a natural law interpretation, the Bible seems to advocate: (1) an appeal to essences, grounded in creation, that all human agents can perceive; (2) given the reality of human nature some kinds of actions are natural and fitting for humans while others are unnatural and inappropriate; (3) both a minimal morality expected of all people, and the fulfillment of the law in the practice of certain kinds of virtues; and (4) that happiness or blessedness is the final *telos* or purpose for human existence.[30]

2.5 Patristic and Medieval Christian Theologians: Augustine and Aquinas

Unquestionably, the most influential theologian of the patristic era was Augustine of Hippo, who managed to combine elements of the great pagan thinkers Plato and Cicero with his own interpretation of the Christian faith. This Christian synthesis of pagan and sacred

30. Even though the Bible does not speak in terms of "essences," "flourishing," "the virtues," and "teleology, it has consistently been argued by both natural lawyers and virtue theorists that the Bible supports, or at least is consistent with this manner of speaking. Cf. Jean Porter, "Virtue Ethics" in *The Cambridge Companion to Christian Ethics*, ed. Robin Gill (New York: Cambridge University Press, 2001), 96–111.

writings can be seen especially in his treatment of moral themes that
include: the goodness of creation, moral illumination, the importance
of love, and the universality of moral knowledge.

Augustine contends that knowledge about the natural world and the
principles that govern it are available to all people regardless of their
religious orientation. God has revealed some truths to all people; and
in a famous passage from *On Christian Doctrine*, he claims that

> if those who are called philosophers, especially the Platonists, have said
> things that are indeed true and are well accommodated to the faith,
> they should not be feared; rather, what they have said should be taken
> from them as from unjust possessors and converted to our use . . . like
> Israel despoiling the Egyptians.[31]

And in another famous passage Augustine acknowledges that "even
the pagans" know basic truths about the world, the seasons, and the
operation of the created world and that Christians should not try to
refute the patently obvious things nature teaches, as this brings the
Christian faith into disrepute.[32]

According to Augustine, the entire universe bears the imprint of
God's creative activity. He encourages his readers to, "let your mind
roam through the whole of creation: everywhere the created world
will cry out to you: 'God made me.'"[33] The knowledge of God is available to every human mind, since it is the divine intellect that has
illuminated the created intellect.

God has also illuminated the human mind with regard to moral
truth. By means of the divine light, God enables all humans to discover
elementary moral truths. In fact, it is by participating in the divine
that humans are enlightened to know moral truths. In a remarkable
flourish of rhetoric that rivals Sophocles and Plato before him, Augustine absorbs their insights into his own Christian understanding
of the eternal law:

> Where indeed are these rules written, wherein even the unrighteous
> person recognizes what is right, wherein he discerns that he ought to
> have what he himself lacks? Where, then, are they written, if not in

31. Augustine *De Doctrina Christiana*, trans. D.W. Robertson, Jr. (Indianapolis:
Bobbs-Merrill, 1976), II, xl.

32. Augustine *De Genesii ad litteram* I, xix.

33. Augustine *In Psalmos* 26 Serm. 2, 12.

the book of Light that is called Truth? Whence every righteous law is copied and transferred . . . to the heart of the person who does righteousness, just as the impression from a ring passes into the wax, yet does not leave the ring.[34]

Combining Platonic metaphysics with Christian theology, Augustine believes that any particular thing must conform to the divine exemplar found in the divine mind. This basic metaphysical principle permeates all of Augustine's thought, with the result that any particular moral law must conform to the eternal law in the divine mind. The eternal law is frequently identified with the divine reason by which God establishes the laws that govern the entire cosmos.

The eternal law illuminates the intellects of all people. Augustine's famous doctrine of divine illumination can be distinguished from Plato's participation theory of the forms by the fact that it is God who illuminates the intellect, not the form of the good. Gareth Matthews says, "The doctrine is appropriately called a doctrine of *divine* illumination because Augustine tells us that it is the light of Christ, or the light of God, by which the mind is said to be able to discern the objects of intellectual vision."[35]

This divine illumination enables all people to know the basics of morality: the difference between good and evil, that punishments and rewards are consequences of free choice, and the idea that each person is due what is owed to him or her. The natural law according to Augustine is that uniquely human ability to know these truths. He says, "By divine providence the natural law is . . . transcribed on the rational soul of man."[36] Accordingly, all people, by virtue of their reason, are able to know the natural law. Vernon Bourke comments on this aspect of Augustine's thought by saying, "Just as the sun's light gives life to all, so does the Augustinian God of Lights shine forth and spiritually enliven all human souls."[37]

It would be a mistake, however, to attribute to Augustine a fully developed theory of the natural law. Rather, Augustine's thoroughly

34. Augustine *De Trinitate* XIV, 15, 21.
35. Gareth B. Mathews, "Knowledge and Illumination" in *The Cambridge Companion to Augustine*, ed. Eleanore Stump and Norman Kretzmann (New York: Cambridge University Press, 2001), 180.
36. *De diversis quaestionibus LXXXIII*, 53, 2.
37. Vernon Bourke, *Wisdom from St. Augustine* (Houston: Center for Thomistic Studies, 1984), 120.

Christian theology focuses on the nature of love not law; or rather we should say that his discussions of law typically take place within the context of his discussions of love. In *De Civitate* Augustine argues that our ultimate end is found in the love of God. Yet since God created us with a communal nature, we should love not only God, but the neighbor and the self as well. The underlying theme throughout is that humans have a specific nature, ordered to God and others, such that some actions always lead to peaceful coexistence and others to social strife. The backdrop to the entire discussion in Book XIX, chapters 12 and 13, is an essentialist understanding of human nature.[38]

Yet no theory that attempts to give a complete account of morality without explicit reference to the Christian God will ever be accurate. Oliver O'Donovan says,

> St. Augustine in the *City of God*, with an inconsistency that is only apparent, explains the success of the Roman empire in terms of traditional Roman virtues and, at the same time, denies that they are virtues at all, since there is no virtue without true religion. Such misknowledge may take the blatant form of idolatry, or its modern non-religious equivalent, ideology.[39]

This theme that one can never have a genuine moral perspective on life apart from God's revelation in Christ shows up more clearly in Augustine than in any of the other natural law thinkers. Yet if God requires more from us than mere obedience to the precepts of natural law, then it follows that, at the very minimum, an account of the virtues—especially the virtue of charity—must have a role, as well as an understanding, of those revealed precepts that the natural law does not address.

By far the most influential natural law theorist was Thomas Aquinas. Although Aquinas spends relatively little space in his *Summa Theologiae* on natural law, his Treatise on Law has become the *locus classicus* for subsequent theorists. According to Aquinas, the natural law is a "participation on the part of the rational creature in the eternal law."[40]

38. The Latin *naturam* is used no fewer than 14 times in chapter 13 alone suggesting that, for all Augustine's criticisms of Cicero's secularist account of ethics, the notion of nature remained an important holdover from the great Roman jurist's thought.

39. Oliver O'Donovan, *Resurrection and Moral Order: An Outline for Evangelical Ethics* (Grand Rapids: Eerdmans, 1986), 89.

40. Aquinas IaIIae.91.2.

Aquinas argues that we can come to understand the natural law by means of a careful consideration of nature: by observing how various creatures act, and what things do, and do not, contribute to their flourishing. For Aquinas, "nature is understood primarily in terms of the natures of specific kinds of creatures, regarded as the intelligible principles of their existence and their causal powers."[41] The human capacity to reason is an *a priori* capacity, but the content of the natural law must be discovered by an inquiry into human nature. Like Cicero before him, Aquinas borrows freely from Aristotle's theory of human nature that distinguishes among the organic, animal, and rational souls. The precepts of the natural law apply universally to all human beings. The approach is the following:

> The order of the precepts of the natural law is according to the order of natural inclinations. . . . First, there is in humans an inclination toward the good they share in common with all substances. . . . Second, there is in humans an inclination toward those things which are in accordance with what humans have in common with other animals. . . . Third, there is in humans an inclination to the good according to the nature of their reason, which is proper to humans. Thus, humans have a natural inclination to know the truth about God, and to live in society; and in this respect, whatever pertains to this inclination belongs to the natural law: e.g., to shun ignorance, to avoid offending those among whom one has to live and so on.[42]

One considers the natural inclinations and determines from those inclinations what kinds of actions must be avoided and what actions must be pursued. However, Aquinas does not intend to say that every natural inclination is to be acted upon in any and all circumstances. Rather, reason reflects on these natural urges and considers how they are to be pursued. For example, the natural desire for sexual reproduction is a good found in our animal nature; however, reason determines that its appropriate context is within marriage. But why? Aquinas believes that the good of the community depends on the order of society and, given the extraordinary emotional attachment associated with human sexuality, he contends that it is only within a stable, lifelong relationship that this kind of activity is appropriate.

41. Jean Porter, *Nature as Reason: A Thomistic Theory of Natural Law* (Grand Rapids: Eerdmans, 2005), 69.
42. Aquinas IaIIae.94.2.

Other creatures act on the basis of instinct alone, but the human creature is capable of self-directed activity. According to Aquinas, the natural law has the following characteristics:

1. It is discoverable by the natural light of reason.
2. It is a participation in the divine *logos*.
3. It is immutable.
4. It is universal.
5. It has been established by God for the common good of humanity.

By the "natural light of reason" humans come to know many things about the creation: that there is a God, that there is an order to creation, and that certain activities are right and others are wrong. This capacity that humans have to know and understand the world was given to humans by God in creation. Although human nature was indeed damaged by "The Fall," humans still retained the ability whereby they could know moral truth. Human nature was weakened and lost its perfection, but it was not destroyed or obliterated or incapacitated with regard to its ability to know the basic moral principles necessary for peaceful coexistence.

The metaphysical and epistemological structure of Aquinas's natural law ethics is a participation metaphysics.[43] He says, "[T]o participate is to receive as it were a part; and therefore, when anything receives in a particular manner that which belongs to another in a universal [or total] manner, it is said to participate in it."[44] Obviously, humans receive their nature from God and "participate" in God's creative activity. It can be said that participation is the means by which Aquinas expresses the radical existential dependence of creatures on God.

Norris Clarke lists three essential elements in Aquinas's participation structure: "(1) a source which possesses the perfection in question in a total and unrestricted manner, (2) a participant subject which possesses the same perfection in some partial or restricted way, and (3) which has received this perfection in some way from, or in dependence on, the higher source."[45] The relation of the natural to the eternal law

43. Craig A. Boyd, "Participation Metaphysics in Aquinas' Theory of Natural Law," *American Catholic Philosophical Quarterly* 79, no. 3 (2005): 431–45.

44. Aquinas *Commentary on the De Hebdomadibus of Boethius*, lect. 2.

45. Norris Clarke, "The Meaning of Participation," *Proceedings from the American Catholic Philosophical Association* (1952): 152.

clearly exhibits these three characteristics. First, the eternal law possesses the perfection of law as it is, the "divine reason." Since law is a dictate of reason, and the Word is the *expressivum et operativum* of the Father, it follows that God, by means of the *Verbum Dei*, establishes the natural law in human nature (Isa. 34:3). The human capacity to reason is therefore a mirror that reflects the divine reason.

The second requirement for participation is that there must be a participant subject which in some partial way possesses the perfection. Humans possess their being directly from God; as John Wippel explains, "In every finite substantial entity there is a participated likeness or similitude of the divine *esse*, that is, an intrinsic act of being (*esse*) which is efficiently caused in it by God."[46] All people participate in the divine *esse* and receive their being from God. As a result of participating in the divine *esse*, all people possess the natural light of reason. Consequently, all humans know the primary precepts of natural law through the natural light of reason, since we are created in the divine image.

The final element of the participation structure is that the participant must have received the perfection from the source in question. In the case of the natural law, the perfection is reason's capacity to know. That participation enables the agent to act freely and to govern her activities in accordance with reason. The *imago Dei* for Aquinas bridges the human and the divine. He says, "That the human is made in the image of God . . . implies that the human agent is intelligent and free to choose and govern itself" (IaIIae, prologue). This intelligence provides the continuity between the human and the divine. Since humans participate in divine reason by being created in God's image, they are thereby enabled to understand that God commands the precepts of natural law because of the way in which God has created humanity.

Aquinas appeals to the scriptures and especially to the passage from Romans 1 in support of his idea that all humans know universally applicable moral principles.[47] The most basic precept of the natural law is that "good is to be done and pursued and evil avoided."[48] Yet

46. John Wippel, *The Metaphysical Thought of Thomas Aquinas: From Finite Being to Uncreated Being* (Washington, DC: Catholic University of America Press, 2000), 131.

47. Fergus Kerr, *After Aquinas: Versions of Thomism* (London: Blackwell Publishing, 2002), says "Thomas's concept of natural law is thoroughly theological, and his appeal is to Scripture (Rom. 2:14; Ps. 4:6), not to philosophical authorities or considerations," 106.

48. Aquinas IaIIae. 94, 2. "Bonum est faciendum et prosequendum, et malum vitandum."

the natural light of reason enables us not only to know these basic moral truths but also to distinguish between those activities that are truly good for us and those that are not.

According to Aquinas, we can distinguish between apparent and real goods (or ends).[49] Apparent goods are those that seem to be good, but do not satisfy our natural and legitimate desires. For example, lying presents itself as an apparent good, as it might help us out of a difficult situation in the short term, but it does not satisfy our natural and legitimate desire to live with others in community. This is so because deception is a practice that breaks down the basic structure of community. On the contrary, real goods are those that truly satisfy our natural desires. As food satisfies my natural hunger, so too knowledge satisfies my natural desire to know. And I need to possess knowledge in order to survive. So we discover that there are objective goods that all people recognize as real goods. Included in the list of real goods are honesty, prudence, and non-malefescence, among others. Those actions that are always and everywhere good Aquinas calls the primary precepts of natural law.

Yet in order to avoid an important misunderstanding here, we should note that the natural law does not exhaust the entirety of Aquinas's views on ethics. The natural law lays down universal principles for human action that all humans recognize as binding. However, ethics properly understood concerns not only "doing the right thing" but acting for the right reason and in the right manner. It is the acquisition of virtue that enables us to act accordingly.[50] For Aquinas, "each person's reason dictates that he should act virtuously." "Reason's dictate" here is the activity of the natural law. The virtues thus provide the agent with a stable character that enable her to act in a habitually good fashion, fulfilling the general precepts of the natural law. Natural law precepts, when considered in isolation from an account of the virtues, result in a hollow, deontological approach that prescinds from human nature, leaving us with a list of "dos" and "don'ts" that have little bearing on who we are as persons who exist in real relationships with God and one another. Yet these primary precepts of the natural law serve the all-important function

49. A more current natural law argument is offered by Mortimer Adler, *Six Great Ideas* (New York: Macmillan, 1981), especially chapter 11. I follow Adler's argument here.

50. I will address this issue in greater detail in chapter 7.

of delineating what kinds of behavior contribute to human flourishing, and which do not.

In contrast to his later, more voluntaristic critics (e.g., John Duns Scotus or William Ockham), who emphasized the divine will and the mutability of the moral order, Aquinas held that the primary precepts of the natural law are immutable and universal. They do not change over time or from culture to culture; rather, they apply to all humans *as* humans. Accordingly, humans must always honor their parents, practice prudence, and treat others justly. Conversely, one may never commit adultery or murder, as these actions frustrate the natural human *telos* to live together peacefully. But the end of living peacefully with others is only part of the natural law; the purpose of human existence transcends the purely terrestrial goods of peaceful communal life and aims at a life of communion with God. In the words of Claude Tresmontant,

> The purpose of creation was not merely to bring about a group of spirits living together peacefully before God in a just and happy society. The purpose of creation, the supernatural goal of creation, according to God's plan as it actually is, is a union, a marriage, a fundamental transformation, a divinization, of human nature.[51]

As the natural law prompts us to pursue the good, we discover that the good to be pursued is the good in itself, God. So it is that the natural law directs us toward God as the goal of all our activity, our ultimate *telos*.[52] This union with God, Aquinas understands, is a kind of participation in the divine nature that truly perfects, or completes, the human soul.

2.6 Early Modern Philosophy: Suarez, Grotius, and Hooker

The Renaissance and Reformation mark the beginning of two radically different attitudes toward natural law morality.[53] The

51. Claude Tresmontant, *The Origins of Christian Philosophy*, trans. Mark Pontifex (New York: Hawthorn Books, 1963), 108.

52. Ibid. "From the standpoint of Christian ontology and anthropology, what defines man precisely is the supernatural destiny offered him by divine grace, for which he is preadapted by creation. . . . The philosopher should be able to discover by philosophical analysis, in concrete human nature as shown to us today, traces and signs which reveal that characteristic preadaptation to a supernatural destiny," 110–11.

53. For a discussion of Luther and Calvin and their adoption of divine command ethics, see chapter 4 on "The Religious Challenge" to natural law morality.

continental reformers Luther and Calvin did not outright reject natural law morality, but they did relegate it to a position of lesser importance when compared to the concept of grace.[54] For the Protestant reformers, nature was a theological category that was at best ambiguous. On the one hand, Christians needed to affirm nature as the good creation of an omni-benevolent God; on the other hand, it could not serve as the starting point for theology since sin had so corrupted human nature as to render its accomplishments mere hubris. Sin's ubiquitous presence not only made nature a problematic starting point for theology; it also radically altered the human capacity to reason. And if human reason had been so radically altered, how could we know with certainty that our apprehension of the natural law was sufficient to the task?

Instead of focusing on the natural law, the reformers tended to focus on the historic revelation of God in Christ, and the moral demands placed upon humanity by this new revelation. As a result, a morality founded upon divine commands tended to dominate the thought of Luther and Calvin with the added emphasis upon the inscrutability of God's wisdom.[55] A correlate of this was the emphasis upon the divine will as the source of moral norms, rather than on the naturally known precepts of natural law.

Natural law theorists in the early modern era began to focus increasingly on how the theory might be applied to issues of domestic and international law. Richard Hooker used the theory as an apologetic for the Anglican Church against the radically fideistic attacks of the Puritan reformers, while Hugo Grotius employed the idea as a basis for international law. As these developments took place, natural law increasingly became untethered from its theological moorings, subordinated to a theory of natural rights, and disengaged from a coherent theory of human nature. We begin this section with the work of Suarez, who could be considered the last of the scholastic natural lawyers.

The Jesuit Francisco Suarez (1548–1617) saw himself as an interpreter of Aquinas and many of his ideas can be traced directly to the

54. Emil Brunner reads Calvin as employing natural law in a significant way by seeing it as an expression of Calvin's natural theology. See his *Natural Theology; Comprising "Nature and Grace by Professor Dr. Emil Brunner and the Reply 'No!'" by Dr. Karl Barth* (Eugene, OR: Wipf and Stock, 2002).

55. I will consider their views on ethics in more detail in chapter 4.

great Dominican. According to Suarez, the natural law is "the natural light of the intellect which represents the will of God, the author of all creation, which compels men to observe the dictates of right reason."[56] In terms of its content he says, "The natural law is the rule whereby each of us is commanded to do to another what he would wish done to himself."[57] One must include in a definition both God's intellect and God's will, since both are necessary conditions for law. For Suarez, law has both a descriptive and a prescriptive function. In its descriptive role, it demonstrates to human beings what is good and what is bad; in its prescriptive role, it commands or impels its subjects to action. A teacher may point out that some course of action is wrong, but this knowledge of the relative moral value of the act in question does not constitute a law. Law requires the further element of obligation, which results from someone in authority commanding the act in question. Thus, for Suarez we can see that law is the command of a genuine authority who both knows and wills the good for a community.

Suarez wants to steer a course between the extreme voluntarism of Ockham who thinks that law is purely the function of divine will, and Gregory of Rimini, who held that the requirements of the law remain even if God did not exist. Gregory contends,

> Even if God did not exist, or if He did not make use of reason, or if He did not judge of things correctly, nevertheless, if the same dictates of right reason dwelt within man, constantly assuring him, for example, that lying is evil, those dictates would still have the same legal character which they actually possess because they would constitute a law pointing out that evil exists intrinsically in the object.[58]

Suarez will have none of this, and sees the need for a position that includes both the requirement of promulgation (as an act of the will) and universal validity (as natural law reflects God's wisdom). He says, "I hold that a middle course should be taken, this middle course being in my mind, the opinion held by St. Thomas and common to all the theologians."[59]

For Suarez nothing can stand over and above God as a metaphysical principle and therefore he agrees, to a limited extent, with the

56. Francisco Suarez, *De Legibus*, II, c.6, n.7.
57. Ibid., II,7,8.
58. Ibid., II, c.6,6
59. Ibid., II, c.6,5.

voluntarists who held that God is free to command what God wills. However there are specific actions, given the manner in which God created humanity, that necessarily contribute to human flourishing, and others that contribute to its destruction. Suarez appeals to the idea of the absolute divine decree in order to preserve both God's freedom and the universal intelligibility of the natural law. God cannot act contrary to God's nature by issuing contrary divine decrees. He says, "If God should move in opposition to an absolute decree, there would be in existence . . . contrary decrees. . . . He would have willed absolutely two contradictories, a conception which is repugnant to reason."[60] But since God has decreed that we should love God and that we have a specific nature, it follows that there are specific kinds of actions that are "intrinsically evil."[61]

In an interesting development of Aquinas's theory of natural law, Suarez sees self-evident precepts in terms of (1) general precepts, (2) specific precepts, and (3) those moral precepts that can be deduced from self-evident principles. The general precepts of the natural law include the idea that "Good should be done and evil should be avoided," as well as "What you do not want done to you, you should not do to another."[62] These principles are so uncontroversial that Suarez says, "about these there is no doubt that they belong to the natural law."

There are also more particular precepts of the natural law; concerning these precepts there is no doubt concerning either their belonging to the natural law or their self-evident nature, which becomes apparent from considering the terms themselves. Included in these precepts are, "Justice should be observed; God should be worshiped; One should live with temperance."[63]

Suarez also claims that we can deduce some precepts of natural law from others. He says that various kinds of activities, including

60. Ibid., II, 6–7.
61. Frederick Copleston says that, "The divine volition presupposes a dictate of the divine reason concerning the intrinsic moral character of certain acts. It is repugnant to reason to say, for example, that hatred of God is wrong simply and solely because it is prohibited by God. . . . God is indeed the author of natural law; for He is Creator and He wills to bind men to the dictates of right reason. But God is not the arbitrary author of the natural law; for He commands some acts because they are intrinsically good and prohibits other acts because they are intrinsically evil." *A History of Philosophy* vol. 3, pt. II (New York: Image Books, 1963), 207.
62. *De Legibus*, II, c.7,5.
63. Ibid., c7.5.

adultery, theft, and other similar kinds of actions can be inferred fairly easily, while others such as usury and lying require a bit more effort. This last type of precept belongs to the natural law essentially and seems to correspond closely to the precepts of the Decalogue, especially those of the second table.[64]

Suarez ties the precepts of natural law to the Decalogue in order to demonstrate that what God speaks by means of special revelation can be confirmed by natural reason. Suarez sees these authorities as converging rather than competing with one another, as more secular theories of natural law would contend later. The beginning of this phase was ushered in, unintentionally, by Hugo Grotius (1583–1645).

As a response to late medieval voluntarism, Grotius argues that law must have a rational basis in the nature of humanity. Law could not merely be understood as the embodiment of the will of the ruler; it had to have a binding force that transcended the will. This fundamental conviction applied not only to human rulers but also to God.

Grotius therefore represents a critical point in the narrative of natural law for two reasons: first, his repudiation of the Reformation and late medieval voluntarists; but second—and more importantly—his arguments lead to the secularization of natural law. The voluntarism of the medieval theologians and reformers seemed to jeopardize the noetic basis for natural law. If morality was merely the arbitrary command of an all-powerful tyrant, then who could know that content, and in what sense could we say that it applied universally?

Natural law requires a stable foundation, but in the midst of a world torn asunder by the Protestant Reformation, appeals to divine will would not fare very well. In contrast to Aquinas, who saw natural law as the uniquely human participation in the eternal law, Grotius makes no such appeal. According to Hendrik van Eikema Hommes, "natural reason was no longer believed to be capable of detecting the principles of natural law and the structure of the state as founded in a divine *lex aeterna*. Law and state had to be constructed by natural reason out of the empirical elements of human society."[65] An understanding of law that appealed to the "naturally known" and universally

64. "For the precepts of the Decalogue are matters of natural law, as is undoubted by all. Yet they do not all contain self-evident principles, but some require a reasoning process." Ibid., II, 7,7.

65. Hendrik van Eikema Hommes, "Grotius on Natural and International Law" in *Netherlands International Law Review* 30, no. 1 (1983): 66.

applicable elements of human nature did not seem to warrant an appeal to the divine origins of the natural law. Like Suarez, Grotius contends that there are moral precepts that are in themselves right and others wrong. There are certain things God can and cannot do. Grotius's famous dictum that "what we have been saying would have a degree of validity even if we should concede that which cannot be conceded without the utmost wickedness, that there is no God, or that the affairs of men are of no concern to Him."[66] Because human nature does not change, no one—not even God—can change the precepts of the natural law. Grotius says,

> Measureless as is the power of God, nevertheless it can be said that there are certain things over which that power does not extend. . . . Just as even God cannot cause two times two should not make four, so He cannot cause that which is intrinsically evil not be evil.[67]

Grotius defends the natural law against the voluntarist critics, like Ockham, who would argue that there is no necessity in the divine command. But for Grotius, the necessity of the natural law is self-imposed by God.

God alone is the author of human nature; God has created human nature and appointed the appropriate ends, and thus it would be irrational for God to act contrary to the creation that God Himself has established.

> The law of nature is a dictate of right reason which points out that an act, according as it is or is not in conformity with rational nature, has in it a quality of moral baseness or moral necessity; and that, in consequence, such an act is either forbidden or enjoined by the author of our nature, God.[68]

The critical element of human nature is our rationality, which assists us in understanding the world as the creation of God and our place in it. Yet Grotius's comment that "even if there were not God" opens the door to a new interpretation of the natural law. Instead of seeing God as the creator and author of our nature,

66. Hugo Grotius, *De jure belli ac pacis*, prolegomena, trans. Louise Loomis (Roslyn, NY: Classics Club Library, 1949).
67. Ibid., 1,1,x.
68. Ibid., 1,1,10,1.

later natural lawyers would see God as just so much unnecessary theological baggage.

Another example of the "political" use of the natural law can be found in the work of Richard Hooker (1554–1600).[69] While Grotius used the natural law to negotiate agreement on international laws that were not tied to theological doctrines, Hooker employed it as a means of establishing Anglican Church polity against those who held that reason could play no role in church polity.[70] For Hooker, the Thomistic idea of "the light of reason" seems to play a central role in his views on the means by which all humans come to an understanding of morality and law. Hooker says that inasmuch as God has created all humans with the natural "light of reason," they all are "enabled to know truth from falsehood and good from evil."[71] Humans are able to make judgments about the created order, as well as the moral order, on account of the "light of reason." Echoing Aristotle and Aquinas, he observes that "the main principles of reason are in themselves apparent."[72] They are known, as the scholastics would say, as "self-evident."

The judgments that we are to pursue certain courses of action and avoid others are called laws. More specifically, a law has reference to human agency. Thus, "the rule of voluntary agents on earth is the sentence that reason giveth concerning the goodness of those things which they are to do."[73] Thus, reason discovers in nature the laws God has promulgated and all people know them to be right. He summarizes the "marks" of the laws of reason: (1) they are good and beautiful and ordered, (2) they do not need the "help of Revelation supernatural and divine," and (3) all people know them.[74]

To say that these laws are good and beautiful and ordered is to assume a basic teleology for all human activity.[75] The aim of all human

69. Richard Hooker, *The Works of Richard Hooker*, ed. W. Speed Hill, Folger Library edition, vol. I (Cambridge, MA: Harvard University Press, 1977–90), 81–93.

70. The Puritans refused to allow reason any role in theological "argument." As they saw it, *only* the Bible provided absolutely pure truth. All authorities, especially reason and tradition, were radically corrupted by the Fall. According to Thomas Cartwright, the whole of scripture is to human reason as "a cleare fountaine is to a filthy puddle." *Confutation, f.2.,f.3* (Leiden: Brewster, 1618).

71. Hooker, *The Works of Richard Hooker*, 84.

72. Ibid., 85.

73. Ibid., 85.

74. Ibid., 89–90.

75. The significance of this is that the nominalism of Luther and Calvin commit them to denying that natural reason can discern any kind of final causality. Frederick

activity is happiness. As all people know that activities such as murder and dishonesty are wrong, they realize that these prohibited actions always work against human happiness. So, any genuine law will direct or "order" the human agent to the good. In contrast to the Augustinianism of the Puritans and the continental reformers, Hooker's views naturally followed the thought of Thomas Aquinas. On the Thomistic model of the cosmos divine reason reigned supreme. God ruled the universe according to the *lex aeterna*. Hooker was in fundamental agreement with this assessment, even though his taxonomy of laws that follows diverged from Thomas. They did agree that God rules all things by the eternal law. He says that "God therefore is a law both to himselfe, and to all other things beside."[76] And he insists that laws are all fundamentally rational in their essence: "Howbeit undoubtedly a proper and certain reason there is for every finite work of God inasmuch as there is a law imposed on it."[77]

The eternal law plays a key role in Hooker's thought. It accounts for all of God's activities *vis-a-vis* creation. It is, in Hooker's own words, "that order which God before all the ages hath set down with himself, for himself to do all things by."[78] This law includes all other laws, both natural laws and divine laws. So, the natural as well as the supernatural come under the purview of the *lex aeterna*. Munz says that "the two realms of nature and supernature co-exist in perfect harmony, because in the last analysis they both flow from God's *lex aeterna*. Hence there can be no real contradiction between reason and faith."[79]

God has created nature with its enduring natural laws such that God's creative activity is not made void by the Fall and human sinfulness. Certainly human nature is damaged, as Hooker readily admits. However, human nature has not been damaged to the radical extent that the continental reformers held. Rather, God bestowed reason on humanity as a gift. While it functions imperfectly, it still is able

---

Beiser says, "Luther undercuts the main premise behind natural theology by denying that it is possible for reason to know *final and efficient* causes of things. All that reason can know, in his view, is their *formal and material* causes." *The Sovereignty of Reason* (Princeton, NJ: Princeton University Press, 1996), 31 (emphasis in the original).

76. Hooker, *Ecclesiastical Laws*, chap. 2, par. 3, 60.

77. Ibid., 61.

78. Ibid., 63.

79. Peter Munz, *The Place of Hooker in the History of Thought* (London: Routledge and Paul, 1952).

to ascertain various truths about God. Hooker seems to think that God can be considered from both the perspective of natural reason and from special revelation. This clearly follows Aquinas, who held that

> There is nothing to prohibit the same things from being considered by the philosophical sciences when they can be looked at in the light of natural reason and by another science when they are looked at in the light of divine revelation.[80]

Contrary to the bifurcating tendencies of Luther and Calvin, Hooker saw reason as being able to discern various final causes in creation that could produce knowledge of God. Moreover, this knowledge was not a vain attempt by humans to penetrate the infinite wisdom of God; rather, it was merely an attempt to utter statements about God that all people knew to be the case.

2.7 Late Modern Philosophy: Locke and Kant

Taking ethics and political thought one step beyond Grotius, John Locke (1633–1704) argued for political arrangements based on the theory of social contract, which was a civil agreement designed to enforce the law of nature. In his early years he wrote a series of *Essays on the Laws of Nature* that were never published in his lifetime.[81] In these early essays Locke argues for the universal validity of the natural law based upon right reason. However, at no point does he ever define the content of the natural law.

In the *Second Treatise on Government*, Locke develops a social contract theory of politics that appeals to the idea of the natural law as a moral foundation for the civil society.[82] Locke contends that prior to the development of social organization all people exist in a "state of nature" that is "governed" by the law of nature. The law of nature indicates that all people are free, equal, and independent agents subject only to the dictum that "No one ought to harm another in his

80. Aquinas, Ia. 1.
81. John Locke, *Essays on the Laws of Nature*, ed. W. von Leyden (Oxford: Clarendon Press, 1978).
82. John Locke, *The Second Treatise of Government*, ed. C. B. Macpherson (Indianapolis: Hackett, 1980).

life, liberty or property."[83] The law of nature is a moral principle that all people recognize independent of the variety of political structures in which they may presently find themselves. This law of nature is known by the "natural light of reason." So far, this language does not depart radically from traditional natural law theory; however, the method Locke uses is thoroughly modernist. The law of nature is a necessary assumption for Locke's modernist agenda: securing the idea of individual natural rights.

The law of nature reveals to all people that each one has a right to life, liberty, and property. These rights are derived from the "fact" that each one recognizes himself as free, equal, and independent. The law, therefore, serves the purpose of establishing the rights that all people have in the state of nature.

In the state of nature, each individual has the right to adjudicate transgressions of the law of nature. As a result, there is a derivative right to punish offenders. Unfortunately, there is also a tendency to make a biased judgment in one's own favor when another has violated the right to property. This problem, combined with the problems of social cooperation, lead people to create a social contract. Locke says that God "put man under strong obligations of necessity, convenience and inclination to drive him into society."[84] The social contract serves as a means of preserving and protecting one's individual rights. Locke says,

> Men being, as has been said, by nature all free, equal and independent, no one can be put out of this estate and subjected to the political power of another without his own consent. The only way whereby anyone divests himself of his natural liberty and puts on the bonds of civil society is by agreeing with other men to join and unite into a community for their comfortable, safe and peaceable living one amongst another, in a secure enjoyment of their properties and a great security against any that are not of it.[85]

When people agree to a social contract they agree to lay down their rights to individual judgment in matters of punishment, as well as other matters that may require an unbiased judge. The contract's primary function guarantees the preservation of the individual rights

83. Ibid.
84. Ibid., 7, 77.
85. Ibid., 8, 95.

to life, liberty, and property, and any government that fails to keep these rights for its citizens is either ineffectual or unjust.

In Locke we see three very modern principles at work in his account of the natural law: (1) the subjugation of natural law to natural rights, (2) the primacy of the individual, and (3) the neglect of nature as a moral category. It is in Locke's account of the natural law that the relative importance of law and right are inverted. In the classical accounts of natural law, right was a relationship that was governed by natural law; that is, a right (*jus*) was understood as a relationship that existed either between two individuals or between the government and the individual. The right itself was regulated by the fact that real relationships, as understood by right reason, existed between and among individuals. These right relationships were determined by a theory of human nature that was expressed in the natural law. Yet in Locke's account of natural law, we find that the law of nature merely serves as an artificial construct for the natural rights. Indeed, the natural rights of the individual are primary. They are the deontological basis for any account of ethics, of which the only kinds of precepts Locke is concerned with are negative prohibitions: do not take another's life, do not infringe on another's liberty, and do not take another's property.

Corresponding to Locke's subjugation of law to rights is his emphasis on the individual. The individual's rights have primacy because a social contract obtains its moral legitimacy only from the individual consent to be governed.[86] Government is an artificial means of keeping individuals happy, or as Locke prefers, "comfortable, safe, and secure." And what do we need to be kept safe from? Why, other individuals who desire our things, of course. On this view, social arrangements are voluntary and consensual, not a natural function of our nature as social beings, which leads us to Locke's neglect of nature as a moral category.

For Aristotle, Cicero, and Aquinas nature played an important role in their thinking about morality and how human nature was a necessary but insufficient condition for a system of ethics. With Locke this changes. He sees human nature primarily in political and economic

86. One could also note that Locke's emphasis on rights and the social contract arose out of a scientific milieu that had by this time already rejected final causes. If there was no natural teleology and no hierarchy of the good, a social contract would be necessary to adjudicate among the competing desires of the citizens.

terms. Humans are acquisitive; they desire property and will take the necessary means to obtain it. Our desires for food and drink are understood as a desire for property; that is, a desire for those things that make our lives safe and comfortable. For Locke, nature is an intellectual construction in which moral agents seek property and security against others, all the while endowed with prohibitions not to kill, rob, or deny basic freedoms to others. The modern natural lawyers all seemed to acknowledge a similar content to the natural law, so in this way Locke is hardly innovative. However, his justification for these principles represents an extraordinarily individualistic attempt which stands in an interesting contrast to the last of the modern natural lawyers, Immanuel Kant.

It may seem peculiar to consider Immanuel Kant (1724–1804) in the tradition of natural law theory, but Kant may represent the zenith of the secular approach to natural law in the modern era. Kant's relationship to natural law is complex and we can only touch on some important themes here, so I will limit my comments to three distinct areas: (1) his use of natural law language, (2) his secularist approach to morality, and (3) his consideration of the natural ends of humanity.

Best known for his articulation of the categorical imperative, Kant harbors deep suspicions about the plausibility of basing any moral theory on human nature or any principle that can be understood as heteronomous. Kant argues that happiness cannot suffice as the supreme principle of morality even though all people desire happiness.[87] There are at least two reasons for this. First, no one agrees on what happiness is. Kant says, "It is a misfortune that the concept of happiness is so indefinite that, although each person wishes to attain it, he can never definitely and self-consistently say what it is he really

87. Immanuel Kant, *Critique of Practical Reason*, trans. Lewis White Beck (Indianapolis: Bobbs-Merrill, 1985). "It is astonishing how intelligent men have thought of proclaiming as a universal practical law the desire for happiness, and therewith to make this desire the determining ground of the will merely because this desire is universal. Though elsewhere natural laws make everything harmonious, if one here attributed the universality of law to this maxim, there would be the extreme opposite of harmony, the most arrant conflict, and complete annihilation of the maxim itself and its purpose. For the wills of all do not have one and the same object, but each person has his own, which, to be sure, can accidentally agree with the purposes of others who are pursuing their own, though this agreement is far from sufficing for a law because the occasional exceptions which one is permitted to make are endless and cannot be definitely comprehended in a universal rule," 27.

wishes and wills."[88] Your happiness may differ from my happiness, and as a result in my pursuit of happiness you may encounter a good deal of unhappiness.

A second problem is that even if we did know what happiness is we couldn't be certain of attaining it. Kant says that in order to achieve happiness we would need to be omniscient. Greek tragedy is full of characters who desired to be happy but whose lives in the end were fraught with pain and misery. In light of this basic fact about our lives, Kant suggests that while we might desire happiness, what we should really hope for is to be "worthy of happiness." That is, happiness may serve as a motive for doing our duty, but it cannot supply the content of ethics. Thus "the practical law, derived from the motive of happiness, I term pragmatic (rule of prudence), and the law, if there is such a law, which has no other motive than *worthiness of being happy*, I term moral (law of morality)."[89]

Since happiness is too slender a thread to support the weight of moral duty, Kant argues that we must appeal to *a priori* principles of morality to ensure that we can be worthy of happiness and know with certainty where our duty lies. His means of accomplishing this is by the famous categorical imperative. Since we must have an *a priori* basis for ethics, Kant says that our duties must be universal and necessary. They cannot vary from one time and place to another, and they cannot apply contingently. Kant formulates the categorical imperative in four famous ways:

Formula 1:
Act only on that maxim through which you can at the same time will that it become a universal law.

Formula 2:
Act as if the maxim of your action were to become through your will a universal law of nature.

Formula 3:
Act in such a way that you always treat humanity, whether in your own person or in the person of any other, never simply as a means, but always at the same time as an end.

88. Immanuel Kant, *Foundations of the Metaphysics of Morals*, trans. Lewis White Beck (Indianapolis: Bobbs-Merrill, 1959), 35.
89. Immanuel Kant, *Critique of Pure Reason*, trans. Norman Kemp Smith (New York: St. Martins Press, 1965), 636.

Formula 4:
All maxims as proceeding from our own making of law ought to
harmonize with a possible kingdom of ends as a kingdom of nature.[90]

In Formula 1 of the categorical imperative, Kant appeals to the criterion of "universalizability": the idea that any maxim (i.e., a subjective
principle of action) must in principle be universalized. For Kant this
means we can universalize the principle of helping those in need, as
we might find ourselves in need on some occasion. However, it would
not include the principle of taking out a loan with no intent to pay
back the loan, since this could not be universalized; banks would
close and it would undermine the fiduciary trust on which banking
is based. The main point for Kant is that the principles of morality
must apply universally to all people as a function of pure practical
reason. A correlative of this is found in his second formula of the
categorical imperative.

In Formula 2, Kant alters the language slightly so that the maxim
could become a universal law of nature. Here Kant appeals to the idea
of the laws of nature as a model for the formula for the categorical
imperative. The Newtonian world with which Kant was fascinated
postulated universal laws that governed all material objects without
exception. Indeed, this is part of the very idea of law: that objects
invariably obey the laws that govern them. Gravity holds without
exception for large bodies. In Kant's epistemology we find that it is
impossible for us to even think without conceiving of some kind of
law-like governing structure for the world of the phenomena.[91] So
too in moral philosophy we must have moral principles that apply
with law-like regularity to our maxims.

The third formula introduces the idea of the human person as
an "end in himself." Kant's concern here is for the rationality of the
self, as well as the principle that all people should be treated equally
under the moral law. Persons are valuable in themselves, not merely
as objects of desire or means to our own or other's goals. The idea
that rational agents are ends in themselves, Kant says, "admits of no
proof"; rather, it is a pure practical idea of reason. That is, we must

90. Kant, *Foundations of the Metaphysics of Morals*.
91. Kant, *Critique of Pure Reason*, 136. He says, "There can be in us no modes of
knowledge, no connection or unity of one mode of knowledge with another, without
that unity of consciousness which precedes all data of intuitions, and by relation to
which representation of objects is alone possible."

think this way, even as we must in terms of the idea of causation, even though causation admits no empirical proof.

In Formula 4, Kant introduces the idea that rational agents must think of themselves as legislating for a kingdom of ends. It is at this point Kant considers the problem of social cooperation, much as Locke considered it under the heading of the social contract. Kant saw the critical connection between moral and political life, and attempted to bridge the two by means of this formula of the categorical imperative.

J. B. Schneewind says that Kant accepted the basic problematic of the modern natural lawyers, the problem of social cooperation. Yet there is more that ties Kant to the natural lawyers. According to Schneewind, Kant "makes the concept of natural law basic and defines other moral concepts in terms of it."[92] And Roger Sullivan contends that "Kant must . . . be counted as belonging in some important ways to the 'natural law' tradition, for he does contend that we must regard ourselves as having natural purposes or ends that we must respect."[93] But what are those "natural purposes," and how can Kant afford to smuggle them into his categorical imperative without jeopardizing its autonomy, since normativity must derive from reason not nature?

Kant makes an important distinction between using nature as a basis for morality—in which case the will would be determined heteronomously—and using nature as providing us with information about our natural construction as persons. We thus see Kant employing two of our previous meanings of "nature." On the one hand, he rejects nature[1] as determining the will heteronomously; it is this sense that he ascribes to earlier natural lawyers whom he believes makes the will heteronomous. They were attempting to base an ethical system on the precarious basis of human nature as empirically understood. However, Kant also employs the idea of nature[3] since he sees that there must be a metaphysical sense in which the term can and should be employed. Nature here refers to two distinct elements of human nature: its essential freedom as a noumenal being, and to those elements of physical nature that must be pursued in order to satisfy the conditions necessary for human cooperative existence.

92. J. B. Schneewind, *The Invention of Autonomy: A History of Modern Moral Philosophy* (New York: Cambridge University Press, 1997), 519.
93. Roger Sullivan, *Immanuel Kant's Moral Theory* (New York: Cambridge University Press, 1989), 181.

Kant contends that the categorical imperative prescribes perfect duties to self; one such duty is the duty to "perfect oneself." This duty derives from the fact that if we fail to do this we have failed to treat ourselves as "ends in themselves." Even though Kant explicitly argues against happiness serving as the grounding of the will, he allows that there is an "indirect duty" to pursue happiness. He says, "To secure one's own happiness is at least indirectly a duty, for discontent with one's condition under pressure from many cares and amid unsatisfied wants could easily become a temptation to transgress duty."[94] From these remarks we can surmise that Kant's own position on happiness is that since humans are not only rational, but also animal, they need the basic goods of life in order to secure for themselves the pursuit of duty, which is indirectly a duty. In addition to pursuing these basic goods, they also have the duty to perfect themselves. Kant here is careful to avoid prescribing the direct pursuit of happiness as a duty—since happiness cannot be defined—as well as noting that to fail to pursue the perfection of ones own talents and gifts is to fail to treat oneself as an end. But although we cannot use happiness as the grounding of ethics, could we not appeal to God and the commands that God gives us?

Kant's reluctance to introduce God into his arguments for the justification of ethics is based on two considerations. First, if the maxim for our action is for the sake of some other principle than that reason prescribes it, then the will becomes heteronomous. Acting for the sake of pleasing God, or because God has commanded an action, makes the will heteronomous. Rather, Kant contends that God desires that we act according to the universal precepts of reason, and in this way we avoid the embarrassing situation of an Abraham thinking he needs to sacrifice Isaac, since this clearly violates all four formulae of the categorical imperative we have considered.

Kant also thinks that some actions are intrinsically disordered and in opposition to nature's ends. Two such kinds of actions are included here: suicide and crimes against nature. Suicide is an intrinsically disordered act because it violates the third formula of the categorical imperative; one uses oneself for one's own purposes and fails to treat oneself as an "end in himself." Kant clearly shows his disdain for divine command ethics at this point by stating,

94. Kant, *Foundations of the Metaphysics of Morals*, 15.

> Suicide is not an abomination because God has forbidden it; it is forbidden by God because it is an abomination. If it were the other way about, suicide would not be abominable if it were not forbidden; and I should not know why God had forbidden it, if it were not abominable in itself. The ground, therefore, for regarding suicide and other transgressions as abominable and punishable must not be found in the divine will, but in their inherent heinousness.[95]

The natural law language reappears, as Kant says that suicide thwarts the natural desire for all ends in themselves to perfect themselves. He contends that there are three basic impulses natural to us which can be identified by moral reason: preservation of the self, preservation of the species, and cultural development. Suicide violates the basic duty we have to ourselves to preserve ourselves. However, we also see the natural law language crop up again in his discussion of "crimes against nature."

In his delicate rhetoric concerning sexual impropriety, a younger Kant argues that the natural purpose for human sexuality is the perpetuation of the species—a very Aristotelian and Thomistic idea—and that behaviors such as homosexual relations, adultery, and bestiality run contrary to nature (*contra naturam*).[96] In this regard, the naturally appointed end of preserving the species has been thwarted. But considered from Kant's perspective, it does not so much violate a naturally known *telos* as it transgresses the categorical imperative. Kant's moral philosophy thus stands as the last gasp of the modernist natural law theory, while simultaneously inaugurating a new era of ethics that saw little need to appeal to either God or nature for its justification.

2.8 Contemporary Philosophy

For much of the nineteenth and into the twentieth century, natural law theory gave way to various forms of Kantian rationalism and utilitarianism, until G. E. Moore presented his linguistic critique of ethics. Many natural lawyers attempted to rehabilitate the theory in

95. Kant, *Lectures on Ethics*, trans. Louis Infield (Indianapolis: Hackett, 1979), 120. He also says that "God is Himself good and Holy because His will conforms to this objective law."
96. Ibid., 170.

a variety of ways: as a political theory, as an analytic theory of the good, or even as a neo-Kantian theory. Alan Donagan articulates this last option. He says,

> If we scrutinize the structure of St. Thomas's theory of natural law, we shall find that the teleology underlying it is not a Christianized version of eudaimonism, but an anticipation of the very same teleology Kant was to arrive at a little more than five hundred years later.[97]

Donagan accepts the challenge of Kantian ethics by rejecting a natural teleology and placing in its stead a deontology more in keeping with his Kantian sympathies. However, the two primary issues of concern for the natural lawyers in the twentieth century turned on the relation of God to morality and the neglect of human nature.

John Finnis's approach has been to recognize religion as one of the fundamental goods of human existence. He includes the good of religion along with education, life, and family, among others. Yet he has stated unequivocally that he does not intend to include theology in any way as a basis for his own theory of natural law. He has said that his approach to natural law is "a rather elaborate sketch of a theory of natural law without needing to advert to the question of God's existence."[98] As such, he hopes to avoid getting into the messy arena of apologetics, thereby complicating his arguments by first proving God's existence and then deriving precepts of natural law from a divine lawgiver. Finnis's reluctance to engage the theological foundations of natural law and Donagan's Kantian theory of natural law represent two perceived problems that natural lawyers faced during the twentieth century.

Ethical theory for the past 100 years has tended to focus on the agenda Moore set for it in his *Principia Ethica*: the avoidance of any notion of ethical naturalism and the exclusive focus on the nature and meaning of moral language. Many, like Germain Grisez, as we shall see in chapter 6, accepted Moore's challenge and attempted to modify traditional conceptions of natural law in order to address the "Is-Ought" problem. Many natural lawyers like Donagan read into

97. Alan Donagan, "Teleology and Consistency in Theories of Morality as Natural Law" in *The Georgetown Symposium on Ethics*, ed. Rocco Porreco (Lanham, MD: University of America Press, 1984), 93.

98. John Finnis, *Natural Law and Natural Rights* (Oxford: Oxford University Press, 1982), 400.

natural law a Kantian universalizing tendency that fails to understand contextual elements and the absolutizing tendencies of previous theories of natural law. Others, like Finnis, develop the theory along the lines initiated by Grotius, as an alternative to various secular political theories. And almost all defenders of natural law avoid developing a theory of nature that seriously considers the developments in scientific accounts of human nature since the time of Aquinas.

I begin my development of natural law with the last of these issues; those who endorse natural law need to develop a theory of nature that addresses important developments in the scientific understandings over the past two centuries, the most important of which is evolutionary theory. A theory of human nature serves as a necessary condition for ethics, but we must guard against the reductionistic tendencies of many scientists posing as moral philosophers.

The development of the theory of human nature addresses two important challenges to natural law theory: the relativizing tendencies of postmodernism and divine command theory's extreme emphasis on divine power to the neglect of other features of morality. Although divine command theory rightly serves to remind natural lawyers of the importance of God as creator, redeemer, and final end of the human creature, it fails to take seriously the importance of the goodness and orderliness of creation. Postmodern thinkers rightly consider the exaggerated claims of what constitutes "nature," and if there even is such a thing corresponding to the term. They point to the fact that language, especially moral language, is unavoidably embedded in power structures.

3 | The Scientific Challenge

Sociobiology and Evolutionary Psychology

Introduction

Without question, evolutionary theory is the most important development in the biological sciences within the last two centuries. Theodosius Dobzhansky declared, "Nothing in biology makes sense except in light of evolution."[1] Some, like Daniel Dennett, have even argued that it is the singular most important scientific development of all time. According to Dennett, "If I were to give an award for the single best idea anyone has ever had, I'd give it to Darwin, ahead of Newton and Einstein and everyone else. In a single stroke, the idea of evolution by natural selection unifies the realm of life, meaning, and purpose with the realm of space and time, cause and effect, mechanism and physical law."[2] Regardless of its ranking in the history of ideas, evolutionary theory of one kind or another is universally accepted by scientists of all stripes. Richard Dawkins has claimed that "it is absolutely safe to say that if you meet somebody who claims not to believe in evolution, that person is ignorant, stupid or insane

1. Theodosius Dobzhansky, "Nothing Makes Sense in Biology Except in the Light of Evolution," *American Biology Teacher* 35: 125–29.

2. Daniel Dennett, *Darwin's Dangerous Idea: Evolution and the Meaning of Life* (New York: Simon and Schuster, 1995), 21.

(or wicked, but I'd rather not consider that)."[3] This is not merely the verdict of notorious atheists like Dawkins, but a generally accepted position by most philosophers and theologians as well.[4] Recently, theologian Terence Penelhum has written,

> It is as well established scientifically as anything is, that the immense variety of species in the world have evolved over millions of years, and that the human species is one example of this evolutionary process. . . . It is only in the darkest intellectual backwoods that it is still denied that the present variety of species is the result of millions of years of evolution and that the human species is also. [5]

Penelhum's attitude is hardly an isolated instance of Christian capitulation to evolutionary theory. As early as the late nineteenth century, American theologian Asa Gray saw that Darwin's theory was an entirely plausible account of how the Creator brought humans into existence.[6] Most notably, however, the popular Christian writer and Oxford don C. S. Lewis apparently had few misgivings about evolution as a scientific account of how God acted as creator when he wrote,

> For long centuries God perfected the animal form which was to become the vehicle of humanity and the image of himself. He gave it hands whose thumb could be applied to each of the fingers, and jaws and teeth and throat capable of articulation, and a brain sufficiently complex to execute all the material motions whereby rational thought is incarnated. This creature may have existed for ages in this state before it became man.[7]

3. Richard Dawkins, "Put Your Money on Evolution," *New York Times*, April 9, 1989.

4. See for example Francis Collins, *The Language of God: A Scientist Presents Evidence for Belief* (New York: Free Press, 2006); Arthur Peacocke, *Creation and the World of Science: The Reshaping of Belief* (New York: Oxford University Press, 2004); Ernan McMullin, ed., *Evolution and Creation* (Notre Dame, IN: University of Notre Dame Press, 1985); Richard Swinburne, *The Evolution of the Soul* (New York: Oxford University Press, 1997); Howard Van Till, "The Fully Gifted Creation," in *Three Views on Evolution and Creation*, ed. J. P. Moreland and John Mark Reynolds (Grand Rapids: Zondervan, 1999), 161–218.

5. Terence Penelhum, *Christian Ethics and Human Nature* (London: Canterbury Press, 2000), 75–6.

6. Asa Gray, *Darwiniana* (New York, 1877).

7. C. S. Lewis, *The Problem of Pain* (London: Centenary Press, 1940), 65. For further study of Lewis's endorsement of evolution, see Gary Ferngren, "C.S. Lewis on Creation

Lewis saw God as the divine architect directing and guiding the evolutionary process that culminates in humanity as rational and moral animal. We find here no protracted defenses of a literal reading of the Scriptures against the onslaught of atheistic scientism, but rather a calmly reasoned metaphysical argument for the moral and ontological creation of human nature that just so happens to include evolution functioning as a secondary cause in the process.

Although many Christian theists like Penelhum and Lewis have alluded to evolutionary theory in their descriptions of human nature and morality, few have taken the theory seriously enough to incorporate it fully into their ethical theories. This is not only a problem isolated to theists like Lewis and Penelhum; it includes all of the natural law moralists of the past century.[8] Anthony Lisska makes one of the very few comments indicating the possibility that natural law theory can be reconciled with evolutionary theory. In his discussion of the primacy of essences in natural law he says, "This analysis of essence is compatible with an evolutionary account postulating the development of essences over time. . . . The set of properties could have come about through evolutionary development, through *rationes seminales* which Augustine proposed, or through another form of divine interaction."[9] Even though Lisska's comment is provocative, he never develops the ideas of an evolutionary ontology as the basis for natural law. Like most other analytic philosophers, he contents himself with epistemological and metaphysical analysis rather than an exploration of recent developments in biology.

The intellectual provincialism of analytic philosophy has apparently prevented contemporary natural lawyers from venturing out into other disciplines that might provide a more helpful landscape

and Evolution: The Acworth Letters, 1944–1960," *Perspectives on Science and Christian Faith* 48 (March 1996): 28–33.

8. It could be argued that Larry Arnhart sees himself as an exception to this claim. However, two issues can be raised against Arnhart's problematic interpretation of natural law theory. First, he makes no references to the decidedly Christian origins of natural law. Second, his metaphysical reductionism is clearly inconsistent with natural law. Rather, as Arnhart acknowledges, his own theory has greater affinities with David Hume. For a critique of Arnhart's attempt to reconcile natural law morality with Darwinism, see Craig A. Boyd, "Was Thomas Aquinas a Sociobiologist? Thomistic Natural Law, Rational Goods and Sociobiology," *Zygon: Journal of Religion and Science* 39, no.3 (September 2004): 657–78.

9. Anthony Lisska, *Aquinas's Theory of Natural Law: An Analytic Reconstruction* (New York: Oxford University Press, 1996), 131.

for a contemporary ontological setting for natural law morality. This chapter is an attempt to rectify the situation by articulating how a theory of natural law is able to incorporate the insights of sociobiology and evolutionary psychology without necessarily embracing the materialistic metaphysic these approaches often have. In many respects, this is similar to Aquinas's selective use of Aristotelian biology and philosophy. Though Aquinas found Aristotle's description of the eternity of the world, the mortality of the human soul, and the lack of providence problematic, he did not see the need for a complete rejection of Aristotle's insights. On the contrary, Aquinas found many useful insights to be gleaned from Aristotle. In Augustine's words, it was simply "plundering the Egyptians."

As I see it, researchers in sociobiology and evolutionary psychology offer helpful insights into human nature and human morality.[10] First, they contend that human nature is universally shared by the entire species. As a result, even though we may anticipate cultural, genotypical, and phenotypical variations, humans will share the same "nature" everywhere.

Second, evolutionary psychologists rightly consider biology as contributing to important elements of human morality. Human nature is not seen as something that must be overcome, or as a potential impediment, as it was for Kant. Nor is it seen as a red herring that distracts us from the nature of moral language, as it has for many analytic philosophers of the twentieth century.[11] Rather, human biology is a necessary condition for any account of human morality.

The history of evolutionary thought from Darwin to Dawkins provides a helpful backdrop for our discussions concerning the specific contributions to moral philosophy that evolutionary psychology has to offer. The difficulties inherent in any such materialist ontology, however, present significant problems for a theory of natural law.

10. Throughout this chapter I will identify sociobiology with evolutionary psychology unless there is a compelling reason to make a distinction. Wilson still retains the term "sociobiology," but others such as John Tooby and Leda Cosmides prefer the term "evolutionary psychology." For a brief discussion of the controversy over naming the discipline, see John Cartwright, *Evolution and Human Behavior: Darwinian Perspectives on Human Nature* (Cambridge, MA: MIT Press, 2000), 25–29.

11. G. E. Moore, *Principia Ethica* (Cambridge: Cambridge University Press, 1903); C. L. Stevenson, *Ethics and Language* (London: Methuen, 1945); R. M. Hare, *The Language of Morals* (Oxford: Clarendon Press, 1952).

Finally, I consider how to incorporate the valuable insights from evolutionary psychology into natural law morality without being metaphysically reductionistic.

3.1 A Brief History of Evolution: From Darwin to Dawkins

In 1859, Charles Darwin published his most important work, *On the Origin of Species*. The book was prompted by a younger colleague, Alfred Russell Wallace, who in 1858 sent Darwin a letter in which he developed the theory of natural selection independently from Darwin. Darwin was stunned, but after negotiation they consented to present the theory jointly. Darwin's book sold out the day it came off the presses. Response was immediate; it was condemned by some as anti-religious since it called into question "divine design" and the uniqueness of humanity, not because it attacked the literalist understanding of Genesis. Religious opinion on the topic was divided between those who saw the theory as a threat to the dignity of humanity and those who considered it a plausible explanation for human origins. Wallace himself remained a devout churchman his whole life, as did Darwin's most prominent American advocate, Asa Gray (a theologian at Princeton).[12]

3.2 Key elements of Darwin's Theory

On Darwin's theory, individual organisms can be grouped together on the basis of such characteristics as shape, anatomy, physiology, behavior, and so on. These groupings are not entirely artificial, as members of the same species, if reproducing sexually, can by definition breed with each other to produce fertile offspring. Horses can breed with other horses and donkeys can breed with donkeys to produce fertile offspring. However, when horses breed with donkeys an infertile animal—the mule—is the result.

Within species, individuals do not possess identical traits but will differ in physical and behavioral characteristics (e.g., puppies from the same litter will differ in color, size, and weight, as well as various

12. For more on this see Mark Noll's *The Scandal of the Evangelical Mind* (Grand Rapids: Eerdmans, 1994).

kinds of behavior, such as aggression). Some of these differences are inherited from previous generations and may be passed to the next. This variation is enriched by the occurrence of spontaneous but random novelty. As a result, a feature may appear that was not present in previous generations, or it may be present to a different degree.

Darwin's own observations of the Galapagos finches provided him with the data for this conclusion.[13] While on his visit to the islands, Darwin observed thirteen different species that had slight modifications in beak size and shape, diet and song. Darwin theorized that each species adapted its beak size and shape to the available food resources on the various islands. And yet, since there were such common features as body mass and color, there must have been some common ancestor to the various species of finches found on islands. "Seeing this graduation and diversity of structure in one small, intimately related group of birds, one might really fancy that from an original paucity of birds one species had been taken and modified for different ends."[14]

Resources required by organisms to thrive and reproduce are not infinite, as Mendel's studies on populations demonstrated; so competition must inevitably arise among members of the same species for the limited resources. Those more adept at acquiring the resources will have an advantage over others, and will subsequently leave more offspring than their weaker conspecifics. For example, slower Thompson's Gazelles will be killed off by lions and hyenas; and if this happens before they are capable of sexual reproduction, they will not confer their genes on further generations.

Since some heritable variations confer an advantage on their possessors, microevolution will gradually change the characteristic of a species, sometimes in significant ways. Those variants that leave more offspring will tend to be preserved and gradually become the norm. If the departure from the original ancestor is sufficiently radical, new species may form (i.e., macroevolution), and natural selection will have brought about evolutionary change.

As a consequence of natural selection, organisms will become adapted to their environments in the broadest sense—of being well suited to the essential processes of life such as obtaining food, avoiding

13. Charles Darwin, *Voyage of the Beagle* (New York: Penguin, 1989).
14. Darwin, *Voyage of the Beagle*, September 29, 1835 entry.

predation, finding mates, competing with rivals for limited resources, and so on.[15] Natural selection, therefore, acts as a lawful constraint on the development of species and their ability to adapt to their environment. Darwin himself summarized this idea at the close of his *Origin of Species*:

> It is interesting to contemplate an entangled bank, clothed with many plants of many kinds, with birds singing on the bushes, with various insects flitting about, and with worms crawling through the damp earth, and to reflect that these elaborately constructed forms, so different from each other, and so dependent on each other in so complex a manner, have all been produced by laws acting around us.[16]

This lawful and yet dynamic theory of speciation produces species that adapt to their ever-changing environments. In contrast to the Aristotelian cosmos, which emphasized the fixity and eternality of species, Darwin's world was one that continually changed, adapted to change, and left those to die that could not change. Ernst Mayr provides a helpful means of considering the central elements of Darwin's theory (Box 1).

Box 1:
Darwin's Five Major Theories of Evolution[17]

1. The non-constancy of species (the basic theory of evolution)
2. The descent of all organisms from common ancestors (branching evolution)
3. The gradualness of evolution (no saltations, no discontinuities)
4. The multiplication of species (the origin of diversity)
5. Natural selection

According to Mayr, there is a basic plasticity in species since survival requires adaptation. Species descend from common ancestors and must adapt to their own unique environments. Those individuals better at

15. Cartwright, *Evolution and Human Behavior*, 33.
16. Charles Darwin, *The Origin of Species by Means of Natural Selection* (New York: Penguin Books, 1985), 459.
17. Ernst Mayr, *What Evolution Is* (New York: Basic Books, 2001), 86.

adapting survive and reproduce, passing on their genes, while those that don't adapt perish without successfully procreating.

The principle of natural selection is one that requires no special teleological explanation.[18] When asked the question, "Does any process in evolution require a teleological explanation?" Mayr responds with an emphatic "No." All kinds of teleological explanations "have been thoroughly refuted, and it has been shown that indeed natural selection is capable of producing all the adaptations that were formerly attributed to orthogenesis."[19] (Orthogenesis is the belief that biological organisms have the tendency to move on to greater degrees of perfection.) However, according to Mayr, no "mechanism could be found to drive" the trend toward perfection and that, "there is no evidence whatsoever to support any belief in cosmic teleology."[20] But on what basis is this statement made? Biological considerations or philosophical? He seems committed to the view that biology cannot make the claim, yet he also wants to give biological analysis precedence over any metaphysical claims made by either philosophy or theology, which creates a critical problem. Does biology rule the other disciplines by its own self-proclaimed superiority; or is Mayr simply practicing philosophy without a license?

Mayr's rejection of philosophy and theology seems to be based on the questionable assumption that these two disciplines stunted the development of the sciences. Specifically, philosophy and theology advocated a view of nature that could be understood as "essentialism." According to Mayr, essentialism was the dominant view on nature from the earliest Greek philosophers until the time of Darwin. The ancient Greek's idea was further developed by Christian theologians who claimed a biblical basis for it (e.g., the references to "kinds" of animals in the Genesis creation narrative). According to Mayr, "each kind, each type, each species is believed to have been separately created and all now living members of a species

18. It is interesting that Darwin himself harbored doubts about evolution destroying final causality. In a letter to W. Graham, as late as 1881, he says that "the existence of so-called natural laws implies purpose. I cannot see that. . . . But I have no practice in abstract reasoning, and I may be all astray. . . . Nevertheless you have expressed my inward conviction, though far more vividly than I could have done, that the universe is not the result of chance." *The Autobiography of Charles Darwin and Selected Letters*, ed. Francis Darwin (New York: Dover Books, 1959), 62.

19. Mayr, *What Evolution Is*, 275.

20. Ibid., 82.

are believed to be the descendents of the first pair created by God. The essence or definition of a class (type) is completely constant; it is the same today as it was on the day of Creation."[21] However, Darwin introduced the idea of variable populations in the place of constant classes. Within each population there is a great variety of heritable traits, which enable some to survive and reproduce. This theory of variable populations "was congenial to most naturalists, who in their systematic studies had discovered that species of animals and plants showed as much (and sometimes far more) variation and uniqueness as the human species."[22] This observed variation in species seemed to call into question the fixity that earlier thinkers advocated. Species gradually adapt and evolve based upon the great variation within each species.

The other key problem, which was closely related to both essentialism and teleology, was "finalism," the belief that "evolution moved necessarily from lower to higher, from primitive to advanced, from simple to complex, from imperfect to perfect" forms of life.[23] The advocates of finalism wanted to introduce into biology a force that aimed at a particular goal. Darwin accepted only mechanistic explanations, and as Mayr points out there seems to be no empirical evidence to suggest these teleological forces are at work in evolution.

Darwin's ideas concerning natural selection were formulated on the basis of artificial selection. He observed that various breeds of domestic dogs were bred for different purposes (e.g., collies for herding, terriers for ratting, hounds for hunting, etc.). The variations were produced by breeders who desired certain traits in the animals (e.g., collies must possess excellent limbic communication skills with non-dogs, terriers must possess excellent hearing skills, and hounds must have superior sight).

Since there is no teleology operative in evolution, evolutionary processes simply conform to the principle of natural selection. As this applies to human beings, we see that human nature is not constant over time but simply a temporary phase in a continually evolving process. Thus, traits that may have helped some humans adapt at an earlier time may not later confer an advantage since climate and environmental conditions may change unpredictably.

21. Ibid., 74.
22. Ibid., 75.
23. Ibid., 75.

3.3 Problems in Darwin's Theory

Darwin recognized that his theory had two basic problems. First, how was it that specific traits could be inherited from one generation to the next? A related question concerned how different traits could be introduced into various populations. Darwin knew that inheritability was true, but he did not know the mechanism for it. Lamarckism was rejected, as it seemed obviously false (e.g., people who lose a thumb in an accident do not beget children lacking a thumb).

Darwin's second problem was that it would seem impossible for apparently altruistic behavior to evolve in a world of scarce resources populated by self-interested organisms. Darwin considered this second issue so problematic that he claimed any trait that evolved for the "good of another would annihilate my theory, for such could not have been produced through natural selection."[24] More recently, Robert Trivers has said, "An altruistic act is one that confers a benefit on someone at a cost to the other. Since cost is measured by a decrease in reproductive success, we know that altruistic acts are opposed by natural selection's working on the actor."[25]

The answer to the first question was not fully answered until Crick and Watson's research in the 1950s. The DNA sequencing of the human gene provided the answer to the question of inheritability. This research also led to various explanations to the second question. If qualities like eye color, for example, could be inherited by genetic transmission, why not behavior patterns like altruism? Two of the primary mechanisms of explanation are kin selection (sacrificial behavior in behalf of one's close relatives) and reciprocal altruism (*quid pro quo* behavior). These ideas will be developed later.

3.4 Evolutionary Relativism

In light of the dynamic theory of speciation, Ian Tattersall has argued that there can be no moral norms derived from nature. The basic dynamics of evolution preclude any kind of universal morality based upon human nature. Any attempt to construe nature as provid-

24. Charles Darwin, *The Origin of Species* (New York: Penguin Books, 1968), 186.
25. Robert Trivers, *Social Evolution* (Menlo Park, CA: Benjamin/Cummings, 1985), 41.

ing moral guidelines for human behavior is mere anthropomorphism. Tattersall says,

> Each society has invented its own ways of coping with economic and social needs, and with the knowledge of individual mortality. What's more, appalled though members of one society may be by ways of doing business in another, no society is intrinsically better or worse than others in any universal sense. We can derive no concepts of morality (a social construct) or of "natural law" (an intellectual construct) from the contemplation of nature.[26]

Here we find a perspective on human nature that denies any universally normative prescriptions regarding human social arrangements and behaviors. As a result, cultural relativism necessarily follows from the dynamically diverse condition that is humanity. Tattersall believes that "as a species, *Homo sapiens* presents a bewildering variety that is next to impossible to boil down to a neat account of anything we could describe as *the* human condition."[27] On Tattersall's view, there can't even be the possibility of a human nature since the evolutionary process in always in flux. David Hull agrees with Tattersall and develops the argument in the form of a hypothetical syllogism. "If species evolve in anything like the way Darwin thought they did, then they cannot possibly have the sort of natures that traditional philosophers claimed they did. If species in general lack natures, then so do *Homo sapiens*."[28] Thus, if evolution is true there can be no such thing as human nature.

Tattersall and Hull have merely selected one aspect of Darwin's theory—the dynamic theory of speciation—and given it primacy. Ethical relativism ineluctably follows from this basic assumption. This classic form of question-begging may suit the more philosophically naïve, but it hardly accounts for two serious objections.

The first argument against Darwinian relativism makes use of the biology that Tattersall and Hull are so eager to employ for their own agenda. There seem to be some behaviors, such as incest avoidance and nurturing the young, that are shared universally by humans, Tattersall

---

26. Ian Tattersall, *Becoming Human: Evolution and Human Uniqueness* (New York: Harcourt Brace and Company, 1998), 198 (emphasis in the original).

27. Ibid., 198.

28. David Hull, *The Metaphysics of Evolution* (Buffalo: State University of New York Press, 1989), 74.

and Hull's objections notwithstanding. If a human society of any kind is to survive—if only as a biological community—these two norms must be operative, given how the facts of genetics affect the offspring of close relatives and given the extraordinary length of time it takes human infants to mature. We will return to these biological factors shortly.

The second objection to Darwinian relativism is the philosophical objection. Philosophers James Rachels and Michael Ruse, both ardent Darwinians, reject relativism on the basis of social cooperation.[29] For social cooperation to take place, there must be universally binding moral principles. According to Rachels, since humans are social animals, at least two moral principles apply necessarily and universally.[30] The first is the principle of non-maleficence, which holds that in order to cooperate, all members of a community must agree not to harm other members of that community. The second principle is the principle of honesty. In order to be members of the community, all must speak truthfully in their promise not to harm others. Without these two principles, no human society is even conceivable.

What we can say, therefore, to Tattersall's suggestion that morality is simply an invention that enables us to cope in different ways is that there are specific constraints on what can and cannot serves as the basis for moral systems. Given the fact that we are social animals, and have evolved various adaptations to cope with our social conditions (e.g., language), it follows that every society must have rules requiring truth-telling and forbidding harm to other members of the community. To suggest, as Tattersall does, that there is no universal basis for our ethical systems, that natural law is a pure fiction, and to focus on the specific differences of cultural norms, rather than on the foundational principles that enable the society to function, is simply to bury one's head in the sand of moral relativism.

3.5 Sociobiology and Evolutionary Psychology

In traditional approaches to natural law ethics, we find a principle of life that directs each organism to its own preservation. Following

---

29. James Rachels, *The Elements of Moral Philosophy* (New York: McGraw-Hill, 2002); Michael Ruse, *Can a Darwinian be a Christian? The Relationship between Science and Religion* (New York: Cambridge University Press, 2001).

30. Rachels, *Elements of Moral Philosophy*, 25–26.

Aristotle, Aquinas saw that the function of each non-human organism was the perpetuation of the species. Even though these organisms do not consciously direct themselves to their own self-preservation and perpetuation of the species, some principle operates to govern this behavior. There is, thus, a teleological principle that functions in all living beings. Since humans are also animals, it follows that there must be principles at work in them that do not rise to the level of consciousness, but yet still operate in such a way as to preserve the individual as well as the species.

In his provocative and controversial work, *The Selfish Gene*, Richard Dawkins contends that all human behavior is based upon genetic foundations.[31] These foundations, Dawkins argues, have a long evolutionary history of survival, and they determine to a large extent how humans behave. After eons of time, proteins evolved from the primordial soup. These molecules copied themselves repeatedly, and eventually various strands of DNA developed. The role of DNA is to copy itself and inform the organism, so that it can perform those tasks necessary for survival. The fundamental rule is that the DNA directs all organisms, from amoebas to apes, for the purposes of adaptation, survival, and reproduction.

Dawkins advanced the thesis that the genes function as "replicators"; these replicators' primary task is survival, by whatever means necessary. So for Dawkins, individual humans simply function as "vehicles" for the replicators' survival. Arguing in a similar vein to Dawkins, E. O. Wilson says of the genes that "the individual organism is only their vehicle, part of an elaborate device to preserve and spread them with the least possible perturbation."[32] Simply stated, human beings do not survive, but their genes can live on and on. Individual creatures come and go, but the genotype endures.

The genotype serves as the basis not only for the phenotype (i.e., the creature's physical characteristics), but also to a great extent the organism's behavior, although geographical context and historical contingencies play a significant part as well. Just as non-human animals act according to the evolutionary development of their own genes, so humans are also subject to the same kind of genotypical tyranny.

31. Richard Dawkins, *The Selfish Gene* (New York: Oxford University Press, 1989).
32. E. O. Wilson, *Sociobiology: The New Synthesis* (Cambridge, MA: Harvard University Press, 1975), 3.

According to Dawkins, our genes have programmed us to compete with other conspecifics for valuable resources. Those more successful at securing food, shelter, and reputation have a greater chance to reproduce successfully. And on the sociobiological account, we will attempt to perpetuate our genes any which way we can. Sexual reproduction provides the simplest means of accomplishing this purpose. However, our genes have also programmed us to avoid sexual reproduction with close relatives.

In the late nineteenth century, the noted anthropologist Edward Westermarck demonstrated that all cultures (with rare exceptions) have taboos on marrying one's close relatives.[33] One could easily argue that evolutionary constraints select against incest for three reasons. First, incest runs contrary to the evolutionary tendency toward fitness, because the offspring of incestuous relationships typically suffer from mental and physical deficiencies. Wilson attempts to demonstrate that cultural taboos on incest are simply normative expressions for avoiding a biologically risky behavior. This taboo, observed across almost all human cultures, seems to be so rooted in human nature that there is a natural aversion to it. Corroborating observations of other primates indicate that incest is exceedingly rare, something observed only in primates with abnormal temperaments. Even though human cultures articulate the taboo in various ways, it appears that there is a natural urge to avoid incestuous relations so that different cultures may vary in the ways they understand "close relatives." There seems to be a universal avoidance of parent-child and sibling-sibling sexual encounters. But what explanation can we give for this natural avoidance? According to Wilson, there are numerous reasons to avoid incest since the resulting offspring often have damaging or deadly deformities.

The harmful consequences of incestuous relations result from the fact that, on any given pair of chromosomes, there will be two potential sites that carry lethal genes. These sites will differ from person to person, but the closer the kinship relation the greater the chances the lethal gene will manifest itself.

> Only one of the two homologous chromosomes in the affected pair carries lethals at the site; the other homologous chromosome carries a

---

33. Edward Westermarck, *The History of Human Marriage*, 3 vols. (New York; Allerton Book Company, 1922).

normal gene, which overrides the effects of the lethal gene. The reason is the lethality itself. When both chromosomes carry a lethal gene at a particular site, the fetus is aborted or the child dies in infancy. . . . The total effect is that early mortality of children born of incest is about twice that of outbred children, and among those that survive, genetic defects such as dwarfism, heart deformities, severe mental retardation, deaf-mutism, enlargement of the colon and urinary tract abnormalities are ten times more common.[34]

Because the risk to potential offspring is exceedingly high, taboos will naturally arise. However, it may also be the case that the high parental investment in deformed offspring also presents a sociobiological account for the incest taboo.[35] Parents who have deformed children must have a higher parental investment in the deformed child than in other children, thus risking valuable resources on this one child. Furthermore, there is a high probability that the deformed child will not survive, or, if it does, it will have a great deal of difficulty in reproducing.

Wilson claims this avoidance of incest reveals an innate tendency to experience moral emotions. These emotions have been shaped and adapted by natural selection with the result that they have become heritable traits all humans possess. The development of various emotions—especially guilt and shame—serves the evolutionary interests of the genes.

Second, since there is this problem of fitness associated with incest, humans, by means of natural selection, tend to feel a sexual aversion for those to whom they are closely related.[36] Third, the natural avoidance of incest results in a moral prohibition on the practice within all cultures.

Various studies on incest seem to confirm Westermarck's views. Arthur Wolf has shown that in China boys and girls raised from childhood together for the purposes of marriage tend to have less sexual satisfaction in their marriages than those who are not raised together.[37] Likewise, Israeli children on the kibbutzim, raised like siblings do not

34. Wilson, *Consilience: The Unity of Knowledge* (New York: Vintage Books, 1998), 188–9.
35. This argument is my own, based upon parental investment theory. Although it is not one of Wilson's arguments in *Consilience*, it is clearly one that can be used by the sociobiologist.
36. Ibid., 190.
37. Arthur Wolf, "Childhood Association and Sexual Attraction: A Further Test of theWestermarck Hypothesis," *American Anthropologist* 72 (1970): 503–15.

marry, as they tend to view their companions as brothers or sisters but not as potential spouses.[38]

Closely related to the incest avoidance issue is the practice of sexual fidelity. From the perspective of sociobiology, it would seem that sexual fidelity is a moral norm that would result from the evolution of sexual strategies. If we turn our attention to how early human societies and sexual strategies developed, we can discover a basis for sexual fidelity.[39] Women would always know that the fetus they carried was their own. However, men would not possess this knowledge. Men would never know whether the child was theirs or whether it belonged to someone else. Therefore, men would fear cuckoldry more than anything else in the marriage relationship. Women would fear abandonment—the fear of a life without a man investing in the lives of the children would create serious difficulties.[40]

One can see then that cultures would develop rules regarding fidelity and marriage to regulate and order the sexual and nurturing desires all humans possess. Adultery would be forbidden for at least two reasons. First, adultery jeopardizes the paternity of the father. Individuals living in societies that practice primogeniture would come to value rules prohibiting adultery, since economic and social status depended on paternity. Polyandry and adultery, if practiced on a grand scale, would have had dire consequences, since men would not know which children were theirs and which were not. As a result, they would not likely invest in children born to their partners. If there was doubt concerning the paternity of the child, there would be greater likelihood of low parental investment; and since children require a great deal of care from both parents, many children might die, or at least be seriously dis-"advantaged" as a result.

A second reason for rules promoting sexual fidelity would be for the benefit of the woman. The custom of the dowry insured the faith-

---

38. S. Parker, "The Precultural Basis of the Incest Taboo: Towards a Biosocial Theory," *American Anthropologist* 78 (1976): 285–305.

39. The use of the term fidelity is intentional, as opposed to polygamy, since polygamy (as well as monogamy) entails the notion of commitment to the spouse. Early human societies may have practiced polygamy, but it may have been due to economic considerations—e.g., a shortage of males who may have perished in military pursuits.

40. In the early evolutionary environment men would obviously not have access to modern methods of paternity testing and women would not have the freedom they now possess.

fulness of the husband and simultaneously facilitated fidelity among other couples in the tribe. Women need not fear abandonment, because the rules of marriage would coerce men to be faithful to their own offspring.

We begin to see the link between norms concerning sexual reproduction and care for the offspring. Humans, like other mammals, are "k-selected." That is, mammals have relatively few offspring, but those offspring require a great deal of parental investment. In contrast, reptiles are "r-selected." They have many offspring, of which only a few will survive. The difference between k-selection and r-selection is one of quality versus quantity. In humans, the infant needs high levels of investment from both parents, for which there seem to be both biological and cultural reasons.

In some mammalian species (e.g., grizzly bears) the male merely contributes the sperm, and the female carries the remaining burden of caring for the young. Human infants, however, are not bears and cannot survive without a good deal of male parental investment (MPI). Stephen Post observes that males help in nurturing the young because

> (1) women have relatively narrow birth canals as a result of the narrow pelvis associated with walking upright; (2) the heads of babies became larger and larger to provide room for the evolving brain; and (3) as a result of (1) and (2), human infants are born very prematurely, requiring intense maternal investment (of the sort that hampers her food gathering). Men with high MPI were necessary for protection and provision.[41]

We can supplement Post's biological arguments for high levels of male parental investment with cultural arguments for male parental investment.

Human children who come from single-parent homes often suffer from disadvantages that children from two-parent homes do not. Numerous studies indicate that children from single-parent households have less education, higher stress levels, and experience economic hardship.[42] From the perspective of natural selection, these factors clearly place children from single-parent homes at a disadvantage.

41. Stephen Post, *Unlimited Love: Altruism, Compassion, and Service* (Philadelphia: Templeton Foundation Press, 2003), 94.

42. Paul R. Amato, "Children of Divorce in the 1990s: An Update of the Amato and Keith (1990) Meta-Analysis," *Journal of Family Psychology* 15, no. 3 (2001): 355–70.

Rules concerning sexual reproduction and the care of the young account for only some constraints on social interaction. Not only do we need to care for those who share our genes, we must also practice tolerance for those with whom we must live.

From the perspective of sociobiology, it can be seen that cultures would create rules prohibiting murder by reflection on two biological tendencies: kin selection theory and reciprocal altruism. Kin selection theory holds that those biological organisms most closely related will practice benevolent behavior toward each other and more hostile behavior toward "outsiders." Indeed, some organisms may even forego reproduction in order to raise the offspring of a close relative. William Hamilton first developed this approach to explain the behavior of *hymenoptera*(i.e., bees, ants, and wasps).[43] For example, a worker bee might act in ways that would not favor its own reproduction, but would favor the reproduction of a close "relative," that is, the queen. Female bees, since they have both mothers and fathers, are distinguished from male bees, which have only mothers. Females will, therefore, have a full set of chromosomes, while males have only half a set. On this view, females have a 75 percent genetic relatedness to their sisters, while they would have only a 50 percent relatedness to their own daughters. Hamilton held that sisters would have a greater evolutionary interest in practicing cooperation with their sisters than with their own daughters, and this prediction was empirically confirmed. Thus, it is possible to see how a "coefficient of relatedness" can anticipate the potential benefit to an organism relative to the cost.

Yet kin selection is not the only explanation for apparently benevolent behavior in animals. Not only will some animals engage in prosocial behavior toward their biological relations, many will practice a *quid pro quo* relationship with others. Two well-known examples in non-humans demonstrate how reciprocal altruism works.

G. S. Wilkinson has shown that vampire bats will share blood meals with other roost mates.[44] Since vampire bats can live only three days without a blood meal, frequent access to blood is critical to their well-being. On any given night, up to 33 percent of juveniles and 7 percent

43. William Hamilton, "The Genetic Evolution of Social Behavior, I and II," *Journal of Theoretical Biology* 7 (1964): 1–52.

44. G. S. Wilkinson, "Reciprocal Food Sharing in Vampire Bats," *Nature* 308 (1984): 181–84; G. S. Wilkinson, "Food Sharing in Vampire Bats," *Scientific American* 262 (1990): 76–82.

of adults will not be successful in locating a blood meal on their own. However, successful bats will share their blood meals by regurgitating blood for their roost mates. One interesting point to note is that this practice is found not only among bats who are related (which is not surprising), but also among those that do not have a significant coefficient of relatedness.

Another example of reciprocal altruism is Frans de Waal's studies of captive chimpanzees.[45] According to de Waal's research, chimpanzees would "exchange" grooming behavior for food. Thus, if one chimpanzee would groom another up to two hours before feeding time, the second chimpanzee would be much more likely to share his food with the "groomer" than if no grooming had taken place. This *quid pro quo* relationship seems to facilitate group cooperation—a critical factor for the survival of any social mammalian species.

We have seen the principle of cooperation at work in non-rational animals. Various social animals must cooperate in order for their herd or pack to survive, but this does not mean that all forms of cooperation are strictly moral. It does, however, mean that cooperation may serve as a necessary condition for morality. On the human level cooperation, in the form of non-maleficence and honesty, serves as the basis for social organization and cohesion. Holmes Rolston has argued that human forms of cooperation must rise above that of non-rational animals, because only rational animals can make a "social contract" and only in this context does the concept of "cheating" begin to take on meaning.

> Yes, one ought to cooperate; yes, that is in fact what produces the greatest good for the greatest number. Yes, if everybody else cheated, one would suffer. If one is caught, one is penalized, is ostracized and loses. But one might not be caught, and so could gain at the expense of others. Left to one's calculating self-interest, "cheating" seems promising, if risky. . . . The selfishness that is deplorable arises when persons are unable to rise from the defense of life proper at the animal level to a moral level proper to human destiny.[46]

45. F. B. M. De Waal, "The Chimpanzee's Service Economy: Food for Grooming," *Evolution and Human Behavior* 18 (1997): 375–86; F. B. M. de Waal, "Food Transfers Through Mesh in Brown Capuchins," *Journal of Comparative Psychology* 111 (1998): 370–78.
46. Holmes Rolston, *Genes, Genesis and God: Values and Their Origins in Natural and Human History* (New York: Cambridge University Press, 1999), 226.

Cheating always presents a temptation to defect. Yet the possibility that one will be caught will dissuade many from cheating. Game theoretic situations present a plausible account of why we should not cheat.

Frequent encounters with other members of a community constitute a salient aspect of reciprocal altruism. Without the expectation of another encounter there is no compelling reason to cooperate with the other. However, if one anticipates frequent encounters, then cooperation becomes an important aspect of communal life.

Game theory, especially the Prisoners' Dilemma (PD), attempts to explain elements of rational choice in situations where cooperation and defection are both available options.[47] The PD occurs when each player pursues her self-interest to the point where self-interest is not maximized. Yet if the player cooperates, she jeopardizes the little she knows she can have. In a PD we imagine that there are two people arrested for the commission of a crime. The district attorney presents both suspects with two options: confess to the crime and defect on one's partner, or refuse to talk to the district attorney and cooperate with the partner in a code of silence. However, if one refuses to talk and the other confesses to the crime, the confessor (or defector) gets off easy, while the partner does hard time. The result of this kind of game theoretic situation is that both players have a dominant strategy to defect.

We see below how a PD is configured. When both players cooperate, they each net 3 units of satisfaction. However, when one player defects and the other cooperates, the defector nets 5 units while the cooperator gets 0. And when both players defect, they each net 1 unit.

Column Player

		Cooperate	Defect
Row Player	Cooperate	**3, 3**	**0, 5**
	Defect	**5, 0**	**1, 1**

47. Game theory has traditionally assumed that rational choice strategies determine the various outcomes of the PD. However, Turner and Chao have isolated an instance of bacteriophages that seem to operate in the same way as "rational agents" in a PD scenario. P. E. Turner and L. Chao, "Prisoners' Dilemma in an RNA Virus," *Nature* 398 (1999): 441–43.

In a non-iterated **PD**, the dominant strategy is to defect and hope the other player cooperates. But in an iterated **PD**, cooperation emerges as a dominant strategy since both players realize that mutual defection is sub-optimal. Seen in terms of an iterated **PD**, cooperation, or a strategy of reciprocal altruism, makes evolutionary sense as it maximizes a player's interests. The elements of cooperation are as follows:

1. avoidance of unnecessary conflict by cooperating as long as the other player does
2. provocability in the face of an uncalled-for defection by the other
3. forgiveness after responding to a provocation
4. clarity of behavior so that the other player can adapt to your pattern of action [48]

Since cooperation is essential for the basis of social harmony, there must be a *prima facie* tendency against conflict. Enlightened self-interest requires cooperation.

Provocability also seems to play a significant role. If one is engaged in frequent encounters with another who will never retaliate, then there seems to be no point in not defecting. There may be an occasional "universal cooperator"—one who always cooperates regardless of what the other does—whom one may take advantage of. However, if the other does retaliate, then the strategy must be adjusted in order to facilitate self-interest.

When defection does occur, forgiveness becomes an important factor, especially when one lives in close proximity with the other and has frequent encounters with the other. The strategy "massive retaliator" fails miserably in game theory competitions because it never returns to cooperation after a defection on the part of the other player.

Finally, clarity of behavior enables others to adjust to the player's practices. When one employs a tit-for-tat strategy, others can expect the player who employs tit-for-tat to always respond "in kind." Defection calls for defection and cooperation calls for cooperation. Consistent practices result in a reputation that others can rely upon.

48. Robert Axelrod, *The Evolution of Cooperation* (New York: Basic Books, 1984), 21.

A strategy of cheating in an iterated dilemma situation makes little sense as there is little likelihood that one can defect consistently and successfully while simultaneously promoting social cooperation. As a result, we see humans making rules for their social interactions. "Be nice to others." "Share your candy with your sister." "Don't be the first one to throw a punch." And so on. The rules we develop governing our relationships with others are cultural products that reflect the synthesis of both culture and nature. We see a convergence of biological factors (kin selection and reciprocal altruism) and cultural influences (moral sanctions) on the evolution of human cooperation.

The application to the issue of murder becomes obvious. In early hominid societies, the community consisted largely of those to whom one was related. The good of the society was critical to the good of the individual member. Thus, prohibitions on arbitrarily taking the life of a valuable member of the community would naturally evolve.

Recent research seems to corroborate these ideas concerning the evolutionary basis for prohibitions on harming one's close relatives. Daly and Wilson, in their study on homicides in the city of Detroit from the late 1970s to the early 1980s, collected data on murder rates and focused upon the relatedness of the murderer to the victim.[49] Their research showed that a homicide victim was much more likely to be unrelated to the murderer than to be one's own kin. Indeed, they determined that a stepchild was 100 times likelier to be murdered by a stepparent than a natural parent. This may suggest that, as advocates of sociobiology would contend, there is a natural disposition to protect and nurture one's offspring, while investing in offspring that are not one's own is foolish from an evolutionary perspective.

However, one could also see the prohibition on murder develop on the basis of reciprocal altruism. One needs to practice benevolence to others in the community in order for others to act benevolently to oneself. Just as vampire bats share blood meals with other bats and later receive the same assistance, and as primates may exchange grooming for food, human practices of benevolence may have developed in an evolutionary process such that murder could never have evolved as a culturally sanctioned activity.

It could be argued that in many early human societies murder was prohibited on the basis of inclusive fitness and reciprocal altruism.

49. M. Daly and M. Wilson, *Homicide* (New York: Aldine de Gruyter, 1988).

The prohibition on killing non-group members would be lifted, as there would be little chance of relatedness as well as little chance of iterated encounters with the non-group members. In any case, it appears that murder is a prohibition that encourages "in-group niceness," while war may be encouraged as a means of "out-group nastiness."[50]

David Sloan Wilson and Elliott Sober have argued that groups of altruists fare better than groups of egoists.[51] Those who practice pro-social behavior within the group will flourish, and so will groups populated by these individuals. In contrast, groups of egoists will suffer, since individual egoists will press their own advantage at the expense of the group; and thus the entire group will be undermined from within. Those groups that tolerate murder and violence toward others within the group will not—one may be inclined to say "cannot"—do as well as those groups that forbid murder.

As we have seen, there are philosophical as well as biological reasons for the adoption of non-maleficence. In addition to the prohibition on harming others, human societies also require honesty. Natural law theory has always maintained that lying runs counter to the common good of society. Is this really so, or is it merely an attempt to gain cooperation from as many others as possible? Although there may be pressures to lie, these can and must be overcome. It appears that two evolutionary principles may account for the enduring need for honesty necessary for human community.

Honesty may have developed as an effect of humanity's social nature. Because humans evolved the capacity for speech, language naturally played a critical role in social interactions. Language became important for many purposes: determining how to organize a hunt, understanding what was wrong with a young child, or locating

50. Craig A. Boyd, "Just War Theory, Natural Law Morality and Evolutionary Psychology" in *Studies in Science and Theology* 10 (2005): 45–57.

51. Wilson and Sober's use of the term "altruist" simply signifies individuals who practice pro-social behavior. See Elliott Sober and David Sloan Wilson, *Unto Others: The Evolution and Psychology of Unselfish Behavior* (Cambridge, MA: Harvard University Press, 1998). "Group selection favors within-group niceness *and* between-group nastiness. Group selection theory does not abandon the idea of competition that forms the core of the theory of natural selection; rather, it provides an additional setting in which competition can occur. Not only do individuals compete with other individuals in the same group; in addition, groups compete with other groups," 9 (emphasis in the original).

a source of food. Those who were more adept at using the language could gain power by their facility with the language. An almost universal principle from the Chinese to the Greeks was that the storytellers had a significant place in these ancient societies.[52]

Another important function of language is the communication of relevant information about one's neighbors. Gossip, that is, "reporting to others in the community what you have been doing," becomes an important factor in human relationships. One can quickly develop a reputation as a bad person if one is caught lying to others and fabricating the truth. Members of a society will cease to converse and interact with those who are untrustworthy, thereby making it difficult for the liar to gain cooperation, secure a spouse, and gain status, among other things. Social stigma places pressure on the members of a community in ways that it is difficult to overestimate.

A second argument for honesty in human communities concerns the role of lie detection. Autonomic responses, such as blushing, averting one's eyes, and voice modulation are telltale signs of deception. Law enforcement officers are trained to look for these giveaway signs in suspects. And yet, it may be possible that in order to avoid detection some individuals may develop the ability to control some autonomic responses. If an individual can convince herself that the lie is the truth, then the deception may work. In the popular sitcom *Seinfeld* the expert liar, George Costanza, explains to Jerry the secret of his success at deception: "It's not a lie, Jerry, . . . if you believe it!" Yet, deception as a *modus operandi* risks all the agent has and may ever get. If the autonomic responses don't reveal the liar for who she really is, then discovery of the lie is still an ever-present deterrent, since the deception may be revealed in other ways. So what do these data tell us about human morality?

It may be the case that, although we may have evolved to take advantage of each and every situation, honesty really is the best policy. Lying carries too many risks. We may give ourselves away by blushing, sweating, or by giving evasive answers under questioning. We

52. Eric Havelock has famously argued that, according to Plato, the greatest threat to ancient Greek education and culture was not the Sophists but the poets, since their abilities with language seemed to shape the entire Greek ethos by means of their positive portrayal of characters that were oftentimes less than admirable. *Preface to Plato* (Cambridge, MA: Belknap Press, 1982).

may be found out by those who really know the truth, even when we don't think that is possible. And in the end, gossip functions as an effective deterrent to prevent us from becoming pathological liars. We risk what may be our most valuable resource—our reputation—when we lie. Once again, we see that evolution may have shaped us in such a way that lying is not only problematic from the adaptationist perspective; it also violates the natural law.

3.6 The Value of Sociobiology and Evolutionary Psychology

Sociobiology and evolutionary psychology provide us with plausible conditions, or at least proximate causes, for why humans evolved specific moral behaviors and codes. It would seem that suicide, lying, murder, and incest, among other behaviors, are neither evolutionarily adaptive strategies, nor are they possible candidates for a moral code in any society. But why?

Given what we know about the drives to survive, to procreate, and to engage in social relations, it would seem that only certain kinds of behaviors could contribute to social cooperation, successful strategies for survival, and procreation. Sociobiology considers the biological element in morality a *sine qua non* for any account of human ethics. If ethics is concerned with "the good," as various thinkers from Aristotle and Augustine to Moore and MacIntyre contend, then we must begin with a preliminary account of the good. No account of the good that excludes the biological can, or should, be taken seriously. Moreover, sociobiology provides a plausible explanation for the source of these biological conditions for morality.

According to Michael Ruse, evolved behavior serves as a "proximate cause" for human morality. Without it human society would not be possible.

> The sociobiological claim is that in the case of humans we are genetically predetermined to think in certain ways, so that in specified situations we will incline to act in certain ways. And the genetic predetermination manifests itself as a moral sense: an awareness of certain rules or guides, which are binding upon us—the prescriptions of normative ethics.[53]

53. Ruse, *Can a Darwinian be a Christian?* 194.

We therefore see how the normative rules for ethics may have evolved. The genetic basis for the evolution of human morality is rooted in the problem of social cooperation. As human beings evolved, they required cooperation as a survival mechanism. Natural selection tended to favor those disposed to cooperation. These dispositions were held to be genetically heritable traits that included such social emotions as sympathy, love, guilt, and shame. Over the passage of time, humans developed rules to regulate behavior based upon the need for cooperation and the concomitant emotions that had evolved. Thus, raw biological emotions were curtailed by rules which rewarded cooperators and punished violators.

On this view, human nature can be seen as a synthesis of genetic predispositions as altered by cultural norms, both of which are the products of an evolutionary process. In addition to our genes and the role culture plays, Wilson says that our nature is further constituted by "the epigenetic rules, the hereditary regularities of mental development that bias cultural evolution in one direction as opposed to another, and thus connect the genes to culture."[54] Sociobiology provides an explanation of why some moral norms may be rooted in human nature, but it does not consider the more complex developments of human culture and rational reflection on the value of those norms. That is, biology may provide a necessary condition for human morality, but it does not constitute a sufficient condition.

These biological prerequisites for morality extend not merely to local human societies; they are adaptive strategies for all humans, regardless of their environmental context. Certainly some behaviors will be unique to various locales and cultural contexts; however, the need for social cooperation, defense of the community, competition for sexual partners, and care for the young are all universal human behaviors. Even though some cultures practice polygamy and others practice monogamy, the basic principle of sexual fidelity remains constant. Sexual behavior must be regulated, given the extraordinary emotional attachment involved, and the considerable importance of paternity. Sociobiologists, in contrast to relativists, claim that human beings must engage in pro-social activities in order to survive and reproduce. However, it is precisely this issue—the human being's primary and only drive for survival and reproduction—that

54. Wilson, *Consilience*, 164.

embroils sociobiologists in philosophical discourse that exceeds their competence.

3.7 The Limits of Sociobiological Explanations

Critics have raised at least two serious problems for sociobiology. First, if all behavior is fitness-enhancing, then how is it possible for humans to practice behaviors that are genuinely altruistic? Second, how is it possible to adjudicate among a variety of natural impulses?

Sociobiological accounts of morality, as presented by Dawkins and Wilson, attempt to be explanations of the entire spectrum of human behavior. But as Stephen Pope has observed, "The primary flaw found in sociobiology is its tendency to see the human organism and not the human person."[55] Wilson's approach is to reduce all moral principles to biological explanations. Although Dawkins believes that human nature is simply the result of millions of years of surviving "replicators," he suggests that humans should resist the power of the genes by appealing to the power of moral inculturation. For both Wilson and Dawkins, the human agent's ability to resist the power of the biological is a problem yet to be solved.

Christian Smith has argued that although kin selection theory may operate nicely in the world of bees and ants, it hardly seems a plausible explanation for non-fitness-enhancing behavior in humans. If kin selection theory worked for humans, "then people would only be altruistic to those who share their genes, and only in rough proportion to the extent that they do share their genes—children would elicit more altruism than, say, nieces and nephews. But that very often is not the case. People frequently do sacrifice themselves in various ways for people who do not share their genes, even sometimes for foreigners and strangers."[56] Moreover, it seems impotent to explain

---

55. Stephen J. Pope, *The Evolution of Altruism and the Ordering of Love* (Washington, DC: Georgetown University Press, 1994), 120.

56. Christian Smith, *Moral, Believing Animals: Human Personhood and Culture* (New York: Oxford University Press, 2003), 35–6; Pope makes a similar point when he says, "Sociobiology here is apparently subject to a refutation by *reductio ad absurdum*: that we should say, care more for a third cousin three times removed than for a nonrelated individual, since we at least share some of the same genes with the former compared to the latter. Kin favoritism is after all only one of the variables in human assistance-giving." *The Evolution of Altruism*, 114.

the self-sacrificial behavior of martyrs and others who risk their lives not only for strangers, but also for enemies.[57]

On a related point, one may also object to the use of game theory as an explanation of human behavior. Although game theoretic structures may prove useful in the world of international diplomacy and strategy, it is difficult to see how it might help explain the behavior of those individuals who are willing to sacrifice their own lives and genetic progeny for a complete stranger, since it assumes that economic notions of rationality dominate all human decision-making.

The third major criticism of sociobiology concerns our competing desires. We can always ask, "How is it that any human creature is able to adjudicate among competing natural impulses?" Is it merely the stronger impulse? If Mary Midgley is correct in suggesting that contemporary defenders of sociobiology follow Hume, then one must wonder if reason really is the slave of the passions: "How is it supposed to know which of them to obey?"[58] If a Christian under persecution had to decide to recant the faith or go into the Coliseum to face the lions, what natural impulse urged her to choose martyrdom? The natural law incorporates the biological tendencies humans have into a coherent account of practical rationality, something sociobiological explanations cannot account for. In this light Leo Elders says, "There is no question of a blind submission to biological structures, but to *human* law. The natural law is not a set of biological principles. It consists in the insight and command of our reason telling us that in a particular field we must act in this way or refrain from performing a particular action."[59] Unless humans do not have the capacity to adjudicate among competing desires (including the organic, biological, and human), then the stronger passion always wins. But this is plainly false, as the recurrence of martyrdom and celibacy proves. What this calls for is a developed human capacity to judge among competing goods, and to deliberate well in various circumstances. In short, what is needed is a theory of virtue.[60]

57. A particularly dramatic example of this is Paul Rusesabagina, whose story is chronicled in Philip Gourevitch's *We Wish to Inform You That Tomorrow We Will Be Killed With Our Families* (New York: Picador, 1998).

58. Midgley, *Beast and Man*, 184.

59. Leo Elders, "Nature as the Basis of Moral Action," *Sapientia* 56, no. 210 (2001): 565–88.

60. I devote all of chapter 7 to a discussion of natural law and virtue ethics.

3.8 Memetic Explanations

Dawkins has particular difficulty in explaining the persistence of non-fitness-enhancing behaviors such as celibacy and martyrdom. He acknowledges that the sociobiological account is limited. "Kin selection and selection in favour of reciprocal altruism may have acted on human genes to produce many of our basic psychological attributes and tendencies. These ideas are plausible as far as they go, but I find that they do not begin to square up with the challenge of explaining culture, cultural evolution and the immense differences between human culture around the world."[61] In order to explain how humans could have evolved in order to resist their genes, Dawkins develops memetic theory.

As genes desire their own survival, so memes (i.e., units of culturally developed ideas) also have a drive to survive.[62] Susan Blackmore has taken Dawkins's idea of the meme and employed it vigorously as an attack on religion, morality, and ontological descriptions that defy genetic explanations. According to Blackmore, "when you imitate someone else, something is passed on. This 'something' can then be passed on again, and again, and so take on a life of its own. We might call this thing an idea, an instruction, a behavior, a piece of information."[63] Indeed, this is what makes humans unique among all the animals—our memetic behavior. Although other animals have the capacity to learn and mimic sounds of other animals, only humans can invent ideas and pass them on to others. Only humans can create systems of ideas, information, and art. This power makes the human species *sui generis*.

Memetic transmission is unique to human culture. Just as human bodies serve as the vehicles for genes, human brains serve as the vehicles for memes. Dawkins says, "Just as genes propagate themselves in the gene pool by leaping from body to body via sperm or eggs, so memes propagate themselves in the meme pool by leaping from brain to brain by a process which, in the broad sense of the term, can be called imitation."[64] As a result, ideas such as God, truth, the

61. Dawkins, *The Selfish Gene*, 191.
62. Ibid., 180.
63. Susan Blackmore, *The Meme Machine* (Oxford: Oxford University Press, 1999), 4.
64. Dawkins, *The Selfish Gene*, 192.

soul, love, and altruism are all memes that have an extraordinarily high capacity to survive and spread from person to person. But the meme for altruism has certain problems that the others don't. There may be a plausible reason for the explanation of the God meme—it was helpful in getting social cooperation from resistant individuals. However, the altruism meme seems to fly in the face of fitness theory. How could a meme that encourages non-fitness-enhancing behavior survive?

On the sociobiological interpretation, there are three possible ways to interpret "altruistic behavior."[65] The first is by appealing to the processes of kin selection theory and reciprocal altruism. Any behavior that benefits another is simply a *modus operandi* for self-interest. Either one's genes benefit, in the case of assisting one's nieces and nephews, or else one's own prospects of survival are enhanced, as in the case of helping another with the expectation to be helped at a later date (i.e., altruistic behavior is an investment in the future).

A second way of interpreting altruistic behavior is by appealing to a capacity that transcends biological and psychological explanation. One can invoke religious or philosophical theories to account for human morality and the apparently altruistic behaviors that they recommend. Sociobiologists like Dawkins and Blackmore, however, view this approach as illegitimate. Blackmore argues that this approach "has been to try to rescue 'true' altruism and propose some kind of extra something in human beings—a true morality, an independent moral conscience, a spiritual essence or a religious nature that somehow overcomes selfishness and the dictates of our genes; a view that finds little favour with most scientists who want to understand how human behaviour works without invoking magic."[66] Apparently, according to Blackmore, philosophy and theology are shamanistic

65. Blackmore and others prefer to use the term "altruistic." According to Blackmore, altruism "is defined as behaviour that benefits another creature at the expense of the one carrying it out. In other words, altruism means doing something that costs time, effort, or resources, for the sake of someone else," *The Meme Machine*, 147. This definition, however, turns out to amount to nothing more than what others have labeled "pro-social" behavior. Genuine altruism, in contrast to Blackmore's definition, seems to amount to something more than kin selection and reciprocity. According to Ralston, "altruism in the ethical sense applies where a moral agent consciously and optionally benefits a morally considerable other, without necessary reciprocation, motivated by a sense of love, justice, or other appropriate respect of value." *Genes, Genesis and God*, 217.

66. Blackmore, *The Meme Machine*, 154.

tools used to control the masses while scientists like herself toil away in the never-ending quest for truth.

The third approach, preferred by Dawkins and Blackmore, appeals to memetics, which occupies the virtuous mean between what they see as the vain speculations of metaphysics on the one hand, and the oversimplifications of biology on the other. Blackmore says, "With a second replicator acting on human minds and brains the possibilities are expanded. We should expect to find behaviour that is in the interests of the memes, as well as behaviour serving the genes."[67] The argument for memetic approaches to morality is a simple one.

1. If people act in altruistic ways, then they will be popular.
2. Others imitate the behavior of popular people more frequently than unpopular people.

Therefore, altruism (as a characteristic of popular people) will spread throughout populations and—*voila!*—morality is born.

The more popular an individual is, the more offspring he or she is likely to leave. Therefore, genes and memes work together in establishing pro-social behavior, which they transmit biologically through their genes, and culturally through their memes.

The memes for morality embed themselves into various religious and moral systems that require allegiance. The memes therefore preserve themselves and transmit themselves to others. Ideas such as the soul, God, natural law, and beauty are all memes. These memes are transferred from human brain to brain, and their survival is predicated upon their ability to function in culturally significant ways. For example, the God meme has the ability to elicit cooperation from people by threatening them with the prospect of hell as a means to gain compliance. Interrelated complexes of memes—God, hell, sin and salvation, for example—can be called "memeplexes."

Among the more insidious memes are memes for "truth" and "reason," since they seem to appeal to some transcendence beyond themselves. By their very nature some memes, such as religion, have a truth meme embedded into the memeplex; that is, into "groups of memes that are replicated together."[68] Yet we need not worry that there is truth in religion or in morality since "truth," like "religion,"

67. Ibid., 154.
68. Ibid., 19.

is merely a meme that has happened to have a very good survival rate.

Blackmore believes that science, like religion, appeals to the "truth" meme. But in the case of science, it really does get at the truth, and the truth is that religions are memes that are false but indestructible. Dawkins has said, "It is fashionable to wax apocalyptic about the threat to humanity posed by the AIDS virus, "mad cow" disease, and many others, but I think a case can be made that faith is one of the world's great evils, comparable to the smallpox virus but harder to eradicate."[69]

In contrast to the fictitious memes of religion, scientific memes actually have a helpful role to play in society. Science is "fundamentally a process; a set of methods for trying to distinguish true memes from false ones. . . . Religions provide nice, appealing and comforting ideas, and cloak them in a mask of 'truth, beauty and goodness.' The theories can then thrive in spite of being untrue, ugly or cruel."[70] Science paves the way for the sure road to truth and enlightenment, while religion subjugates its adherents to lives of cruelty and perpetual falsehoods. And yet, strangely, science has not been able to eradicate the religion memeplex.

Sociobiologists argue that it is possible for memes to enable humans to resist the power of the genes. A specific instance of the meme's ability to resist biology is the issue of celibacy. Since a gene for celibacy cannot survive (since it cannot be inherited), we must give some account of its persistence. According to Dawkins and Blackmore, it must be transferred mimetically. Some religious groups expend vast amounts of energy praising the value of celibacy and extolling its eternal value; in this way the meme survives from one generation to the next, not genetically, but mimetically. But do memes really have the explanatory power that Blackmore and Dawkins claim they have?[71]

69. Richard Dawkins, *The Humanist* (1997) vol. 57, no. 1.

70. Blackmore, *The Meme Machine*, 202–3.

71. Alister McGrath, *Dawkins' God: Genes, Memes, and the Meaning of Life* (Malden, MA: Blackwell Publishing, 2005), offers four critical objections to meme theory. "There is no reason to suppose that cultural evolution is Darwinian, or indeed that evolutionary biology has any particular value in accounting for the development of ideas. There is no direct evidence for the existence of 'memes' themselves. The case for the existence of the 'meme' rests on the questionable assumption of a direct analogy with the gene, which proves incapable of bearing the theoretical weight that is placed

Behaviors like celibacy and martyrdom continue to endure, and have not been weeded out by selection. Appealing to memes, however, is a metaphysical position that seems subject to a number of criticisms. First, it begs the question concerning the existence of such elusive entities as God and the soul. Dawkins begins by assuming that they are merely fictions, and in the end he "argues" that they really don't exist—indeed, given his own materialist metaphysic they can't exist. Dawkins' memetic theory is subject to the same criticisms as any other naively reductionistic materialism.

A second problem for meme theory is what we might call sociobiology's "anthropological dualism." That is, there seem to be two kinds of inheritance, genes and memes. But they are entirely different kinds of entities. Moreover, it is difficult to understand just how they correspond. Jeffrey Schloss raises a critical problem with this dualistic approach when he writes, "[I]t is not clear how biology gives rise to something that resists or contravenes biology."[72] That is, how could evolution operate in such a way as to promote non-fitness-enhancing characteristics such as celibacy and martyrdom? It is contradictory to suggest that biology evolves in ways in order to resist itself. A house divided against itself cannot stand.

The third and most devastating criticism of memetic theory is that it is self-defeating. How do we know which memes are true if "truth" and "science" themselves are simply memes? According to Blackmore, science is a better meme than religion because the science meme really conveys the truth; but how can she know this if all she has to work with are the memes themselves? Is there some "super-truth" meme that only she and others like her are able to know? What this reveals is that she either has to equivocate on the word "truth" or face an embarrassing dilemma.

1. If truth is simply a meme then it has no objective reference.
2. If truth is more than a meme then there is objective truth to be discovered.

---

upon it. There is no reason to propose the existence of a 'meme' as an explanatory construct. The observational data can be accounted for perfectly well by other models and mechanisms," 121.

72. Jeffrey P. Schloss, "Emerging Evolutionary Accounts of Altruism: 'Love Creation's Final Law,'" in *Altruism and Altruistic Love: Science, Philosophy and Religion in Dialogue*, ed. Stephen G. Post, Lynn G. Underwood, Jeffrey P. Schloss, and William B. Hurlbut (New York: Oxford University Press, 2002).

3. Either truth is a meme or more than a meme.
4. Therefore, truth either has no objective reference or it can be discovered.

If there is no truth available to anyone, then all the appeals to argument and references to "scientific truth" are vacuous.[73] Yet if there is truth—the hidden operative assumption of meme theorists—then one should employ all the resources science and philosophy have to offer. Summarily dismissing truth when one's opponent disagrees with your views may work for the intellectual bully or the infantile, but it hardly passes muster in serious academic debate. What this dilemma demonstrates is that reductionists like Blackmore and Dawkins either greatly underestimate the intelligence of their audience, or are simply philosophically ignorant themselves.

Blackmore and Dawkins want to argue that truth in religion is merely a mask for power, greed, and corruption. "Truth" seems to cover a multitude of intellectual sins and superstitions; or, to use Blackmore's term, religion is simply "magic." On this view, only science can attain the trans-memetic truth that enables us all to see the hoax of religion and conventional morality for what it is—a sham. What Blackmore, Dawkins, and Wilson all fail to understand is that human reason must be understood to have some normative power that transcends the merely biological. Otherwise, we are left with the silliness of the memes or some other warmed-over reductionistic rhetoric that has failed for centuries.[74]

A related problem for sociobiological understandings of ethics is that the approach conflates nature[1] with nature[3]. Sociobiology takes as its starting point the theory of evolution and its narrative of natural selection and human development. This scientific theory yields plausible accounts of how humans developed various capacities, and why some capacities have flourished and survived while others have not. As a scientific approach to human nature, sociobiology provides explanations of the evolutionary development of the human creature.

73. This point is accepted by the postmodernist, an issue we will address in further detail in chapter 4. Dawkins and Blackmore want to avoid this kind of epistemological relativism since they really believe their own views are true.

74. Cf. C. S. Lewis, *Miracles* (New York: Macmillan, 1946) for an argument against purely naturalistic explanations of reason; Victor Reppert has recently resurrected Lewis's "argument from reason" in his *C. S. Lewis's Dangerous Idea: In Defense of the Argument from Reason* (Downers Grove, IL: Intervarsity Press, 2003).

However, when sociobiologists such as Dawkins, Blackmore, and E. O. Wilson attempt to use their own reason to explain evolutionary theory; or, more significantly, when they attempt to provide arguments against religious and philosophical explanations and on behalf of their own dubious theories for memes, they have moved beyond an understanding of nature[1] and have unwittingly engaged nature[3]. The key problem is that they have failed to realize that an explanation of efficient causality, such as the one sociobiology provides, does not exclude other causal explanations, such as final or formal causality.

A more intelligent and metaphysically sophisticated understanding of nature appeals to the power of human reason and human choice, one that does not commit itself to the reductionistic tendencies of sociobiology. The wisdom of Aquinas, and others like him, was that he could see the normative power of "the true, the good, and the beautiful." These transcendentals, so conceived, did not constitute unreal Platonic universals. Rather, they operated in ways that enabled humans to perceive, to judge, and to test their insights into nature. In other words, nature[3] enables us to make judgments about the adequacy of nature[1].

3.9 Natural Law, Sociobiology, and the Normative Use of Reason

Natural law has the resources to incorporate recent research from sociobiology into its own account of human nature. In fact, one can argue that the organic and biological powers of the human agent are simply the philosophical terms for the sociobiological drives for survival and procreation.

In Dawkins's work a principle (i.e., the genotype) functions in a profoundly similar way to how advocates of natural law ethics see the organic powers of the soul. Self-preservation is a principle of organic life that humans share with all other forms of life. Although Dawkins, Wilson, and other defenders of sociobiology contend that the only *telos* operating in the genotype is self-replication, one may say that the genetically-based drive to preserve the self plays a part in all biological organisms; but it is not the only possible teleology, at least from a philosophical perspective. Dawkins's arguments clearly move from the empirical to the philosophical without the slightest hesitation.

From the sociobiologist's perspective, the taking of one's own life runs counter to the basic urge to survive and reproduce. The natural law theorist can say that this basic organic tendency provides the data for the prohibition on suicide. The defenders of natural law acknowledge that suicide runs counter to the natural urge that all life has toward self-preservation. Since life is a basic good, there is an obligation to preserve it. However, there may be occasions when risking one's life may take precedence over self-preservation (e.g., defending the life of one's children or of one's community). But in these examples the intention is not, strictly speaking, the seeking of one's own death but rather seeking some greater good. What is strictly forbidden is the act of suicide (i.e., the intentional destruction of the self), as this runs contrary to the natural impulse toward self-preservation.

Sociobiological research also seems consistent with natural law ethics with respect to sexual norms. Since humans have a natural drive to reproduce, rules necessarily apply to the issues of how and with whom this activity takes place. In human societies marriage plays the mediating role. From the standpoint of natural law, marriage functions for three purposes: procreation, raising the young, and companionship. Since marriage has these three purposes, it follows that specific behaviors will be prescribed while others will be prohibited. Because procreation is so critical, marriage serves an important cultural function in regulating sexual activity. Promiscuity is forbidden by natural law, as it undermines the paternity of the child (which would result in males failing to provide for the children). That is, if women engage in sexual relations outside the bonds of marriage, men will not have the assurance that the child who is born will be theirs and not another's. Thus cultures develop and enforce specific behaviors regarding sexual reproduction.

Marriage also serves as the institution within which raising the young takes place. Again, sociobiology and natural law ethics converge on this issue under certain conditions; animals may occasionally raise other closely related infants, but usually parents—especially primate parents—raise only their own offspring. In human culture the institution of marriage serves this purpose.

Marriage and the family provide the most basic of all human relationships. Sexual attraction and the desire to nurture our young provide necessary conditions for human morality. Furthermore, these desires also point to the fact that we are social creatures. Mothers are not left on their own to raise the infants—fathers, elder siblings, grandparents, and a web of others in the local community also facilitate this process. Marriage and familial relationships enable us to pursue the biological goods, and also serve as a prototype for our relationships with others within our human communities.

With reference to the human goods, we see yet another convergence concerning the two primary normative rules that all human societies require for their stability: non-maleficence and honesty. Research in sociobiology demonstrates that prohibitions on murder would evolve due to kin selection theory and considerations of reciprocity. No society can tolerate the indiscriminate killing of its members who contribute to the well-being of the community. Again, a primary precept of natural law is that murder is prohibited on the basis of the good of the community.

All creatures have a natural drive to preserve their own being, and interference in the natural *telos* is unwarranted. Although it may be permissible to kill nonrational animals for various reasons, we find a strict *prima facie* prohibition against killing humans, since they are ordered both to the common good of society and to God as their ultimate end. The killing of rational animals thwarts their divinely appointed *telos*, but it also disturbs their role in the common good.

Since the human community is like a natural organism, it follows that no individual good can be separated from the common good of society. Humans need each other. Children need parents for their care and nurture. Parents need their children in their declining years. Since no individual is self-sufficient, each member of the community needs the others. Human societies are natural and, therefore, one who murders "deprives the community of a greater good."[75] Communities depend on their members to promote the common good by sharing the burdens of the community. To indiscriminately kill members of the community is to act contrary to the common good.

Although sociobiology provides important elements for a natural law theory, it fails as an "explanation for everything." Natural lawyers, however, have adequate means to resolve these problems; that which pertains to the natural law as proper to humans is knowing the truth,

75. Aquinas IIaIIae.64,6,ad2.

pursuing virtue, and living peacefully in society.[76] These ends, proper to humans *qua* human, and apprehended by the intellect, point us toward that which is truly perfective of our nature. Moreover, any operation of the intellect toward the good is properly related to the natural law. So it is that the intellectual appetite pursues the truly human goods. These human goods transcend the purely biological and organic goods, because no purely animal power can endow its possessor with the capacity to grasp "the truth" or to "desire God." Commenting on this unique human capacity, Aquinas says that it is "by the intellectual appetite we may desire the immaterial good, which is not apprehended by sense, such as knowledge, virtue, and the like."[77]

This reference to the acquisition of virtue is especially important to our discussion.[78] Natural law serves as the basis for our moral drives, yet it does not spell out the details of moral behavior. Indeed, this is the reason natural law ethics requires a theory of the virtues. I postulate that anything that pertains to reason's pursuit of the good is a matter of natural law. And since the acquisition of virtue is a function of reason, it follows that the human agent's pursuit of virtue would be prescribed by the natural law. "Since the rational soul is the proper form of the human, there is thus in every human a natural inclination to act according to reason; and this is to act according to virtue. Thus, all the acts of the virtues are prescribed by natural law, since each person's reason naturally dictates to that one to act according to virtue."[79] The key point here is that all the acts of the virtues fall under the sphere of the natural law, since they are prescribed by reason. However, the natural law does not dictate precisely how one is to act according to reason. The natural law simply determines what specific kinds of actions are *per se* good, and what kinds are evil. Aquinas does not indicate in his views on natural law just how one goes about determining what kind of behavior is required, since

76. Of course, many natural lawyers include pursuing the truth about God in this list as well. Most sociobiologists would reject this as a natural desire. However, David Sloan Wilson allows for "religion" as an evolutionary adaptive strategy. If it is adaptive, then one could argue that religious practices (and possibly beliefs as well) might have their roots in evolutionary biology.

77. Ia.80.2.ad2.

78. I develop a more detailed account of the relationship between the natural law and virtue in chapter 7. At this point, I simply attempt to show why it is that the precepts of natural law, which are directed toward the human good, require the virtues.

79. IaIIae.94.3

the natural law simply indicates what Aquinas calls the "object of the act."[80] However, one must not only know what kind of act is required in any given moral situation, one must also act for the right purposes and in the right circumstances. So it is that natural law does not simply prescribe certain kinds of actions; it also requires the development of virtue, which enables a person to act consistently for the right reasons and in the right circumstances. We find a discussion of how one deliberates well and acts virtuously in Aquinas's question "On Martyrdom."

According to Aquinas, the practice of martyrdom is an act of virtue.[81] Since virtue's purpose is to "preserve a person in the good as proposed by reason," it follows that martyrdom is a human good that apparently conflicts with the organic and biological goods of self-preservation and the flight from danger. Aquinas is aware of the conflict when he says that

> A person's love for a thing is demonstrated by the degree to which, for its sake, one puts aside the more cherished object and chooses to suffer the more odious. It is manifest that among all the goods of this present life a person loves life itself the most, and on the contrary, hates death the most, and especially when accompanied by the pains of physical torture—from fear of these even brute animals are deterred from the greatest pleasures, as Augustine says.[82]

Since there is this conflict, how is it that one would willingly sacrifice his life for his faith? Martyrdom is not simply enduring suffering and death for the sake of some vaguely defined religious principle. Rather, martyrs endure death for the sake of the truth (i.e., a human good). But it is not merely any truth; it is "the truth involved in our obligation to God."[83] That is, martyrs willingly choose to die rather than renounce their faith or commit some serious offense against God (e.g., apostasy, blasphemy, or some egregious crime against humanity).

This appeal to God demonstrates the hierarchy of impulses in action. Even though we have obligations to preserve our own lives and to flee harm, we also have a greater obligation to God. Since God is the Good Itself, we recognize that no created good, even life itself, can compete

80. IaIIae.18.1
81. IIaIIae.124.1
82. IIaIIae.124.3
83. IIaIIae.124.5

with the possession of everlasting goodness. The natural hierarchy of goods that natural law requires, and human virtue enacts, enables the individual to judge among the many goods that vie for her attention. If strict sociobiological accounts were true, celibacy and martyrdom could not survive. And since we can safely reject meme theory as a plausible explanation, it seems to follow that the human capacity to reason enables the agent to act as the situation demands— against the organic and biological goods—for the sake of a higher good.

Conclusion

In this chapter I have argued that a theory of natural law may use the findings of sociobiology with reference to various organic and animal goods. Sociobiology seems to provide ample evidence for drives for self-preservation, marital practices, and prohibitions on murder that fit well with the principles of natural law. We may say that sociobiology is compatible with some versions of natural law; yet there seem to be areas of natural law ethics that transcend purely sociobiological explanations. Sociobiology encounters two significant problems as it attempts to explain non-fitness–enhancing behaviors—that is, behaviors that cannot be accounted for by appeals to inclusive fitness or reciprocal altruism.

Explanations of rational and moral behavior necessarily move beyond merely scientific explanation and must invoke philosophical explanations. Dawkins's appeal to memetic theory is the most obvious example of the move from the empirical to the philosophical. However, sociobiology's explanations now become simply one of a number of competing philosophical theories. And their value as philosophy is suspect. As Henry Plotkin has argued,

> Underlying all the biological and social sciences, the reason for it all, is the 'need' (how else to express it, perhaps 'drive' would be better) for genes to perpetuate themselves. This is a metaphysical claim, and the reductionism that it entails is . . . best labeled as metaphysical reductionism. Because it is metaphysical it is neither right nor wrong nor empirically testable. It is simply a statement of belief that genes count above all else.[84]

84. Henry Plotkin, *Evolution in Mind: An Introduction to Evolutionary Psychology* (Cambridge, MA: Harvard University Press, 1998), 94.

Plotkin's analysis of sociobiology's metaphysical reductionism is surely on target. However, one need not endorse Plotkin's skepticism regarding all metaphysics. Simply because metaphysical views are not "empirically testable," it does not mean that some are not closer to the truth than others.

An alternative philosophical theory to the one offered by sociobiology is that of natural law theory. On this view, biology plays a central role in explaining any account of human behavior. Yet the analysis of human morality is not limited entirely to the realm of biology. Natural law includes "human goods," or rational goods, in addition to the goods of our biological nature.

4 | The Religious Challenge

Divine Command Ethics

Introduction

One of the most difficult questions any theory of natural law must face concerns the relationship between the precepts of natural law and the various divine commands found in almost every religious faith. Or, in other words, what is the nature of religious authority based upon some kind of special revelation vis-a-vis the authority of the natural law as a kind of "natural revelation"? Are actions morally right because God commands them, or does God command certain actions because those actions are right in themselves? Conversely, is it God's prohibition that makes an act wrong, or is it that the act is wrong in itself? These questions have plagued devoutly religious persons since the time of Plato. Indeed, Plato's earliest dialogue, the *Euthyphro*, addresses precisely this question.[1] The dilemma that results from this disjunction can be seen in the following argument:

1. If God's command *makes* an act right, then morality is arbitrary.
2. If God commands an act *because* it is right, then God's command is not essential to morality.

1. Plato, "Euthyphro" in *Plato: The Collected Dialogues*, ed. Edith Hamilton and Huntington Cairns, trans. Lance Cooper (Princeton, NJ: Princeton University Press, 1961), 169–85.

3. Either God's command makes an act right, or God commands an act because it is right. Therefore,

4. Either morality is arbitrary, or God's command is not essential to morality.

Many religious believers have found this dilemma troubling. The person of faith finds herself torn between wanting to affirm an "objective foundation" for morality and the need to affirm God's sovereignty over all creation. Those who subscribe to divine command theory hold that the rightness of an action is determined primarily by the command of God.[2] William Frankena summarizes the divine command theory by noting "that what ultimately *makes* an action right or wrong is its being commanded by God and nothing else."[3]

On this view, God's omnipotence is not subject to some "external" standard of moral correctness. God is completely free to command whatever God chooses. And as a result, the command of God alone serves as the obligation for human creatures. Furthermore, to advance a theory of natural law is to preclude God from any significant role in ethics. Carl F. H. Henry objects that

What it excludes is a distillation of moral law from the transcendent supernatural, that is, from divine revelation. What it affirms is that all human beings share a set of ethical norms and imperatives that they commonly perceive without dependence on supernatural disclosure and illumination. Humanity, in short, universally knows a body of morally binding laws that shape a common pattern of social behavior, and

2. Defenders of divine command theory include theologians such as Emil Brunner, *The Divine Imperative: A Study in Christian Ethics*, trans. Olive Wyon (London: Lutterworth Press, 1937), and Helmut Thielicke, *Theological Ethics* vol. 1 (Philadelphia: Fortress Press, 1966); and philosophers such as Robert Merrihew Adams, "A Modified Divine Command Theory of Ethical Wrongness" in Paul Helm's *Divine Commands and Morality* (Oxford University Press, 1981), and his *Finite and Infinite Goods: A Framework for Ethics* (New York: Oxford University Press, 1999); Philip Quinn, *Divine Commands and Moral Requirements* (Oxford: Oxford University Press, 1978); John Hare, *God's Call: Moral Realism, God's Commands and Human Autonomy* (Grand Rapids: Eerdmans, 2001).

3. William Frankena, *Ethics* (Engelwood Cliffs, NJ: Prentice-Hall, 1973), 29; Adams says that "according to such a theory, God's commands are the standard, conformity to which constitutes the ethical validity of human social requirements, and the correctness of the one against another when they disagree." Robert Merrihew Adams, "The Concept of a Divine Command," in *Religion and Morality*, ed. D. Z. Philips (London: Macmillan, 1996), 59–60.

moreover knows these imperatives without reference to transcendent revelation.[4]

Defenders of divine command theory want to maintain that natural law theory abandons religious and biblical sources for ethics and replaces these sources with secular substitutes. As a result, the Bible plays a central role in the theory, as supported by the historical developments of elements in Augustine, and by his late medieval and Reformation interpreters. In what follows, I explore the origins of divine command theory, its contemporary articulations, and how a natural law theory might plausibly incorporate the important insights from an ethic of divine commands without suffering the weaknesses inherent in the latter theory.

4.1 The Divine Command Tradition

Like the tradition of natural law morality, divine command theory also traces its origins to the Bible, since most Christians believe it to be a critical source of authority.[5] Since God speaks through the scriptures, their prescriptions and prohibitions must always be taken seriously. This of course does not mean that scripture is immune from interpretation, or that some precepts that were entirely social constructs still apply. Rather, what we mean is that if God—whom Christians take to be personal—communicates to believers in and through the scriptures, then we must assign these commands a special place of authority that may transcend the political or private spheres.

In the Hebrew Scriptures we find God making various kinds of demands on people. God commands Adam and Eve, "do not eat of the fruit in the middle of the garden," and tells Abraham not only to "go to a land that I will show you," but also to "take your son, your only son Isaac to Mt. Moriah and offer him there as a sacrifice to me."

4. Carl F. H. Henry, "Natural Law in a Nihilistic Culture," *First Things* 49 (January 1995), 55.

5. Although many laypeople may consider the Bible to be the central revelation of God to humanity, it becomes clear after little reflection that Jesus Christ is the key source of revelation since "in Him the fullness of God was pleased to dwell" (Col. 1:19). No such claims are found anywhere in scripture referring to its own authority. As Luther said, "The scriptures are the cradle of the Christ-child."

The authority of God alone seems to count as a reason for engaging in (and avoiding) all sorts of behaviors.

Some of the commands seem reasonable and contribute to the well-being of society: such are the prohibitions on murder, theft, lying, and adultery as found in the Decalogue. As we have seen, these kinds of behaviors seem to evolve in groups of people who have pro-social dispositions. Yet other commands seem to be simply arbitrary: "don't eat shellfish or pork," "circumcise your male children," and "sacrifice only unblemished animals." And yet there is still one more set of commands, however rare, that seem to violate the first kind: "sacrifice your son Isaac," "destroy all the people of the land," and "stone the idolater."

In the New Testament, Jesus also gives commands that, at the very least, defy Aristotelian practical reason. His commands include: "take up your cross and follow me," "do not repay evil with evil but repay evil with good," and "love your enemies and pray for those who persecute you." The centrality of Christ and his teaching are central to many Christian defenses of divine command theory, since no investigation of nature, human virtue, or common sense would ever seem to yield these kinds of prescriptions. Philipp Quinn articulates the concern here when he says,

> The love of neighbor of which Jesus speaks is unnatural for humans in their present condition. It does not spontaneously engage their affections, and so training, self-discipline, and, perhaps, even divine assistance are required to make its achievement a real possibility. For most of us most of the time, love of neighbor is not an attractive goal, and, if it were optional, we would not pursue it. It must therefore be an obligatory love with the feel of something that represents a curb or check on our natural desires and predilections.[6]

On Quinn's view, Jesus's command to "love your enemies and pray for those who persecute you" rests not upon some naturally known principle of morality but upon God's desire to redeem a sinful humanity. The reality of human sinfulness and the relationship of revealed

6. Philipp Quinn, "The Primacy of God's Will in Christian Ethics," in *Philosophical Perspectives, vol. 6: Ethics*, ed. James E. Tomberlin (Atascadero, CA: Ridgeview, 1992), 504. Quinn assumes a particular understanding of nature here that reflects a decidedly Reformed understanding; that is, nature, as adversely affected by sin, cannot function as a reliable guide to how we should behave.

commands to naturally known principles of morality continued to occupy Christian thinkers in the patristic and medieval eras.

4.2 The Christian Tradition

A central question in the development of medieval theology from the high Middle Ages on, focused upon the role of intellect and will in the nature of law.[7] In contrast to the pagan Greek philosophers like Aristotle, Christian theologians believed God acted in the world and had personal characteristics. And with Augustine's development of the theory of the will, we find that God not only knows the creation but chooses to act in decisive ways within that created order. As a result, many theologians in the Middle Ages wanted to explore the relationship between God's knowing and God's willing. Much of their attention focused on the theory of law since, at least in human affairs, law requires that the lawgiver not only knows what he is doing but also chooses that some laws will be promulgated while others won't. Those thinkers who held that law derived primarily from an act of the intellect were known as intellectualists, Aquinas being their primary representative. In contrast, those who held that the will was primary were known as voluntarists, with John Duns Scotus and William Ockham representing this view. Even though this may seem an arcane and subtle scholastic argument, the result of placing one faculty above the other has far-reaching consequences.[8] Briefly, if one sees the divine intellect as superior, then it follows that ethics might seem to be primarily about *knowing* the good rather than about *choosing* the good. In this light, some thinkers like Aquinas understand that human nature has a better capacity to understand the good than to do the good. Accordingly, Aquinas believes that sin has affected us more with regard to "the desire for the good than the knowledge of the truth."[9] However, if one places the will above the intellect, then ethics is primarily about choosing the right course of action with the

7. An excellent treatment of this issue can be found in Thomas Davitt, *The Nature of Law* (St. Louis: Herder, 1951).

8. The distinction between intellect and will in God was only a mental distinction for the medievalists, since they all believed in divine simplicity. However, this language served as a means of sorting out the various ways in which God could be understood in light of human analogies and God's relationship to other beings.

9. Aquinas IaIIae.70.1

right intent. Well known voluntarist Peter Abelard held that the will's willing the end was the only determinant in assessing the value of an agent or her act.[10] This emphasis upon the will derived its legitimacy from Augustine, who employed and developed the term for a number of purposes.

The figure of Augustine looms large over both natural law morality and divine command theory since his writings are so diverse and contextualized. But as he aged, he gradually moved away from his earlier emphasis on the intelligibility of the natural order to the sovereignty of God and an emphasis upon God's freedom.[11] As we have seen, he explicitly borrows natural law language and content from Cicero and modifies it to suit his own Christian ethical perspective. Yet it is his development of the theory of will that begins a long and controversial period of medieval discussion of human morality.

One of Augustine's early works, *De Libero Arbitrio*, attempts to answer the perennial problem of evil by an appeal to the concept of the will.[12] Augustine argues that God did not create evil, but created human beings with free will; free will was a gift from a good and generous God who desired them to use it to love God. However, humans used it to promote their own selfish desires, and as a result evil entered into the world. Evil is, therefore, the consequence of a poor choice of the free will. As Albrecht Dihle observed, Augustine is the first to develop and utilize the idea of will as a means of explaining evil as well as attributing to it the power of free choice.[13]

Years later, in *De Civitate Dei*, Augustine continues to use the idea of will as a means of explaining evil, but also as a criterion by which we can distinguish between the just and the unjust. He says, "We see then that the two cities were created by two kinds of love: the earthly city was created by self-love reaching the point of contempt

10. Peter Abelard, *Ethical Writings: Ethics and Dialogue between a Philosopher, a Jew, and a Christian*, trans. Paul Vincent Spade (Indianapolis: Hackett, 1995).

11. For a discussion of this shift in emphases in Augustine's writings, see Vernon Bourke, "The Political Philosophy of St. Augustine," *Proceedings of the American Catholic Philosophical Association*, vol. 7 (1932): 45–55.

12. Augustine, *The Problem of Free Choice*, trans. Dom Mark Pontifex (Mahwah, NJ: Paulist Press, 1978).

13. Albrecht Dihle, *The Theory of Will in Classical Antiquity* (Los Angeles: University of California Press, 1982); also Vernon J. Bourke, *Will in Western Thought: An Historico-Critical Survey* (New York: Sheed and Ward, 1964).

for God, the heavenly city by the love of God carried as far as contempt of self. In fact the earthly city glorifies in itself, the heavenly city glories in the Lord."[14] Genuine believers consistently place the love of God ahead of self-interest. These individuals, the members of the "heavenly city," freely will the good, while those members of the "earthly city" consistently and freely will their own selfishness. Thus, the difference between good and evil human creatures rests entirely on what they will.

The legacy of Augustine lay primarily in his emphasis on the will, but late medieval theologians would also emphasize the divine will; since God must be omnipotent, there can be no independent standard of morality apart from God. One of the most notable scholastics to develop Augustine's theory of the will in a voluntarist fashion was John Duns Scotus (1266–1308).[15] Scotus contends that the will is the source of obligation because in God the will reflects divine power. For God to command in accordance with some standard of goodness apart from God is blasphemous, for it amounts to saying that God is under obligation to some other entity; and if this is so, God cannot be God.

Scotus therefore contends that God can will anything that does not involve a contradiction. God cannot will that 5+7=11, since this is contradictory; nor can God command us to hate God, since this also would require us to engage in contradictory behavior. But why? On Scotus's view, God is the ultimate object of our desire; or, in other words, God is supremely lovable. Indeed, human creatures are created for the primary purpose of loving God. Scotus says,

> I say that God is no debtor in any unqualified sense save with respect to his own goodness, namely that he love it. But where creatures are concerned he is debtor rather to his generosity, in the sense that he gives creatures what their nature demands, which exigency in them is set down as something just, a kind of secondary object of this justice,

14. Augustine, *City of God*, trans. Henry Bettenson (New York: Penguin, 1984) XIV, 28.

15. I have chosen to include Scotus under the rubric of divine command theory since this is the customary way of considering his work. However, one could argue that he could be considered a natural law moralist since (1) natural law plays a significant role in his consideration of ethics, and (2) he sees the demands of morality as rooted in human nature, albeit in an interesting way that differentiates his thought from Aquinas.

as it were. But in truth nothing outside of God can be said to be definitely just without this added qualification. In an unqualified sense where a creature is concerned, God is just only in relation to his first justice, namely, because such a creature has been actually willed by the divine will.[16]

It would therefore be contradictory for God to command that one not love that which is the object of one's love. But if God cannot do this, are there other restrictions on God's power?

A standard question among the high and late medieval scholastics concerned the relationship of the precepts of the Decalogue to the precepts of the natural law. For Aquinas they overlapped; but for Scotus and the later Franciscans the relationship was not entirely clear, because there were obvious exceptions in the scriptures to the natural law. God tells Abraham to sacrifice Isaac, which would constitute murder since Isaac is an innocent person. God tells the Israelites to despoil the Egyptians, which constitutes theft. And God tells Hosea to marry Gomer the prostitute, which constitutes adultery. These three cases not only seem to violate the precepts of the natural law but are also violations of the precepts of the Decalogue. So how is it that God can simply dispense with these precepts?

In typical scholastic fashion, Scotus contends that there are at least three ways in which a precept of the Decalogue may belong to the natural law: a strict fashion, a general fashion, and one that doesn't seem to fit.[17] The first two commandments of the Decalogue belong to the natural law in a strict manner. He says these must apply to all people and at all times, since they direct the human creature to God as the proper object of their desire. God cannot dispense with these precepts, since it would be contradictory for the reasons we have seen above.

The commandment concerning "keeping the Sabbath" on a particular day of the week is puzzling for Scotus. Since, on the one hand, keeping the Sabbath seems to direct us to God it would seem that God cannot dispense with it; but, on the other hand, we can always ask, "Why *that* day and not another?" Quite clearly, God *must* be honored—

16. John Duns Scotus *Ordinatio* IV, dist.46.
17. John Duns Scotus *Ordinatio* III, suppl., dist.37 in Alan Wolter, *Duns Scotus on the Will and Morality* (Washington, DC: The Catholic University of America Press, 1997).

since God is our natural *telos*—but Scotus isn't sure whether this must take place on a particular day of the week or not.

The second table of the commandments concern our relationship to our neighbors (taken in an inclusive sense our parents are also our "neighbors"). They belong to the natural law only in a general sense, and God can dispense with them as needed (as in the case of Abraham and Hosea). God could have commanded adultery if God so desired. Scotus argues that in some circumstances polygamy was desirable, as, for example, in the Old Testament. These other precepts of the Decalogue do not depend on some Platonic or Aristotelian essentialism, but owe their obligatory status solely to the will of God. "Anything other than God is good because God wills it and not vice versa."[18] Yet we need not worry that God will command actions that are absurd, or contrary to the divinely mandated *telos* of the human soul toward God, since "God wills in a most reasonable and orderly way."[19]

Picking up on the Augustinian theme that there are two "cities" of people distinguished by their two loves, Scotus develops his own account of moral psychology. The will can determine itself to an object in one of two ways: either as desiring its own benefit or as desiring that which is appropriate. Scotus calls these powers of the will the affection for the advantageous (*affectio commodi*) and the affection for justice (*affectio iustitia*).[20] According to Allen Wolter, the affection for the advantageous "inclines one to seek whatever perfects the nature of the agent, either as concretized in this individual or as concerning the species to which it belongs."[21] This affection for the good is a natural desire of the will for the good which perfects the nature, as the object is presented to the will by the intellect. However, if we want to avoid an account of moral psychology that avoids a will that cannot resist the lure of the good—in which case we have no moral accountability—we need to posit another capacity on the part of the will. Wolter says the affection for justice is "free will's congenital inclination towards the good in accord with its intrinsic worth or value rather than in terms of how it may perfect self or nature."[22] The

18. Duns Scotus *Opus Oxon.*, III, 19.
19. Duns Scotus *Opus Oxon.*, III, 32,6.
20. Duns Scotus *Ordinatio* IV, 49.
21. Wolter, *Duns Scotus on the Will and Morality*, 39.
22. Ibid.

affection for justice therefore has the capacity to restrain the affection for the advantageous, and in this way it is possible for the will
to resist the intellect's presentation of the good. In this way, Scotus's
account of the will gained ascendancy over Aquinas's emphasis on
the intellect. Yet this assignment of the priority of the will would be
taken to its radical extreme with the work of William Ockham.

Like Scotus a generation before him, William Ockham (1285–1349)
placed a premium on the role of the will. But where Scotus subscribed
to the more traditional Aristotelian realism, Ockham abandoned
the realist metaphysics for a radical nominalism. On the nominalist perspective "universals" do not refer to real entities, either in the
particular object or to the real concepts in the mind. Ockham also
rejects the traditional Augustinian notion of divine ideas. Rather,
universals play the role of signifiers in our language; they are a
convenient means of identifying groups of individuals. There is no
universal human nature, either in Adam or in the mind of God (or
any other mind). If there were, then God would necessarily need
to create Adam in accordance with that nature, and God's freedom
would thereby be restricted.

Ockham also held that God could do anything that did not involve
a logical contradiction; but for Ockham this opened up new vistas of
power for God, since Ockham rejected the kind of realism found in
both Scotus and Aquinas. As a thoroughgoing nominalist who rejects
any and all "natural kinds," Ockham realizes that the phenomenal
world relies entirely on the creation of God; radical ontological contingency permeates the cosmos. As such, the notion of "necessity"
applies neither to any sort of created being and its so-called "nature,"
nor to any kind of precept directed to that creature. Ockham says,
"No act is necessarily virtuous."[23] Necessity, *qua* necessity, applies
only to logical, not empirical, relationships.

This radical nominalism finally achieved the kind of power for
God Ockham thinks appropriate for the divine being. No longer held
captive by artificially imposed constraints such as "natural law," God
now freely commands what God desires. Ockham proclaims, "By the
very fact that God wills it, an act becomes just."[24] This completely
untethered freedom enables God to command even what we think

23. Ockham *Quodlibeta III*, 13.
24. *Sent., I.* q. 17.

may seem absurd: the ability to command creatures to hate God.[25] Although Ockham says God has this ability, it is not clear that any creature would have the ability to obey the command.[26]

The entirety of the Decalogue depends solely on the divine will, since there is no intrinsic ordering of the creature to God. Rather, with Ockham's account of the divine will we see the zenith of medieval voluntarism and its excessive emphasis on God's unrestricted freedom, with its resultant rejection of "natures" and natural law.

In the work of Martin Luther (1483–1546), we find continuity with the nominalist tradition's emphasis on the divine will, as well as a new concern with human sinfulness.[27] The tendency among the continental reformers was to see nature in terms of a fallen nature that contrasted with the grace of Christ.[28] As a result, a theory of natural law was suspect, since it appealed to a post-fall conception of nature; instead, the grace of Christ and the inaccessibility of God's wisdom took center stage.

Keeping with the voluntarist emphasis on the power and inscrutability of the divine will, Luther claims that the will of God is autonomous and needs no appeal to anything other than itself.

> God is He for whose will no cause or ground may be laid down as its rule and standard; for nothing is on a level with it or above it. . . . What God wills is not right because He ought or was bound so to will; on the contrary, what takes place must be right, because He so wills.[29]

God, as the supreme legislator, commands what God wills and we, as loyal subjects, obey because God has thus commanded.

25. Ibid., IV, q. 16, "Sed Deus potest praecipare quod voluntas creata odiate eum."

26. Lucan Freppert, *The Basis for Morality According to William Ockham* (Chicago: Franciscan Herald Press, 1988).

27. Heiko Oberman, *Luther: Man Between God and the Devil* (New Haven: Yale University Press, 1989). Oberman argues that Luther was thoroughly steeped in the nominalist tradition, and this was one reason he rejected much of the medieval realism of Aquinas. At one point Luther even refers to Ockham as his "dear master."

28. James M. Gustafson, *Protestant and Roman Catholic Ethics: Prospects for Rapprochement* (Chicago: University of Chicago Press, 1978), observes that Luther and Calvin misread the natural law theory of Aquinas since they fail to see that "the moral law was grounded in creation, and thus was a gift of grace," 12.

29. Martin Luther, *Martin Luther: Selections from His Writings*, ed. John Dillenberger (Garden City, NY: 1961), 195–6.

Yet we also find another theme in Luther that hearkens back to Augustine: the doctrine of human sinfulness. According to Augustine, God created humans "able not to sin and able to sin" (*posse non peccare et posse peccare*). However, after the fall all humanity found itself in the condition of *non posse non peccare*, "unable not to sin" or "without the ability to keep from sin."[30] The human incapacity to avoid sin means that our natural desire to set up moral systems based upon our fallen nature is doomed from the start. As a result, Luther emphasizes God's commands and human love, rather than a system of natural law that would seem to lend itself to the domestication of God.[31]

Like Luther, Calvin also emphasized the inscrutable wisdom of God and the sinfulness of the human creature. According to Calvin,

> God's will is so much the highest rule of righteousness that whatever he wills, by the very fact that He wills it, must be considered righteous. When, therefore, one asks why God has so done, we must reply: because He has so willed, you are seeking something greater and higher than God's will, which cannot be found.[32]

The human intellect may be capable of asking such questions, but there is no other answer than "*Deus vult*."

The fall of Adam for Calvin, as in Luther, destroys the capacity for human goodness and deeply damages the *imago dei*. For Aquinas, the *imago dei* has been stained by original sin, but still retains the capacity to know the basic precepts of natural law. However for Calvin the image is deeply flawed and "darkened," so that it can barely understand even the most basic rules for civic cooperation.

Although Calvin recognizes St. Paul's account of the law in Romans 1, the reformer focuses not on humanity's noetic capacity to grasp the law, but on the resultant perversions that follow from turning away from the law. Calvin says the human mind is "so shrouded in the darkness of errors" that one cannot use the law as a reliable guide to morality. Rather, the law can become a hindrance to us. Calvin

---

30. Augustine, *Handbook on Faith, Hope and Love*, 28.

31. A recent work that challenges this traditional reading of Luther is Antti Raunio, "Natural Law and Faith: The Forgotten Foundations of Ethics in Luther's Theology," in *Union With Christ: The New Finnish Interpretation of Luther*, ed. Carl E. Braaten and Robert W. Jenson (Grand Rapids: Eerdmans, 1998), 96–124.

32. John Calvin *The Institutes of the Christian Religion*, III, 23, 1.

delineates three uses of the law. First, the law increases the transgression on the part of the sinner, since it shows us both what the law requires and that we cannot fulfill these requirements on our own. Second, law restrains the wicked by threatening them. In this light, we see that the law assumes, as it were, our own unrighteousness. That is, the righteous have no need of the law; it is given for the wicked. And third, it can teach the elect to know their duty more clearly. But none of this is any good apart from a redeemed heart. Calvin says natural law is "that apprehension of the conscience which distinguishes sufficiently between just and unjust, and which deprives men of the excuse of ignorance, while it proves them guilty by their own testimony."[33] The law, then, increases human responsibility but does not enable or assist in the actual doing of the good. Only grace—and grace alone—can fulfill the requirements of the law. It is, therefore, no surprise that Calvin makes little use of the natural law.

The work of Søren Kierkegaard (1809–49) represents one of the last developments in the long line of Christian theists who chose to defend the divine command theory. As one might expect, Kierkegaard does not approach divine command theory in any conventional manner; he places his own unique stamp on the doctrine that resists easy classification. The scholastic defenders of divine command theory sought to understand divine commands in the context of a philosophy of God that emphasized the divine power. The reformers saw divine commands as the inscrutable dictates of a Holy God to his sinful and disobedient children. In contrast to these approaches, Kierkegaard sees the divine commands as intensely personal commands from God to develop our capacity to love God, ourselves, and others in an appropriate way. C. Stephen Evans sees Kierkegaard's contribution to divine command theory as combining the direct address of a personal God with the divinely mandated *telos* for each individual. Evans says, "We have . . . a divine command ethic in which the fundamental command is that a person become what God intends. What God intends for each of us is that we become like him in loving. The most fundamental obligation is the obligation to love God. Tightly linked to this love of God is the command to love our fellow human beings as our neighbors."[34]

33. Ibid., II, ii, 22.
34. C. Stephen Evans, *Kierkegaard's Ethics of Love: Divine Commands and Moral Obligations* (New York: Oxford University Press, 2004), 29.

For Kierkegaard, we must come to see Christ as our contemporary who addresses us personally in the midst of our life. He gives us the great command which is to "love the Lord your God with all your heart, soul, mind and strength, and your neighbor as yourself." The command to love our neighbor is difficult since it requires us to transcend our own preferences for the self in our own favor, and to love the neighbor as a necessary corrective to our sinful self-love. The divine command curbs our naturally selfish and egocentric tendencies and forces us to turn our attention toward our neighbor.

Genuine love must, therefore, be a command, since it conflicts with our natural urges and affections for friendship and *eros*. Genuine love does not change but remains constant and steadfast. Friendship and *eros* may change, as the friend may cease to be a friend and the lover may lose her loveliness, but genuine love remains what it always was and is. Kierkegaard says, "To be sure, you can also continue to love the beloved and the friend no matter how they treat you, but you cannot truly continue to call them the beloved and friend if they, sorry to say, have really changed."[35]

In the Christian tradition from Augustine to Kierkegaard, three themes emerge as dominant strains in divine command theory. First, divine command theory attempts to preserve the autonomy and freedom of the divine will such that it is not beholden to any "external" principle or rule. Second, divine command theory emphasizes the inscrutability of God and God's precepts. Since God and humans are so radically different in kind, it is impossible for humanity to judge the wisdom of God's decrees. Third, divine command theory attempts to provide a necessary corrective to human sinfulness, especially the inappropriate and excessive regard for the self.

4.3 Neo-Orthodoxy and Divine Command Theory

Heavily indebted to the existential philosophy of Kierkegaard, the neo-orthodox theologians in the twentieth century represent the last sustained theological consideration of divine command theory. For these thinkers, two theological objections to natural law figure prominently in the discussion. The first approach sees natural law

35. Søren Kierkegaard, *Works of Love*, trans. Howard and Edna Hong (New York: Harper and Brothers, 1962), 76.

morality as a kind of hubris which attempts to domesticate God and God's commands; it is articulated by both Karl Barth and Emil Brunner.[36] The second approach is to see natural law morality as a kind of perpetually elusive conceptual framework that has a place in secular ethics but no place in the church; Helmut Thielicke represents this more moderate approach.[37]

For Karl Barth, the starting and ending point of all theology is the revelation of God in Jesus Christ. Natural theology has no place in Barth's ethics, nor does natural law morality. He claims that "we must reject any fitness of man for cooperation with God on the basis of this (natural) orientation to him."[38] The reason we reject any and all continuity between humanity and God is because sin has so decisively destroyed any possible relationship between humans and God apart from the grace of Jesus Christ. In fact, Barth goes so far as to say that even "access to the knowledge that he is a sinner is lacking man because he is a sinner."[39]

Such is the pervasive and extreme consequence of sin, that only a divine encounter with God incarnate can restore the human creature to a state of noetic integrity. Only Christ can overcome human sin. "Man is a being that has to be overcome by the Word and the Spirit of God, that has to be reconciled with God, justified and sanctified, comforted and ruled and finally saved by God."[40]

Although Brunner concedes—where Barth does not—the possibility of natural theology and natural law, he believes that humans can only fully understand it after justification. Even though there is a remnant of God's creative activity left to the human person in the "state of nature," it cannot communicate the grace of God, nor can it save. Moreover, any attempt to understand God or the demands of

36. Karl Barth, *Ethics*, ed. Dietrich Braun, trans. Geoffrey W. Bromiley (New York: Seabury Press, 1981); Emil Brunner, *The Divine Imperative: A Study in Christian Ethics*, trans. Olive Wyon (Philadelphia: Westminster Press, 1937).

37. Helmut Thielicke, *Theological Ethics: Foundations*, vol. 1, ed. William H. Lazareth (Philadelphia: Fortress Press), 1966.

38. Barth, *Ethics*, 32.

39. Karl Barth, *Church Dogmatics: The Doctrine of Reconciliation*, vol. IV, pt. I, trans. G. W. Bromiley (Edinburgh: T and T Clark, 1956), 360–61; later in the same volume, Barth exclaims that "there can be no disputing the assertion of the totality of human sin and guilt," 498.

40. Karl Barth, "No!" *Natural Theology: "Comprising Grace and Nature" by Professor Dr. Emil Brunner and the Reply "No!" by Dr. Karl Barth* (Eugene, OR: Wipf and Stock Publishers, 2002), 126.

morality on the basis of natural reason inevitably results in a skewed and corrupted perversion of what humans were originally created to be. Brunner claims,

> There is no such thing as an "intrinsic Good." The hypostatization of a human Good as the "Idea of the Good" is not only an abstraction in the logical sense; it is due to the fact that man has been severed from his Origin, to that original perversion of the meaning of existence, which consists in the fact that man attributes to himself and his ideas an independent existence—that is, that man makes himself God.[41]

Since there is an original alienation of humanity from its origin, any attempt to develop an ethic based upon either "nature" or "the good" is a sinful endeavor based upon a merely human construction; it is the moral equivalent of building the Tower of Babel.

Thielicke considers the noetic consequences of the Fall in greater depth than either Barth or Brunner, and makes more circumspect evaluations than either one of his predecessors. Thielicke sees the Roman Catholic tradition of natural law as building upon a conception of nature that contradicts itself. On the one hand, the concept of nature preserves the original order of creation and, as such, it provides an infallible guide to how we should conduct ourselves. On the other hand, nature is problematic because we live in a fallen world and can't know the precepts as we should. Natural law theory operates in an unavoidably equivocal fashion. He says, "To try to make a 'direct' transfer from the primal state (of original justice) into our own world is as ridiculous as the man who tries to drive his automobile down the lines of longitude from the North Pole to the South. In the concrete world in which we live longitudes are artificial abstractions."[42] So too, we cannot move from the abstract idealized world of nature prior to the Fall, to our own messy world where we only encounter sinful natures.

Our sinful nature and its necessary limitations imply that we cannot truly perceive the nature of humanity. Since we cannot perceive humanity correctly, we cannot know how to render to others what is their due. As a result no natural ethics is possible. Thielicke says, "Our main objection to Roman Catholic natural

---

41. Brunner, *The Divine Imperative*, 114.
42. Thielicke, *Theological Ethics*, 405.

law is that it ascribes a false rank to the *suum cuique*, regarding it as an imperative, the expression of a given and knowable order."[43] For Christians who have the full revelation of God in Christ, a natural law approach is surely a regression. But for pagans who do not have Christ, then natural law suffices for the political organization of society to prevent the worst harms. It clearly does not function as "an order of salvation" or substitute for the personal address of God.[44]

In all three thinkers we find the same recurrent themes: (1) sin so damages the human capacity for knowledge and relationship that no natural knowledge of the "good" is available to anyone apart from grace, (2) the only adequate knowledge of the "good" we find is the revelation of God—Jesus Christ, and (3) natural law is construed as a competitor to divinely revealed imperatives. However, the most significant recent work in the development of divine command theory has not taken place among the theologians of the twentieth century, but among the philosophers.

4.4 Contemporary Philosophical Defenses of Divine Command Theory

The most notable contemporary philosophers who defend divine command theory include Janine Marie Idziak, Philip Quinn, John Hare, and Robert Merrihew Adams.[45] Idziak is especially helpful in delineating the reasons why one would prefer a divine command theory to other competing normative theories.[46] She writes, "Generally speaking, a 'divine command moralist' is one who maintains that the content of morality (i.e., what is right and wrong, good and evil, just and unjust, and the like) is directly and solely dependent upon the commands and prohibitions of God."[47]

The proponents of divine command theory argue that it is their view which best preserves the specifically religious nature of Christian

43. Ibid., 428.
44. Ibid., 447.
45. Janine Marie Idziak, "In Search of Good Positive Reasons for an Ethics of Divine Commands; A Catologue of Arguments" in *Faith and Philosophy* 6, no. 1 (January 1989). See note 2 as well.
46. Idziak, *Divine Command Morality*, 9–10.
47. Idziak, *Divine Command Morality*, 1.

ethics.[48] That is, the advocates of divine command theory contend that their view is most consistent with the Christian ideas of God's omnipotence, God's freedom, and a right emphasis upon the divine will as the source for moral norms. They believe that if morality is somehow autonomous and independent of God's will, then God becomes superfluous to any specifically Christian account of morality. This would result in God's ceasing to be the focus of our supreme loyalty. Thus, in order to preserve the radical dependency of all creation on God (including the moral order), one must maintain that ethics is constituted by whatever God wills.

Traditional divine command theory has been attacked by Christian and non-Christian thinkers alike. Indeed the insights of non-Christian thinkers such as James Rachels and Kai Nielson are instructive: taking the Euthyphro Dilemma and applying it to a Christian account of divine command theory, James Rachels offers the following refutation of divine command theory based upon the *Euthyphro* Dilemma:

1. Suppose God commands us to do what is right. Then *either* (a) the right actions are right because he commands them *or* (b) he commands them because they are right.
2. If we take option (a), then God's commands are, from a moral point of view, arbitrary; moreover, the doctrine of the goodness of God is rendered meaningless.
3. If we take option (b), then we have admitted there is a standard of right and wrong that is independent of God's will.
4. Therefore, we must *either* regard God's commands as arbitrary, and give up the doctrine of the goodness of God, *or* admit that there is a standard of right and wrong that is independent of his will, and give up the theological definitions of right and wrong.
5. From a religious point of view, it is undesirable to give up the doctrine of the goodness of God.
6. Therefore, even from a religious point of view, a standard of right and wrong that is independent of God's will must be accepted.[49]

48. Idziak, *Divine Command Morality*, 8–10.
49. James Rachels, *The Elements of Moral Philosophy* (New York: Random House, 1986), 44.

The common response of many religious believers who wish to affirm the "objectivity" of morality while rejecting the apparent arbitrariness of divine command theory, is to opt for a moral theory based upon natural law. Even though Rachels's argument appeals to our common moral intuitions, he (like many of those who reject divine command theory) holds that "a standard of right and wrong that is independent of God's will must be accepted."

Rachels's argument calls into question the epistemological basis defenders of divine command theory have for calling God "good." The key issue Rachels raises regards how we know God is good. Consider whether torturing innocent children is wrong or not. It is always and everywhere wrong, and we have no need of a divine command to tell us that it is wrong. William Frankena notes that some ethical beliefs may be grounded on religious beliefs, but even religious beliefs must be rationally justifiable.[50] He asks, "Does the conclusion 'It is wrong to kill,' necessarily depend on the premise 'God commanded us not to kill'?"[51] The obvious answer is "No."

As a response to this critique of traditional divine command theory, some philosophers have developed weaker versions of the theory they hope are immune to these kinds of criticism. As a result, we can distinguish two kinds of divine command theory, a strong version and a weak version. The terms "strong" and "weak" do not refer to the power of the argument but rather to the kind of power God has in mandating morality. As we have seen, the medieval thinker William Ockham defended a strong version of divine command theory, according to which God could command any activity that did not entail a logical contradiction. On the strong view, God could command the torture of innocent children for its own sake and we would have to obey. This wildly counter-intuitive position logically follows from the absolute freedom from constraint God allegedly possesses. Most contemporary defenders of divine command theory reject this approach and opt for a weaker version of the theory.[52] In what fol-

50. William Frankena, "Is Morality Logically Dependent on Religion?" in *Divine Commands and Morality*, ed. Paul Helm (New York: Oxford University Press, 1981), 14–33.

51. Ibid., 23.

52. Adams prefers to use the terms "unmodified" for what I call the "strong" version and "modified" for his version of what I call the "weaker" version. One could also characterize Duns Scotus, John Hare, and C. Stephen Evans arguing for the weaker version of the theory.

lows, I consider two kinds of weak arguments for divine command theory: Robert Merrihew Adams's "modified theory" and John Hare's "supervenient" account of an ethic based upon divine commands.

Adams presents three different options regarding the relationship of God to morality. The first view is that of natural law, which he attributes to Aquinas, wherein "it is logically impossible for God to command cruelty for its own sake" because, as Adams says, "what is right and wrong is independent of God's will, *and*" because "God always does what is right by the necessity of His nature."[53] The second view is one Adams attributes to Ockham, wherein "it is logically possible for God to command cruelty for its own sake" and it would be wrong for us to disobey God.[54]

The third view is one that Adams defends. He holds that it is *logically* possible for God to command acts of cruelty for their own sake, but that this is not *really* a possibility since God is believed to be loving and good. Moreover, if God were to command cruelty for its own sake we would be justified in refusing such a command. Adams says,

> The modified divine command theorist agrees that it is logically possible that God should command cruelty for its own sake but he holds that it is unthinkable that God should do so. To have *faith* in God is not just to believe that He exists, but also to trust in His love for mankind. The believer's concepts of ethical wrongness or permittedness are developed within the framework of his (or the religious community's) religious life, and therefore within the framework of the assumption that God loves us.[55]

God's will is a good and loving will; therefore the religious believer should have no qualms about obeying God's will or understanding it to be the supreme rule for ethical behavior.

53. Adams, "A Modified Divine Command Theory," 85. The attribution of this view to Aquinas is clearly mistaken, as Aquinas never suggests that there can be a moral standard independent of God's will. See Craig A. Boyd, "Is Thomas Aquinas a Divine Command Theorist?" in *The Modern Schoolman* vol. 74, no.3 (1998): 209–26 (emphasis is in the original).

54. Ibid.

55. Adams, "A Modified Divine Command Theory," 88 (emphasis original). In *Finite and Infinite Goods*, he rephrases this slightly and claims, "I should probably identify moral wrongness, not simply with the property of being contrary to commands of God, but rather with the property of being contrary to commands of a certain kind of God. Perhaps I should say specifically: contrary to the commands of a *loving* God," 281.

When religious believers use the phrase "X is morally wrong," what they mean is that "X is contrary to the commands of God." This judgment of ethical wrongness, or being forbidden by God, produces various intentions and emotions that lead religious believers to avoid such actions. A reason for this avoidance is that a violation of God's command is understood as an act of sin; that is, activity contrary to the expressed will of God which ruptures the relationship between the believer and God. Adams says that "ethical wrongdoing is seen and experienced as *sin*, as rupture of personal or communal relationship with God."[56] The desire to maintain relationship with God provokes believers to ask the question, "Is X forbidden by God, or contrary to God's will?" This phenomenological approach to divine command theory reveals that for many it becomes a "nonnaturalist objectivism" about ethical wrongness.[57] Adams says,

> According to the divine command theory (even the modified divine command theory), in so far as they are nonnatural and objective, they consist in facts about the will or commands of God. I think this is really the central point in a divine command theory of ethical wrongness. This is the point at which the divine command theory is distinguished from alternative theological theories of ethical wrongness, such as the theory that facts of ethical rightness and wrongness are objective, nonnatural facts about creatures.[58]

For Adams, the advantage of divine command theory is that it resists being construed in naturalistic terms and is thus immune from accusations of the "naturalistic fallacy." However, it also seems to preserve the idea that God's will is not determined by natural properties inhering in objects, or "essences subsisting eternally in God's understanding."[59]

A second key element of Adams's weak version of divine command theory concerns his insistence that one can simultaneously affirm that morality depends on the commands of God, and also that it is logically possible for a believer to disobey a command that she finds repulsive. He says that one key reason for a believer to disobey a divine command to torture innocent children is because "the modified

56. Ibid., 90.
57. Ibid., 91.
58. Ibid., 91.
59. Ibid., 92.

divine command theory clearly conceives of believers as valuing some things independently of their relation to God."[60] But this may lead to a common objection that there must be a prior conception of right and wrong that determines which commands are to be obeyed and which are to be disobeyed. In other words, "the believer must have a prior, nontheological conception of ethical right and wrong, in terms of which he judges God's commands to be acceptable—and to admit that the believer has a prior, nontheological conception of ethical right and wrong is to abandon the divine command theory."[61]

Adams responds by distinguishing between valuational judgments that are ethical, and those that aren't. Ethical judgments certainly play an important role in divine command theory, but they do not account for every judgment the believer makes. Sometimes the believer makes judgments based upon aesthetic taste, and at other times based on interpersonal relations. Thus, Adams says that one might refuse to obey a divine command based upon its horror (i.e., the believer finds the act in question revolting). Or conversely, the believer may choose to obey God out of gratitude. In both situations Adams contends that the judgments are independent of the ethical, and as a result he attempts to preserve the assertion that morality is based upon God's commands.

A central feature of Adams's weak divine command theory is that it depends upon the prior conception of a good God (i.e., a God who acts in loving ways on behalf of His creatures). Adams has further weakened his divine command theory by abandoning the idea that the theory is about the nature of the good and is instead about the nature of the obligation. On this weaker version of the weak interpretation of divine commands, the good—which is identified with God and known by all people—provides the basis of value, while the divine commands God gives provides the basis of moral obligation.[62] Adams's theory therefore requires assumptions about the nature of God, and the ways in which the believer has been shaped by her religious community such that all people can have access to knowledge of the good. But this theory of the good—as a value—smacks of natural law assumptions concerning what we can know and the limits on what God can command.

60. Ibid., 93.
61. Ibid., 93.
62. Adams, *Finite and Infinite Goods*, 255.

Another approach to the weak version of divine command theory is offered by John Hare, who instead of focusing on the assumption of God's goodness and the human creature's option of disobedience turns his attention to human sinfulness and the concept of supervenience.

Like Adams, Hare accepts a traditional definition of divine command theory when he says that, "what makes something obligatory for us is that God commands it."[63] The need for a divine command theory is that human sinfulness so permeates our judgments and moral perception that we are incapable of formulating the good and following it. Hare appeals to both Iris Murdoch's secularist account of human evil as well as what he thinks is a biblical account. On Murdoch's view, the "fat relentless ego" dominates the self in such a way that humans are invariably selfish, biased, and incapable of making accurate moral judgments. Furthermore, Murdoch also claims, in an appeal to Plato's "Cave Allegory," that we are so bound by our inabilities to judge accurately that we often confuse the fire inside the cave with the sun in the external world. Hare says that natural law theory "confuses the fire and the sun (that is, we confuse what we aim at with what is in fact good). In Calvinist terms, it does not take seriously enough the Fall."[64] A prime example is Aristotle, who attempts to deduce the good from what we do indeed desire.[65]

Hare appeals to the work of Duns Scotus in his defense of divine command theory by taking note of Scotus's distinction between the affection for the advantageous and the affection for justice. As we have seen, Scotus used this distinction to distinguish two powers of

63. Hare, *God's Call*, 49. Like Adams, Hare contends that his theory is also about the nature of obligation rather than the nature of the good.

64. Ibid., 55.

65. Hare also attributes this view to some theories of natural law, and he is correct in assigning this perspective to various Enlightenment and modern conceptions of the theory. However, as Jean Porter and Pamela Hall argue, Aquinas's theory of natural law is not a *deduction* of the principles of natural law from an *a priori* conception of human nature, but an *interpretation* of moral principles in light of scriptural, philosophical, and historical considerations. Cf. Jean Porter, *Nature as Reason: A Thomistic Theory of the Natural Law* (Grand Rapids: Eerdmans, 2005); Pamela Hall, *Narrative and the Natural Law: An Interpretation of Thomistic Ethics* (Notre Dame, IN: University of Notre Dame Press, 1994). This also seems to be Stanley Hauerwas's interpretation of natural law in Aquinas. *Truthfulness and Tragedy: Further Investigations in Christian Ethics* (Notre Dame, IN: University of Notre Dame Press, 1977).

the will and the ability to resist what one naturally desired (affection for the advantageous) by means of choosing that which is intrinsically good (affection for justice). However, Hare employs the distinction as an explanation for human sinfulness. Prior to the Fall, the affection for justice held primacy in the human soul and the affection for the advantageous was subordinated. After the Fall, the appropriate ordering was reversed and now humans have an invariable desire first to seek the advantageous. Yet the reversal of the ordering of the affections is not the only consequence. In addition, our affection for the advantageous distorts our ability to *perceive* the good as well as our ability to do the good. So how are we capable of not only knowing the good but of doing the good as well?

Again, by appealing to Scotus, Hare sees two kinds of goodness at work, primary and secondary. Primary goodness refers to a being's natural ability to exist and act in accordance with its natural desire to exist. Secondary goodness "always involves a relation." Moral goodness is a kind of secondary goodness; namely, a human creature's relationship to its appropriate end, God. But the precise nature of moral goodness is further elaborated by the concept of "supervenience."

According to Hare, we can describe an act in question as well as consider the moral quality of the act. Torturing innocent children is a description of an act but the moral quality of "evil" supervenes on the act. That is, we can distinguish between the description of the act in question and its moral value; the description of torturing innocent children does not entail an evaluative judgment, nor does the evaluative judgment entail the description. The reason for this is that descriptions as descriptions do not employ prescriptive language.[66] Yet, because torturing innocent children has certain properties (e.g., the pain caused by the torture), we can say that it is morally wrong. Why is this the case? Because descriptions *as* embedded in an evaluative context call forth moral judgments precisely because of the nature of the description. Hare prefers his account of the supervenient nature of ethical language to one that sees ethics as deducible from human nature.

We can make an important distinction between *deducing* morality from nature and seeing it as grounded in nature. Certainly our nature has some part to play in any consideration of human goodness, but we must

66. Whether this is really so is an issue I address in chapter 6 on the "Is-Ought" fallacy.

be careful how we understand the role of nature. According to Hare, "even God is required (by God's justice) to love God. God is not required to create us. But if God does create us, the requirement of justice is that we be created such that union with God is our final end."[67] Our nature is such that we require union with God as our *telos*, but Hare is quick to point out that the union in question may be achieved in a variety of ways, and that there is no necessary connection between the created nature we have and the means by which God orders us to him.

What Hare wants to avoid is a deduction of moral precepts from nature wherein we observe nature, reflect upon the urges therein, and conclude that specific moral precepts always and everywhere apply. Hare says,

> What I am objecting to is the *deduction* of the ten commandments from our created nature. In some versions of natural law theory, if we know the truths about our nature, the injunctions *follow*. . . . The point is that there is no necessary connection between our created natures and the way we reach our final end.[68]

In order to prove a conceptual disjunction between our created natures and the precepts that allegedly follow from reflection on these natures, Hare appeals to an imaginary scenario wherein we are asked to imagine that "God could have willed that we kill each other at the age of eighteen at which point God would immediately bring us back to life."[69] Hare's reliance on this thought experiment at its root appeals to a basic intuition he has about the relationship of our created natures to the will of God. For him, there is no necessary connection—that is, no deduction—between the precepts of the second table of the Decalogue and our created natures. However, it could be argued that there are no imaginary worlds such that he suggests. It may be the case that the moral necessity of the prohibition on murder is not merely because God has willed it, but because there lies in the human person something that requires the respect of all other persons; and what we recognize as the *imago dei* is a created nature that forbids the killing of innocent persons.[70]

67. Ibid., 66.
68. Ibid., 68–9 (emphasis is in the original).
69. Ibid., 68–9.
70. Notably absent from any of Hare's discussion is the idea of the *imago dei*. It would seem that this could provide a necessary connection between the prohibition

There is indeed a connection between nature and the commands of God, but the connection is not a necessary connection. He says, "There are innumerable ways God could have ordered us towards union, even given the nature with which we are created. The route God has in fact chosen is binding upon us because God has chosen it. But we can still say that the route is good *because* it takes us to our final end."[71] God creates us for a loving relationship with the divine Trinity; and the commands that God gives us fit our nature but are not strictly deducible from it, since in different situations God may call us to some kind of activity that seems to violate the "normative" moral precepts.

As Hare develops his theory of divine commands, he prefers to use the idea of the "call" of God since command seems to evoke the notion of power rather than love, which is an element Hare wants to emphasize. The call of God to the good has a "magnetic lure" or attraction to it. The lure of the good is important to Hare because it preserves us from our own attempts at defining the good, and also from the dangers of deducing the good from our wants. The call of God thus enables us to transcend our sinful biases as well as avoid the eudaimonistic tendency to put ourselves at the center of moral discourse. Hare thinks that all forms of eudaimonism are unacceptably self-serving.[72]

Hare argues that any naturalistic ethical theory fails to consider the problem of the "gaps" between our performance and the demands of morality.[73] Hare contends that all Western traditions of morality recognize this problem, and he says that it "describes a gap between the moral demand and the capacities we are born with and naturally

---

on murder and our created nature. Indeed, scholars who study the Hebrew Bible indicate that the primary reason why murder was prohibited was because any assault on a being created in the image of God was a direct affront to God himself. Gordon J. Wenham says, "Because man is God's representative, his life is sacred; every assault on man is an affront to the creator," *Genesis: Word Biblical Commentary* (Waco: Word Books, 1987), 32. Gerhard von Rad concurs with this assessment and maintains that the prohibition on murder is an apodictic command because of the *imago dei. Genesis: A Commentary* (Philadelphia: Westminster, 1972), 132.

71. Ibid., 77 (emphasis is in the original).

72. Ibid., 79.

73. John Hare, *The Moral Gap: Kantian Ethics, Human Limits, and God's Assistance* (Oxford: Clarendon Press, 1997), and John Hare, "Is There an Evolutionary Foundation for Morality?" in *Evolution and Ethics: Human Morality in Biological and Religious Perspective*, ed. Philip Clayton and Jeffrey Schloss (Grand Rapids: Eerdmans, 2004), 187–203.

develop."[74] There are, according to Hare, three different strategies for dealing with the gap without appealing to God's assistance. He says,

> The first strategy is to hold our natural capacities where they are . . . and then to reduce the moral demand in order to fit them. The second strategy is to keep the moral demand where it is . . . and then exaggerate or puff up the capacity to meet this demand. The third strategy is to hold the demand and our capacities constant, and then find some naturalistic substitute to do God's work in bridging the gap.[75]

The gap theory that Hare presents is reminiscent of the traditional arguments that appeal to human sinfulness as the reason why we need divine commands. Hare's approach is more sophisticated, however. He contends that we have some understanding of the human ideal (a claim that more traditional Reformed thinkers would question); the problem lies in our inability to meet the demands on our own natural capacities.

A common thread running through weak versions of divine command theory as presented by Adams, Hare, and Evans is the claim that it is a theory of "moral obligation," not a "theory of the good."[76] In fact, Evans explicitly concedes this point and wants to focus on the idea that what makes an act morally obligatory is the fact that it is commanded by God. And why has God thus commanded? Because our nature, as God has created it, requires such commands. We should point out that for Evans God also desires that we become the kinds of persons God intends and that this may, and does, require specific moral commands to do and act in specific ways consistent with, but not contrary to, our created nature. The binding force of moral obligation rests upon God's command, which in turn has a view to the human good.

4.5 Natural Law Theory Without God

Some divine command theorists have rightly criticized those versions of natural law morality that relegate God to the status of an anachronistic embarrassment. Larry Arnhart and Anthony Lisska are two examples of contemporary thinkers who believe that introducing

---

74. Hare, "Is there an Evolutionary Foundation for Morality?" 189.
75. Ibid., 191.
76. C. Stephen Evans, *Kierkegaard's Ethics of Love*, 118.

God into the discussion unnecessarily complicates issues for natural law theory.[77] Lisska attempts to recover from Aquinas the ethical core of natural law without the theological baggage: "Since most contemporary meta-ethics is agnostic at least, any theory entailing a relation to a divine being is suspect theoretically. Furthermore, this claim amounts to an interpretation rendering of Aquinas's moral theory an instance of theological definism."[78]

There seem to be two issues here: first, Lisska wants to avoid the impression that Aquinas is a "theological definist," that is, a divine command theorist. He thinks that appeals to the eternal law or the introduction of a theological basis for natural law come dangerously close to divine command theory—in other words, theological definism. And here he is certainly correct in maintaining that Aquinas does not subscribe to divine command theory. Lisska claims,

> One need not know the eternal law prior to gaining knowledge of the natural law, because one need not know that God exists prior to acquiring knowledge of an essence or natural kind. If this were not the case, then in principle an atheist or an agnostic could not acquire knowledge of an essence. Aquinas would find this claim incomprehensible.[79]

Aquinas states that the primary precepts of the natural law are known to all humans regardless of their religious affiliations.[80] But if religion does not provide the epistemological basis for natural law ethics, what does?

According to Lisska, "Aquinas did not first ask his readers to accept the existence of God before understanding the concept of natural law. Rather, he asked them to consider the possibility of a metaphysics of natural kinds."[81] As a correlative principle, we see that religious epistemology really adds nothing to the content of morality or to one's conception of human nature. Arnhart says, "Religion does not change human nature. Rather, it reinforces with divine authority

77. Anthony Lisska, *Aquinas's Theory of Natural Law: An Analytic Reconstruction* (New York: Oxford University Press, 1996); Larry Arnhart, *Darwinian Natural Right: The Biological Ethics of Human Nature* (Albany, NY: State University of New York Press, 1998), and his "Thomistic Natural Law as Darwinian Natural Right" in *Social Philosophy and Policy* 18 (Winter) 2001: 1–33.
78. Lisska, *Aquinas's Theory of Natural Law*, 116.
79. Lisska, *Aquinas's Theory of Natural Law*, 127.
80. Aquinas IaIIae.94.1.
81. Lisska, *Aquinas's Theory of Natural Law*, 126.

the teachings of natural reason as to the conditions for securing the fullest satisfaction of human longings."[82]

This second issue, which Lisska emphasizes, places the episte-mological notion of *what* a thing is in the center of the discussion rather than *whence* it originates. An abbreviated account of Aquinas's epistemology can be seen in the following.[83] A substantial form can be known through the unaided power of the agent of intellect apart from special revelation. Lisska says, "The natural law, in the mind of Aquinas, is nothing more than the determination of ends—read final cause—of the dispositional properties of the essence—read formal cause—of the human person. By using theoretical reason, the moral agent comes to understand the content of human nature. This content, in terms of essential properties, is determined by the form. The agent then determines that actions need to be undertaken in order to develop these dispositions."[84] Once the agent is able to determine the formal nature of an object, she can also determine what actions will contribute to its flourishing, and what actions won't. No appeal to divine power is necessary in this epistemologi-cal process.

Human nature, he says, is "determined by a set of synthetic a priori causal connections."[85] That is, humans possess a set of properties that comprise their essence, and this essence is necessarily a part of their nature. The investigation of these causal connections is the primary concern of natural law morality. Although Lisska makes little effort to list the precepts of natural law, Arnhart has twenty rules for human nature ranging from parental care and sexual mating to war and political rule.[86] Second order metaphysical issues concern the origins of eternal and natural law. Lisska says, "Aquinas included the divine mind only because it provided the ultimate . . . explanation of his ontology. God as the 'necessary being' accounts for why there is something rather than nothing."[87] As a result, he contends that God plays no direct role in Aquinas's natural law morality.

82. Arnhart, *Darwinian Natural Right*, 275.
83. Aquinas considers these epistemological issues at Ia.84–87.
84. Lisska, *Aquinas's Theory of Natural Law*, 124–5.
85. Ibid., 128.
86. Arnhart, *Darwinian Natural Right*, 31–6.
87. Ibid., 130. Lisska also remarks that, "the existence of a divine being is neither centrally important nor a necessary condition for an awareness of the content in Aquinas's epistemology," 137.

The theological dimension of Aquinas's ethics falls into this category of second order issues. Here, Lisska points to the fact that Aquinas distinguishes between the imperfect form of happiness that humans can achieve in this life and the perfect happiness of the blessed in heaven. Concomitantly, grace enables one to live the completely virtuous life and receive the vision of God, who is beyond our natural perception, while the natural law enables us to coexist peacefully in this life. In this way, the theological dimensions of Aquinas's ethics are neatly relegated to issues of secondary importance, as they have no direct bearing on our understanding of what constitutes the substantial form of human nature.

4.6 The Value of the Divine Command Critique

Divine command theorists like Hare, Adams, and Quinn rightly object to the interpretation of natural law morality offered by thinkers like Lisska and Arnhart. If natural law can provide a complete account of morality without an appeal to God, then the result is that religious convictions and theological commitments can play no substantive role in moral discourse— Euthyphro's dilemma appears once again on the scene. If this is true, then the charge of "methodological atheism" can legitimately be leveled against the defender of natural law.[88] A purely "naturalistic" understanding of natural law must be rejected by any serious theist since she must admit that, at the very minimum, God establishes the moral law and requires that we not merely act in accordance with our desires. As we have said throughout, nature is a necessary condition for morality but not a sufficient condition. The problem with naturalist theories like the ones presented by Lisska and Arnhart is that they reverse this order—they see nature as a sufficient condition for morality.

This is precisely why Hare's criticism of Arnhart is so devastating. Hare contends that Arnhart's approach to ethics is merely a case of "reducing the demand" of morality. On Arnhart's account, natural desires themselves are a sufficient condition for morality. The twenty natural laws he lists account for the entirety of ethical reasoning, and thus there is no demand other than limiting one desire for the benefit

88. This is the objection Idziak raises in her "Divine Commands are the Foundation of Morality."

of another. Yet there is more to ethics than a consideration of our natural desires; we must have some means to adjudicate our competing desires which is not merely one more desire. Arnhart's thinking, like Hume's two hundred years ago, is flawed by its vicious circularity. Desire *de facto* does not count as a sufficient condition for morality; nature must be guided by some principle that transcends itself.

A divine command theory raises another important consideration with regard to overly naturalistic explanations of ethics. As we have seen, the believer has a desire to follow the dictates of the scriptures in discerning how to act. That is, the scriptures play an important role with regard to authority in the believer's life, and these precepts—like the Decalogue and the Beatitudes—guide and shape her character in important ways. What this reveals is that divine command theorists want to claim: (1) that divine commands provide important *epistemic* resources for the believer, and (2) these commands cannot be reduced to the "demands of desire."[89]

4.7 The Arbitrariness Problem

As we have seen, in response to the problem of the possibility of God commanding the torture of innocent children, many defenders of the divine command theory argue that this does not present a problem, as we know that God is good and loving. According to Adams, a loving and good God would not command such a thing.[90] However, this argument either begs the question or it fails to tell us anything significant about God's character— it tells us nothing about God because it has abandoned any independently meaningful standard of goodness.

From the perspective of divine command theory, it seems *prima facie* that God could indeed command the torture of infants, a position Adams is willing to grant, at least logically. Since divine command theorists maintain that God is not bound by any extrinsic principles of morality, the command to torture innocents is clearly a possibil-

89. Later in this chapter I address the first point by arguing that there is no inconsistency between natural law and divine command ethics with regard to the epistemic source of the commands. The natural law approach I defend contends that the ontological question, however, is more central. The second issue I consider in chapter 7.

90. Adams, "A Modified Divine Command Theory of Ethical Wrongness," 86.

ity and seems to salvage the divine freedom. The defender of divine command theory contends, however, that there is no need to fear that God will give this command, since she believes God is good. But it seems as if our standard of goodness is based upon "prior" notions of goodness. In his critique of "theological subjectivism," a form of divine command theory, Norman Kretzman notes:

> But do not suppose that the adherent of theological subjectivism can extricate himself from this terminal embarrassment with the pious rejoinder that God is good and can be relied on not to approve of moral evil. The only standard of moral goodness supplied by theological subjectivism is God's approval; and so to say within the context of theological subjectivism that God is good comes to nothing more than that God approves of himself—which is easy to grant but impossible to derive any reassurance from.[91]

Kretzman's point here is simply that if we say "God is good," what is the basis for our assertion? How do we know that God is good? We know that God is good because God does good things (e.g., loving his creation). But this goodness of which we speak is dependent upon an objective basis of goodness, and a human agent's prior understanding (in at least some form) of this goodness. If God were to command the torture of innocent children, then obviously God would not be good. If God is not good, then God is not God. In his consideration of divine goodness, popular Christian author C. S. Lewis argues that God must be bound by some notion of goodness that is intelligible to His creatures. Lewis says,

> [I]f God's moral judgment differs from ours so that our "black" may be His "white," we can mean nothing by calling Him good; for to say "God is good," while asserting that His goodness is wholly other than ours, is really only to say "God is we know not what." And an utterly unknown quality in God cannot give us moral grounds for loving or obeying Him. If He is not (in our sense) "good" we shall obey, if at all, only through fear—and should be equally ready to obey an omnipotent Fiend. The doctrine of Total Depravity—when the consequence is drawn that, since we are totally depraved, our idea

91. Norman Kretzmann, "Abraham, Isaac, and Euthyphro: God and the Basis of Morality" in *Hamartia: The Concept of Error in the Western Tradition*, ed. Donald Stump and others (New York: Edwin Mellen Press, 1983), 35.

of good is worth simply nothing—may thus turn Christianity into a form of devil-worship.[92]

For Lewis, we must have some idea of what constitutes moral goodness; this conception of moral goodness need not be a fully developed account, but it must be consistent with our most basic moral intuitions, such as forbidding the torture of innocent children. While we can admit that God's goodness does indeed differ from ours, there must be continuity in how divine and human goodness are understood. Divine goodness is not entirely different from human goodness, yet, as Lewis says, "[I]t differs from ours not as white from black but as a perfect circle from a child's first attempt to draw a wheel."[93] There is indeed continuity; yet our apprehension of God's perfect goodness is incomplete and imperfect. But without that continuity we would not be able to speak meaningfully about God being "good." If God did violate what we might call an analogous concept of goodness, then God would not be worthy of worship (and thus not God) or we would have to abandon using the term "goodness" with reference to God. Even our most primitive understanding of goodness prevents us from conceiving of a God who would not forbid the torture of innocent children. Lewis's argument shows that Christians must have an interest in maintaining a natural law morality, as the divine command theory sacrifices God's goodness in the interest of God's omnipotence. Furthermore, to obey out of fear may indeed count as prudential behavior, but it does not count as moral behavior. In the end, God becomes the cosmic bully (or wearied parent) who threatens us to do the right thing or we shall be punished for refusing. As Leibniz observed,

> If we say that things are good by no rule of goodness beyond the will of God alone, we thoughtlessly destroy, I feel, all the love and glory of God. For why praise Him for what He had done if He would be equally praiseworthy for doing the opposite? Where will His justice and His wisdom be, if all that remains of Him is some

92. C. S. Lewis, *The Problem of Pain* (New York: Macmillan, 1962), 37–8. It may seem that Lewis is unusually harsh in his criticism of the divine command theory and the doctrine of total depravity. However, Lewis's point that we *must* have some sense of "the good" that is congruent with God's seems to be accurate. Otherwise, how could we possibly know that God's commands were good?
93. Ibid., 39.

kind of a despotic power, if His will takes the place of reason, and if, by the very definition of tyranny, what pleases the Almighty is *ipso facto* just?[94]

Power alone does not suffice as a moral reason to obey.

This point has been elaborated by Alasdair MacIntyre, who argues that we must first know whether or not the God who desires our loyalty is good.[95] Only a just God is owed obedience. Therefore, we must distinguish between the true God (i.e., the omnibenevolent God who is worthy of worship) and those that are pretenders (e.g., the ancient Roman's Jupiter or William Blake's Nobodaddy). In order to do this, we must possess at least a preliminary knowledge of the good before we can judge which God ought to be obeyed. A divine command alone cannot suffice for our allegiance to God, and so we must know what kind of God is giving the command. MacIntyre says, "[A]ny account of divine commands as foundational to morality, as antecedent to and partially or wholly definitive of justice, such as we are offered in one version by Occam, in another by Adams, has to fail."[96] Once again, our conception of goodness determines the manner in which God can meaningfully said to be "good." We can develop an argument that spells this out clearly:

1. If the weaker version of divine command theory sees obligation as parasitic upon the good, then God commands what is good for us.

94. G. W. Leibniz, *Discourse on Metaphysics and Related Writings*, trans. R. N. D. Martin and Stuart Brown (New York: Manchester University Press, 1988), 40.

95. Alasdair MacIntyre, "Which God Ought We to Obey and Why?" in *Faith and Philosophy* 3, no. 4 (October 1986): 359–71. A corollary of this question, "Which God ought we to obey?" is "Which religion is right?" Frankena argues that ethical beliefs cannot be logically grounded on religious beliefs, since there is even more dispute concerning which religion is true than what moral principles apply to human nature. Bringing religious disputes, as divine command theorists wish to do, into the domain of ethical discourse is to muddy the waters even further. This, he says, is hardly to "encourage hope that mankind can reach, by peaceful and rational means, some agreement on moral and political principles. It also encourages ethical and political skepticism in those who do not or cannot accept the required religious beliefs. That is why it strikes me as important to reject the view that all morality is logically dependent on religion and to leave open the possibility that at least some important ethical judgments can be justified independently of religion and theology," in "Is Morality Logically Dependent on Religion?" 30.

96. MacIntyre, "Which God Ought we to Obey?" 364.

2. If God commands what is good for us, then there must be an underlying ontology of human nature; otherwise it makes no sense to speak of "the good."

3. God is free to command only those actions that are for our good, either:

    a. Generically: that is, those commands that apply to all human beings (e.g., "love one another," "do not murder," "honor your parents").

    b. Specifically: that is, those commands that fall under a generic rule (e.g., "give $100 to the needy," "take your family and go to a land that I will show you," "come and follow me").

    c. But if God can only really command those actions that contribute to our flourishing, then there is no compelling reason to prefer divine command theory to natural law morality.

If this argument is valid, then we see that a divine command theorist holds, at least implicitly, an account of the good that presupposes the "natural kinds" found in natural law morality. God may freely will those actions consistent with our nature and those actions that may contribute to the development of a mature relationship with God, but these particular divine commands will always lie within the parameters of what contributes to genuine human flourishing—which God established in creation.

4.8 Creation and Natural Law

Our happiness is found in God and it is the natural law, placed in us by God at creation, which prompts us to pursue happiness. In the Christian tradition from Augustine to Aquinas to C. S. Lewis, we find Christian thinkers consistently affirming the fundamental idea that all humans desire happiness.[97] Furthermore, the only happiness that can ever truly satisfy the human soul is the God who created us. The *Catechism of the Catholic Church* asserts this boldly at the very beginning of the profession of faith: "The desire for God is written in

97. Of course, others who do not attempt to tie ethics to theology have also affirmed this. See Aristotle, *Nicomachean Ethics*, trans. Terence Irwin (Indianapolis: Hackett, 1984); and John Stuart Mill, *Utilitarianism*, ed. Roger Crisp (New York: Oxford University Press, 1998).

the human heart, because man is created by God and for God; and God never ceases to draw man to himself. Only in God will he find the truth and happiness he never stops searching for."[98] Echoing this basic Christian affirmation, Lewis offers an interesting analogy:

> God made us: invented us as a man invents an engine. A car is made to run on gasoline, and it would not run properly on anything else. Now God designed the human machine to run on Himself. He Himself is the fuel our spirits were designed to burn, or the food our spirits were designed to feed on. There is no other. . . . God cannot give us a happiness and peace apart from Himself, because it is not there. There is no such thing.[99]

So God *must* command creatures to worship Him. God cannot command any creature not to direct itself to God. To do otherwise would violate God's very creation that God has established for the good of humanity.[100] Aquinas remarks on this idea:

> As the Apostle says, 'God continues faithfully, He cannot deny Himself.' But He would deny Himself if He were to do away with the very order of His own justice, since He is justice itself. Therefore, God cannot dispense a man so that it be lawful for him not to direct himself to God, or not to be subject to his justice, even in those matters in which men are directed to one another.[101]

So there is at least one thing God must do as determined by both God's nature and by God's relation to the creature's nature. Michael Peterson observes that "the divine will cannot totally arbitrarily declare the shape of human morality. What God can will about human morality is constrained by the very kind of being we are—and this in light of the fact that God created the kind of being we are. Given that

98. *Catechism of the Catholic Church* (New York: Image Books, 1997): Profession of Faith I, 26.

99. C. S. Lewis, *Mere Christianity* (New York: Macmillan, 1952), 54.

100. What we must assume here is that agents have both interests and genuine goods that truly fulfill their nature. If we carry Adams's view that God is loving further than Adams himself does, we see that love involves a genuine interest in the good of the other. This assumes "objective standards as to what our interest are, standards that provide God reasons for commanding certain acts and not others." Robert Westmoreland, "Two Recent Metaphysical Divine Command Theories," *International Journal for Philosophy of Religion* 39, no. 1 (1996): 22.

101. IaIIae.94,5, ad2.

we are this kind of being, certain moral considerations necessarily pertain to us."[102] Thus, the nature which humans have been given determines the moral constraints upon God. The distinction here is between God's *potentia absoluta* and *potentia ordinata*.[103] God's absolute power refers to the divine ability to create any possible order, while God's ordinate power refers to God's ability to do whatever can be done within the actual created order. Thus,

> There is no reason why something should not be within divine power which God does not will, and which is no part of the present order he has established . . . as for what lies within power as such, God is said to be able to do it by his absolute power. And everything in which the character of being can be preserved is of this kind. . . . As for what lies within his power as carrying out the command of his just will, he is said to be able to do it by his ordinate power. Accordingly we should state that by his absolute power God can do things other than those he foresaw and predestined that he would.[104]

As God is the author and creator of human nature, God has determined what behaviors contribute to human flourishing and which do not.[105] Consequently, if God were to change the basic precepts of morality, God would first have to change human nature. Reminiscent of Lewis's "car analogy," Carlton Fisher offers his own:

> Consider, if you will, the operation manual for a new car. In it we find instructions to guide our relationship to the car. Don't do this, that, or the other. Do this and that. Commands for behavior. These are the right things to do. Now, let's ask Plato's question in this context. Are

102. Michael Peterson, "Creation, Ethics, and Education" in *Faculty Dialogue*, Winter (1993), no. 19:24.

103. For a helpful discussion on the nature of power in God, see Lawrence Moonan's *Divine Power: The Medieval Power Distinction up to its Adoption by Albert, Bonaventure, and Aquinas* (New York: Oxford University Press, 1994), especially chapters 6 and 7; also Craig A. Boyd, "Is Thomas Aquinas a Divine Command Theorist?" in *The Modern Schoolman* 55 (March 1998): 209–26.

104. Ia.25.5,ad1.

105. IIaIIae.104.4,ad2: "God never acts against nature, because it is the nature of all things to have God acting within them. He does however at times act contrary to the customary course of nature. Similarly, God is not able to command anything contrary to virtue since the meaning of virtue and the rectitude of man's will consist principally in conformity to God's will and in responding to His command, even when this is against the normal mode of virtue."

these instructions right because General Motors commanded us to do them? Or did General Motors command us to do them because they are right? If you will allow me the assumption that General Motors knows what they are doing, I think you will agree that the answer is rather obvious. They are so commanded because these are the right things to do in caring for the car.[106]

Fisher applies the car analogy to the commands in scripture: "The instructions which *are* in Scripture are there, not because God made them up, but because they *belong* in our instruction manual."[107] That is, God commands on the basis of what God has created. The created order determines that which is right, not because God arbitrarily imposes commands on us but because God has created us with a specific nature. We could extend Fisher's argument further:

1. Granted that God knows what God is creating (based on the doctrine of divine omniscience),
2. Granted God's benevolence,
3. God commands only those actions that are befitting our nature as humans.

We could briefly summarize the natural law morality as follows:

1. All humans know that specific activities are right and others wrong.
2. This knowledge is derived from our observation and reflection on the ends of human activity.
3. Given the way humans act for specific ends (viz., happiness), and the nature of our rational faculties, these moral obligations necessarily apply to all humans.

    Thus, given this world (including the manner in which God has created humans), God cannot change the precepts of natural law, as they are rooted ontologically in the creation.

It is in this way that natural law morality seems to make sense of common and general moral intuitions across cultures. As we have

106. Carlton Fisher, "Because God Says So," in *Christian Theism and the Problems of Philosophy*, ed. Michael D. Beaty (Notre Dame, IN: University of Notre Dame Press, 1990), 361–2.
107. Fisher, 365.

said, according to natural law morality all people know the primary precepts of natural law. The reason why all people know this is that there is an identifiable, universal human nature. Through what Aquinas called the "natural light of reason," all people could come to some knowledge about morality. By a kind of moral induction, all people discover that certain actions are always wrong and others are enjoined. So, one should not murder one's neighbor and one should honor one's parents. One need not have special revelation from God, nor does one need to do this simply because God commands it.

The reason why many can recognize these moral truths is that God has created humans with specific natures. These natures, as Aristotle observed, have specific purposes. The purpose, or *telos*, of a thing is grounded in its nature. From a Christian perspective, the *telos* of human nature is union with God; or, in the words of the *Catechism of the Catholic Church*, "God, infinitely perfect and blessed in himself, in a plan of sheer goodness freely created man to make him share in his own blessed life. For this reason, at every time and in every place, God draws close to man. He calls him to seek him, to know him, to love him with all his strength." [108] And so, accepting an account of morality based upon natural law does not result in committing one to the autonomy thesis; rather, a true understanding of natural law morality reveals that God is the *sine qua non* of the natural law.

Conclusion

Some natural lawyers have attempted to provide secular theories that appeal to all people regardless of their prior theological commitments. In so doing, they often relegate the theological dimension of natural law morality to the arena of private opinion or to an issue of secondary importance. These theorists wish to emphasize the universal appeal of natural law morality at the expense of its historic and theologically legitimate origins. In response to these kinds of natural law theories, divine command theorists have objected that if God is to play any part in morality, surely it will have to be an important part and not merely one that is subordinate to culturally acceptable rhetoric.

Two theories of divine command ethics have developed as responses to secularist theories of natural law morality. The strong theory which

108. *Catechism of the Catholic Church*, prologue, I.1.

holds that God command anything whatsoever collapses from the weight of its absurd consequences—that God could command the torture of innocents. However, weaker versions have held that since we know God is good, then these consequences do not follow. Weak theories of divine command ethics share with natural law the idea that created order plays an important role in ethics, but tend to stress either the incapacity to meet the demands of morality or argue that God's loving character is sufficient to meet any epistemic objections.

The natural law morality that I have defended has the advantage of acknowledging the importance of God as creator, and the real possibility of divine commands playing a role in the life of the believer. However, God's commands always lie within the broad parameters of natural law morality. God cannot command the murder of innocents, mass suicides, or the torture of children, since these run contrary to any possible genuine obligation. Thus, natural law morality places a curb on religious fanaticism that divine command theory cannot accommodate without either capitulating to the natural law conception of the good, or agreeing that God did indeed command these immoral activities.

5 | The Cultural Challenge

Postmodernist Relativism

Introduction

According to Stephen Pope, postmodern antirealism represents a critical challenge to natural law ethics, since postmodernism rejects the essentialism which is the epistemic basis for natural law's conception of human nature. Pope writes, "If there is no such thing as 'human nature' at all, then the notion of natural-law ethics is nonsense."[1] As we have seen, natural law has historically held that there are morally binding principles that all rational persons can recognize, and that these principles are discovered by reflection upon a nature that is shared by all people in all cultures. Historically, an essentialist ontology has provided the basis for natural law theory, since without a theory of essences natural law is subject to postmodern criticisms that human nature is merely a cultural fiction.

According to the postmodernists, the cultural fiction of natural law derives from a mistaken meta-narrative which sees the enduring task of philosophy as a search for transcendent truth. Yet meta-narratives are all subject to what Nietzsche called a "genealogy of morals," and

1. Stephen Pope, "Natural Law and Christian Ethics" in *The Cambridge Companion to Christian Ethics*, ed. Robin Gill (New York: Cambridge University Press, 2001), 91.

161

once the deconstruction of the meta-narrative is complete, essentialist assumptions of the meta-narrative can be scrapped.

In this chapter I argue that natural law can plausibly be reconstructed in spite of these criticisms. Accordingly, I contend that natural law morality depends upon a realist epistemology that explicitly denies the skeptical assumptions of postmodernism. In contrast, I hold that there are "natural kinds" of things that can be discovered by any normally functioning human intellect, and that human nature is one of these natural kinds. Moreover, natural law theory holds that all humans have behaviors that are appropriate to them *as* human.

5.1 Postmodernist Arguments Against Natural Law

The postmodern attitude is notoriously difficult to define, since it comprises a wide variety of perspectives. The most succinct characterization of the postmodern approach is captured by Jean-Francois Lyotard, who says "I define postmodern as incredulity toward meta-narratives."[2] This definition captures two key elements of the postmodern attitude: a basic skepticism about knowledge and a rejection of meta-narrative. Expanding on this preliminary definition, we could say that there are three interrelated themes that seem to express the attitudes and agendas of various postmodern writers from Friedrich Nietszche to Richard Rorty. The concerns of postmodern writers constitute intertwined attacks on traditional linguistic, epistemic, and metaphysical approaches to philosophy. The following three themes are central to postmodern philosophy: (1) a genealogy, or deconstruction, of linguistic expressions, (2) an attack on essentialism, and (3) a complete rejection of meta-narratives.[3]

2. Jean-Francois Lyotard, *The Postmodern Condition: A Report on Knowledge*, trans. Geoff Bennington and Brian Massumi (Minneapolis: University of Minnesota Press, 1984), xxiv.

3. Some may object to my characterization of postmodernism as well as the selection of thinkers discussed. To the former objection I say that the list simply reflects my own characterization of postmodernism from a natural law perspective; as a result, it is only natural that I develop those themes that directly challenge natural law. To the latter objection I maintain, for example, that although Rorty explicitly rejects Sartre's account of human agency as an instance of objectivism, both thinkers contribute to the stream of continuing antirealistic epistemology to which postmodernism has given birth. One might add that Martin Heidegger's rejection of the "onto-theological" tradition of Western metaphysics is a central idea in the history of postmodernism,

5.2 Nietzsche's Genealogy

One could argue that Nietszche's attack on conventional morality signaled the beginning of the antirealist approach to ethics that
eventually gave birth to postmodernism. Nietszche's iconoclastic
rhetoric and passionate rejection of Enlightenment epistemology and
morality paved the way for other like-minded thinkers who had grown
tired of the conventional modern attempts at grounding morality in
a universal and objective concept of reason. He asks,

> What then is truth? A mobile army of metaphors, metonyms, and an-
> thropomorphisms—in short a sum of human relations, which have
> been enhanced, transposed, and embellished poetically and rhetori-
> cally, and which after long use seem firm, canonical, and obligatory
> to a people; truths are illusions of which one has forgotten that this is
> what they are; metaphors which are worn out and without sensuous
> power; coins which have lost their pictures and now matter only as
> metal, no longer as coins.[4]

Language has lost its power to persuade, since it no longer has the
ability to convince us that there are objective referents that correspond
to our names. Nietzsche is the boy who is bold enough to declare that
"the emperor has no clothes." Once we realize this state of affairs,
we are well on our way to dismantling the Enlightenment project of
objective knowledge.

The idea of "truth" is merely a construct of our language, and so
there exists no overarching philosophical system that transcends
constructions of our own making. Any attempt at a systematic representation is a fundamental denial of reality. Nietzsche proclaims,
"I mistrust all systemizers and I avoid them. The will to a system is
a lack of integrity."[5]

In the wake of his criticisms of the Enlightenment, Nietszche advocates the morality of the *Übermensch* whose will to power and creative

---

but the inclusion of Heidegger in this chapter would make the analysis of postmodernism even more diffuse. Analytic philosophy as well has given rise to various forms
of antiessentialism, as found in, for example, Ludwig Wittgenstein's *Philosophical
Investigations* (New York: Oxford University Press, 1959).

4. Friedrich Nietzsche, *The Portable Nietzsche*, ed. Walter Kaufmann (New York:
Viking, 1954), 46–7.

5. Ibid., 470.

genius forges his own morality; or, rather, "he creates values."[6] As a result, there is no meta-narrative other than the one the *Übermensch* creates for himself. Arthur Holmes observes, "With no moral world order, no God, and no unchanging human nature in common to all, no grounds remain for universal values apart from our own making."[7] The Christian virtues of faith, charity, justice, and humility are trampled by the will to power, and natural law is rejected simply as the *ressentiment* of the weak and banal masses.

The history of humankind and its values, according to Nietszche, consist in the conflict between the slave morality of the masses (or the herd morality) and the creative genius of the masters. The herd morality appeals to "universal" moral principles in order to keep the powerful from exercising their genius. By inverting the natural powers of the creative soul, Christianity is a prime example of the slave morality at work. But Christianity grows out of the soil of Judaism, and here Nietzsche gives free reign to his contempt for the slave morality.

> It was the Jew who, with frightening consistency, dared to invert the aristocratic value equations good=noble=powerful=beautiful=happy= favored of the gods and maintain, with furious hatred of the under-privileged and impotent, that "only the poor, the powerless, are good; only the suffering, sick, and ugly, truly blessed."[8]

In the herd morality we see an assumed superiority of the slave, the assumed self-righteousness of the one who is capable of resisting his natural urges. The slave is the one who simply says "no" to the world and to all that is beautiful and creative. But this "no" is directed most clearly to the master morality. Robert Solomon says that "the attempt to define and defend morality against all objections and alternatives, is first and foremost the attempt to utterly discredit master morality."[9] This vehement rejection of master morality is based upon *ressentiment*.

6. Nietzsche, *Beyond Good and Evil*, 201. In a rare glimpse of rhetorical transparency, Frederick Copleston reveals his own belief that the *Übermensch* is "all that ailing, lonely, tormented, neglected Herr Professor Dr. Friedrich Nietzsche would like to be." *A History of Philosophy*, vol. 7 (New York: Image Books, 1967), 414.

7. Arthur F. Holmes, *Fact, Value and God* (Grand Rapids: Eerdmans, 1997), 160.

8. Nietzsche, *Genealogy of Morals* I, 7.

9. Robert Solomon, "Nietzsche ad hominem: Perspectivism, Personality, and *Ressentiment* Revisited" in *The Cambridge Companion to Nietzsche*, ed. Bernd Magnus and Kathleen Higgins (New York: Cambridge University Press, 1996), 201.

Ressentiment is the essence of "slave morality," and is created by those who fear the powerful, creative *Übermensch* in their attempt to keep him constrained.[10] Nietzsche explains, "The slave revolt in morality begins when *ressentiment* itself becomes creative and gives birth to values."[11] The herd invents moral principles (e.g., honesty and humility) as a reaction to the creative genius of those who are "beyond good and evil." According to this interpretation, Christianity and natural law represent two prime examples of *ressentiment* at work. The appeal to a "universal" morality is really a device to keep the powerful in their place. Solomon observes that "universality, according to Nietzsche, is thus not so much a logical feature of moral judgments, as philosophers from Kant to R. M. Hare have argued, but rather a strategy of the weak to deny the significance of the nonmoral virtues and impose their own morality on others."[12] But in their appeal to words like "universality" and "necessity," the defenders of the slave morality fail to see that words simply do not have the power that they think they have.

Nietszche contends that all moral systems, from Aristotle to Kant, appeal to the slave morality and its mistaken emphasis upon the universal. Kant, in particular, receives much of the criticism. His appeal to rationality and its fictional ideas of freedom and responsibility are akin to the attempt to "pull oneself up into existence by the hair, out of the swamps of nothingness."[13] Appeals to freedom, universal moral principles, autonomy, and objectivity are all exercises in futility.

For Nietzsche, the fact that there are no values in nature means that we necessarily impute values where there are none. We create values in order to give meaning to our existence and to the world we inhabit. "Because we have for millennia made moral, aesthetic, religious demands on the world . . . and abandoned ourselves to illogical thinking, this world has gradually *become* so marvelously variegated,

10. According to Jorg Salaquarda ("Nietzsche and the Judaeo-Christian Tradition," *The Cambridge Companion to Nietzsche*), *ressentiment* "designated a psychological disposition (although, according to his later analysis this disposition is physiologically conditioned). It is motivated by weakness and the often self-deceptive lust for revenge. Resentment is essentially *reactive*, and it is this reactive character of any morality based on resentment (particularly Christianity) that Nietzsche rejected," 103–4.

11. Nietzsche, *Genealogy of Morals* I, 10.

12. Solomon, "Nietzsche *ad hominem*," 206.

13. Nietzsche, *Beyond Good and Evil* I, 21.

frightful, meaningful, soulful, it has acquired colour—but we have been the colourers."[14] All attribution of value to the world is really self-description.

> When you speak so rapturously of a conformity to law in nature you must either assume that all natural things freely obey laws they themselves have imposed on themselves—in which case you are admiring the morality of nature—or you are entranced by the idea of a creative mechanic who has made the most ingenious clock. With living creatures upon it as decorations. Necessity in nature becomes more human and a last refuge of mythological dreaming through the expression of "conforming to law."[15]

Design, finality, and essences in nature are merely quaint holdovers from an early mythological era. The only values that we find are the ones that we have surreptitiously placed there.

5.3 Sartre's Rejection of the Natural Law's Essentialism

The rejection of the grand meta-narrative of Western ethical theory, its ever-present essentialism, and the articulation of a post-Enlightenment relativism is brought together most clearly in the thought of Jean-Paul Sartre. For Sartre, the Enlightenment did away with the necessity of God as an explanatory entity but made the mistake of retaining the notion of a universal morality. Yet the idea of transcendent universal moral principles should be jettisoned as well, since Nietzsche had shown it too was no longer needed.

Sartre's critique of natural law begins with what he takes to be its assumption that human nature must pre-exist in the mind of God, like the idea of a paper knife must pre-exist in the mind of a human artisan. Just as the paper knife has a specific teleology, so too does human nature (e.g., to live peacefully with others and to know and love God). The essence of the paper knife precedes its existence just as the essence of human nature precedes its existence. God is therefore conceived of as the cosmic artisan making humans "according to a procedure and a conception, exactly as the artisan manufactures a

14. Friedrich Nietzsche, *Human, All Too Human: A Book for Free Spirits*, trans. R. J. Hollingdale (New York: Cambridge University Press, 1996), vol. I,16.
15. Nietzsche, *Human, All Too Human*, vol II, 1, 9.

paper knife."[16] God provides the formal and final causes for the human agent. Yet the idea that God was required as a necessary condition for the establishment of human nature gradually disappeared in the Enlightenment, with the result that by the end of the twentieth century God was superfluous to both science and ethics.

Although many nonreligious people still cling to the idea that there must be universal essences that serve as the cornerstone for morality, Sartre counters that this is not so. Humans create their own essences. In the words of the famous expression, "existence precedes essence." But what does this mean? Sartre explains,

> Man [sic] first of all exists, encounters himself, surges up in the world—and defines himself afterwards. If man as the existentialist sees him is not definable, it is because to begin with he is nothing. He will not be anything until later, and then he will be what he makes of himself. Thus, there is no human nature, because there is no God to have a conception of it. [17]

If we leave aside for the moment the *non sequitur* with which the argument concludes and turn our attention to the claim that there is no human nature, we find Sartre professing that humans create themselves *ex nihilo*.

If essence precedes existence, then we are bound by some principle alien to our own basic freedom, which means we are sentenced to practicing "bad faith." For Sartre, bad faith is the attempt of the human agent to appropriate to itself a false sense of identity. That is, it is simply conforming to various expectations that the self has not freely chosen. Here we see the absolute centrality of freedom to Sartre's conception of human nature. The self is condemned to be free. To abdicate this responsibility and let anyone, or any institution, take on that responsibility for the self is to act on the basis of bad faith.

The key to understanding the human condition is in our ability to create ourselves and exercise our freedom. Therefore, existence *must* precede essence in order to vouchsafe human freedom from those who would relegate it to subservience. Seen in this light, God and the

16. Jean-Paul Sartre, *Existentialism and Humanism*, trans. Philip Mairet (London: Eyre Methuen Limited, 1973), 27.
    17. Ibid., 27.

church can play no role in human morality since their authorities usurp human freedom. As a result, Sartre confesses that,

> The existentialist finds it extremely embarrassing that God does not exist, for there disappears with Him all possibility of finding values in an intelligible heaven. There can no longer be any good *a priori*, since there is no infinite and perfect consciousness to think it. It is nowhere written that "the good" exists, that one must be honest or must not lie, since we are now upon the plane where there are only men.[18]

Sartre agrees with Dostoevsky's dictum that "if there is no God, then anything is permissible." Sartre embraces this fully and proclaims, "everything is indeed permitted if God does not exist, and man is in consequence forlorn, for he cannot find anything to depend upon either within or outside himself."[19] Since there is no basis for morality either found in human nature—as natural law theorists maintain—or in divine commands, we see that Sartrian existentialism is not the Enlightenment rationalism that wants to reject God and retain universal essences. Rather, it is the desire to be rid of both once and for all.

5.4 The Rejection of the Natural Law Meta-narrative: Foucault and Derrida

Postmodernism's first task is to rob language of its fundamentally intuitive realism. Nietzsche's approach is to give a "genealogy" of moral terms, and in his attempt to lay bare the original meanings of terms such as "right" and "good" he claims that they merely reflected the *ressentiment* of the masses. Like Nietzsche, Foucault uses the method of genealogy to unravel the great meta-narratives of Western civilization. In this process, truth claims come to be seen as nothing other than "masks" for power. Any tradition, whether science, religion, or culture, that requires universal assent is hiding its own power agenda, which may have been the suspicion lurking behind Nietzsche's mistrust of "systemizers."

One such meta-narrative is the "fiction" of human nature. Foucault goes beyond Sartre's existentialist proclivities to freedom and pro-

18. Sartre, *Existentialism and Humanism*, 33.
19. Ibid., 33–4.

claims that human nature is simply an invention of human culture dating back to the seventeenth century. On Foucault's view, Sartre is as guilty as all the rest of reinforcing the fiction of human nature. In Sartre's case, he has simply replaced essences with freedom. Human nature is merely a fiction that seemed useful to the philosophers of the day. Now we see that the focus of knowledge is not on humanity but on the linguistic devices that constitute the idea of "humanity." Humans are constructed primarily through linguistic means, and so the idea of a "human nature" is pure fiction based upon a spurious anachronism. Accordingly, Foucault chides, "To all those who still wish to think about man . . . to all those who still ask themselves questions about what man is in his essence, to all those who wish to take him as their starting-point in their attempts to reach the truth . . . to all these warped and twisted forms of reflection we can answer only with a laugh."[20] Foucault's mockery of philosophical anthropology rests upon his charge that there is no continuity in human history because there is no point from which one could possibly have objective knowledge. There is no extra-historical consciousness that enables one to write an objective history. All history is written from within the historical consciousness, and from within the discourses that shape that consciousness.

Three basic problems lie at the root of the meta-narrative that we have naively assented to.[21] First, we have believed that an objective body of knowledge exists. As we have seen, for Foucault this simply is impossible. The second mistake is that we can have genuine knowledge that is value-neutral. Third, the pursuit of knowledge benefits all humanity, not just one specific class. These last two points deserves special attention.

For Foucault, the idea that knowledge benefits all humanity is merely a lie which the powerful have used to deceive the masses. Knowledge and power are intimately linked by a desire for control. He says, "Knowledge does not slowly detach itself from its empirical roots, the initial needs from which it arose, to become pure speculation subject only to the demands of reason. . . . Rather, it creates a

20. Michel Foucault, *The Order of Things: An Archaeology of the Human Sciences* (New York: Pantheon Books, 1971), 342–3.
21. Sheldon S. Wolin, "On the Theory and Practice of Power," in *After Foucault: Humanist Knowledge, Postmodern Challenges*, ed. Jonathon Arac (New Brunswick, NJ: Rutgers University Press, 1988), 181.

progressive enslavement to its instinctive violence."[22] Foucault recognizes what Nietzsche saw before him, that the will to power is what drives the slave morality in its pursuit of control. He believes that the drive is a "will to knowledge," since the possession of knowledge is required for power.

Institutions develop skills in discourse which enable appeals to so-called "objective" knowledge. This knowledge is simply what the power structures have found useful and subsequently inculcated in their adherents. Truth, therefore, is dependent on the interests of the institution and the methods by which the institution develops discourse. In this way, Foucault argues that our perceptions of reality are merely the products of sophisticated rhetoric embedded in systems of power.

History is a good example of how institutions create a discourse for the purposes of exercising power. Political parties rewrite history with a view to establishing their own moral legitimacy. However, genealogy serves as the corrective for this attitude of the powerful. A genealogy uncovers the link of power to knowledge and refuses to submit to the caprice of the hegemonic power structures.

It was Nietzsche's postmodern disciple Jacques Derrida who developed genealogy into "deconstruction." Briefly, deconstruction is the intentional unraveling of realist linguistics. According to Derrida,

> Deconstruction cannot limit itself or proceed immediately to a neutralization: it must, by means of a double gesture, a double science, a double writing, practice an *overturning* of the classical opposition *and* a general *displacement* of the system. . . . Each concept, moreover, belongs to a systematic chain, and itself constitutes a system of predicates. There is no metaphysical concept in and of itself. There is a work—metaphysical or not—on conceptual systems. Deconstruction does not consist in passing from one concept to another, but in overturning and displacing a conceptual order.[23]

God, the soul, truth, and morality are all collective illusions created by human culture expressing nothing other than the interests of those

22. Michel Foucault, "Nietzsche, Genealogy, History," in *Language, Counter-Memory, and Practice: Selected Essays and Interviews*, ed. Donald F. Bouchard (Ithaca, NY: Cornell University Press, 1977), 163.

23. Jacques Derrida, *Margins of Philosophy*, trans. Alan Bass (Chicago: University of Chicago Press, 1982), 329.

who use the words. Religion is a human construction that employs terms (e.g., God, the soul, and hell) for the purpose of maintaining its own power. In order to get compliance from its followers, the religious system must utilize a realist epistemology. Those who become part of the religious institution must really believe in the soul, God, and hell as having real ontological existence, otherwise the fear that gives religion its power will be lost. Thus once the realist epistemology fails, the entire system can be deconstructed.

Derrida sees words as inadequate and inaccurate since they can never encompass the reality of the object. The object is always in flux, and so to use a static signifier for a dynamic reality is pointless. Yet our preoccupation with the discovery of essences has led to a point where words now have an illegitimate priority over their referents, and thus the meta-narratives have endured.

Since language is a human construction, it can also be deconstructed. And because we can only think within the confines of our culture, it follows that the limits of our language set the parameters for our conceptual framework. Hence we can have no genuine knowledge of the world as it is, since we are sentenced to inhabiting a world of our own making with no access to an extra-cultural linguistic reality. The only possible route left open to us is that of competing interpretations, none of which can claim priority. This epistemological attitude is known as "perspectivism," and claims that there is no one point of view that grasps all reality—that there is no "God's- eye view" of things. Consequently, we can never know the world as it is; we can only know our perspective since we are necessarily limited by religion, culture, family, and so on. The result for morality is that there can be no universal standard to which we can appeal to adjudicate moral differences.

The deconstruction of language and its concepts inevitably results in a rejection of essentialism. If language can only be understood within its own web of meaning, there is truly nothing outside the text. Truth does not reflect reality but is merely a convention, or rather an *invention*. Derrida says that the great mistake Western philosophers have made is their belief that all language is representational. Their basic orientation he calls "logocentrism," which assumes that words signify realities "out there." The idea that there is some meta-linguistic reality that corresponds to our words leads us on a quest to uncover the structure that undergirds our conceptions of reality. This quest has resulted in the grand meta-narratives of Western culture, which we are now able to see as the fictions they always were.

5.5 Rorty's Ironic Method and Solidarity

Imbibing from both the traditions of Nietzsche, Foucault, and Derrida, on the one hand, and American pragmatism on the other, Richard Rorty also sees the rejection of a transcendence of language as a critical stage in the successful development of philosophy.[24] For too long, philosophy has been the victim of a Babylonian captivity to realist conceptions of epistemology and ontology. The realist, on Rorty's redescription, believes in two philosophical fictions: (1) there is an objective extra-linguistic reality that transcends our language, and (2) truth is correspondence between our language and extra-linguistic entities. When applied to morality, we see that the realist believes in a universal human nature that somehow stands as the ultimate explanation for why others are owed respect and consideration. The paradigm of this view is natural law ethics. According to Rorty, "this tradition dreams of an ultimate community which will have transcended the distinction between the natural and the social, which will exhibit a solidarity which is not parochial because it is the expression of an ahistorical human nature."[25] Natural law on Rorty's view embodies the key elements of Enlightenment objectivism, since its realist metaphysics and referentialist epistemology attempt to "point to" an objective morality.

At the heart of realist moral theory lies a fear that led to the positing of "real essences." The realist sees natures as useful moral concepts without which it would be impossible to ensure basic rights for all peoples. But Rorty asks, "do we really need essences to know that it is wrong to torture innocent children?" The answer is "no," we merely need adequate inter-subjective agreement and dialogue that result in our acknowledgment that it is wrong to treat children in such a manner.

24. Rorty has recently resisted being labeled "postmodern" in his "Introduction: Pragmatism and Post-Nietzschean Philosophy," *Essays on Heidegger and Others: Philosophical Papers*, vol. 2 (New York: Cambridge University Press, 1992), 1. However, in his earlier work he saw it as an acceptable self-description. See his "Postmodernist Bourgeois Liberalism," *Journal of Philosophy* 80 (October 1983).

25. Richard Rorty, "Solidarity or Objectivity," in *Objectivity, Relativism and Truth: Philosophical Papers*, vol. 1 (New York: Cambridge University Press, 1991), 22.

But this quest to transcend the self's particularity in order to achieve an objective ahistorical understanding of ethics is a perverse desire that requires not satisfaction but eradication. In contrast to the realist conceptualization of philosophy, Rorty offers his own neo-pragmatic account. On this view, natures play no significant role in either ontology or ethics since they have no "cash value."

If philosophy is to survive, we must directly face the fact that we are inescapably bound by our language. The basic principle Rorty appeals to is what he calls the "linguistic turn," according to which "one cannot transcend language; that is, one cannot find a point of view outside of all linguistic frameworks from which the world will appear 'as it is.' One can't think without thinking in a language."[26] For Rorty, postmodernism does not consist in denying that there is an extra-mental world, but in the idea that we can obtain a transcendent understanding of that world apart from our linguistic constructions. Thus,

> We need to make a distinction between the claim that the world is out there and the claim that truth is out there. To say that the world is out there, that it is not our creation, is to say with common sense, that things in space and time are the effects of causes which do not include human mental states. To say that truth is not out there is simply to say that where there are no sentences there is no truth, that sentences are elements of human language, and that human languages are human creations.[27]

Philosophy therefore becomes a dialogue, a conversation among participants rather than a quest for transcendent principles of nature. Truth no longer refers to the correspondence between our minds and reality, as it had in the classic tradition of realist epistemology. Rather, it is simply a linguistic expression we use to facilitate the continuing conversation. He says, "For the pragmatist . . . 'knowledge' is, like 'truth,' simply a compliment paid to the beliefs which we think so well justified that, for the moment, further justification is not needed."[28] If truth consists solely in pragmatic utility, then traditional conceptions

26. Richard Rorty, "Realism, Categories, and the 'Linguistic Turn'" in *International Philosophical Quarterly* 2 (1962): 310.

27. Richard Rorty, *Contingency, Irony and Solidarity* (New York: Cambridge University Press, 1989), 5.

28. Rorty, "Solidarity or Objectivity," 24.

of science—based as they are on realist representationalism—are likewise subject to the postmodernist's critique.

According to Rorty, science is not concerned with understanding reality as it is. Rather, science is technology, and its purpose is to help us cope with the world. Conceived in this way things do not have real identifiable properties; rather, they have more or less predictable tendencies which can be anticipated. Summarizing Rorty's inversion of modernist referentialism, Stanley Grenz says that "properties do not inhere in isolated objects; rather, a thing's properties are dependent on the language we use to describe them."[29] For Rorty, science is simply a pragmatic activity specific to Western cultures that enables people to control their lives and their environments more efficiently.

But how is it that science fails as a realist account of the world? A ready example for the postmodernist is the issue of quantum physics. From the seventeenth through the early twentieth centuries, Newtonian mechanics, with its "universal" laws, dominated the field of physics. But with the advent of quantum physics the world became suddenly strange. The subatomic world did not operate in the anticipated ways that the Newtonians expected. Rather it resisted realist descriptions. The Heisenberg Uncertainty Principle states that we can determine the momentum of an electron but not its position, or we can determine its position but not its momentum. Defenders of postmodernism saw this as a means of calling into question the necessity of realist descriptions of the world. They claimed that there were simply different language games that operated in different forms of life, to use Wittgenstein's terms. Therefore the scientific enterprise could be construed as just another meta-narrative. Scientists' claims for universality and hegemonic dominance are doomed to the same fate as all other meta-narratives.

Since postmodernists deny any and all meta-narratives, natural law can simply be dismissed as just one more logocentric construction. Appeals to universal human nature or natural law can be dismissed as naïve, anachronistic invocations of discarded Western meta-narratives. In addition to these criticisms, we can see that a rejection of realism entails that there can be no "laws" or "natural kinds," since the scientific enterprise is likewise compromised by its realist assumptions that cannot account for the diversity and complexity of the world. And

29. Stanley Grenz, *A Primer on Postmodernism* (Grand Rapids: Eerdmans, 1996), 185.

so Nietszche warns, "Let us be on guard against saying that there are laws of nature."[30] Reflecting on the postmodern challenge to natural law, Pope notes that "if there is no properly rational practical reason, but only a raw human capacity for enculturation and socialization, then it makes no sense to talk about a natural-law ethic."[31]

5.6 The Value of the Postmodern Critique

The postmodern critique of natural law ethics has three valuable features: (1) it reveals the fact that too often moral rhetoric has often been the mask of political interests, (2) it demonstrates that convention has often been confused with enduring eternal moral principles, and (3) it serves as a corrective to the overly-ambitious Enlightenment project of establishing a universal reason.

A claim that both postmodernists and Marxists have made repeatedly is that moral language merely masks private interests. The list of abuses is a long one. "Manifest destiny" was the shibboleth that justified the stealing of land in America from its rightful occupants. The supposed "survival of the German state" was used to justify Hitler's murder of millions of Jews. The so-called "natural superiority of men over women" has been used for centuries to relegate women to subservience and to the status of property. "Self-defense" is a common excuse for unbridled international aggression. It certainly seems unquestionable that moral rhetoric does in fact function in the way postmodernism describes, and that the rhetoric in question assumes an objectivity beyond critique. Objective morality in the hands of the rhetorically sophisticated becomes a dangerous tool for exploitation. However, we can ask whether or not this is a necessary feature of moral language, or simply an abuse of it.

Natural law ethics has often made sweeping universal judgments to justify what, in retrospect, were merely social conventions; slavery and the subjugation of women are two ready examples of this. The feminist critique provides a clear example of how natural law has endorsed a morality of gender inequity. As Simone de Beauvoir observed, the natural law tradition, tracing its roots from Aquinas

30. Friedrich Nietszche, *The Joyful Wisdom*, trans. Thomas Common (New York: Frederick Ungar Publishing, 1960), 152.
31. Pope, "Natural Law and Christian Ethics," 91.

back to Aristotle, consistently emphasized the inferiority of women. She notes that Aristotle considered women "defective," and Aquinas saw women as "imperfect" men. She writes,

> Legislators, priests, philosophers, writers and scientists have striven to show that the subordinate position of women is willed in heaven and advantageous on earth. . . . They have made use of philosophy and theology as the quotes from Aristotle and St. Thomas have shown.[32]

She observes that at one point Aquinas claims that "it is unchangeable that woman is destined to live under man's influence."[33] Esther Reed has voiced the objection of many feminists to natural law ethics when she writes, "Vast tracts of Aquinas' writings . . . are texts of horror which perpetuate misogyny."[34] The natural law apologist must demonstrate that the theory is capable of being recontextualized, in order to reflect the present understanding of human nature without abandoning natural law's primary precepts. This requires both a noetic humility as well as an understanding of human nature that is, in some sense, stable.

A third important issue postmodernists raise concerns the idea that the Enlightenment project was overly ambitious in its attempts to secure objective knowledge. There simply is no "God's-eye view" of the world, or a perspectival-less orientation to the problems of nature and morality. Although many modernist versions of natural law appeal to Enlightenment conceptions of reason, it does not follow that all natural lawyers are committed to Kantian *a priori* conceptions of reason.

5.7 Critique of the Postmodernist Agenda

The perennial problem for postmodern philosophy of any kind is the difficulty of self-referentialism. If we grant that the postmodern perspective does in fact offer a genuine criticism of traditional epistemology, how seriously should we take that criticism? There

32. Simone de Beauvoir, *The Second Sex*, trans. H. M. Parshley (New York: Vintage Books, 1997), 22.
33. As quoted in de Beauvoir, *The Second Sex*, 129.
34. Esther Reed, "Pornography and the End of Morality?" *Studies in Christian Ethics*. 7, no. 2 (1994): 86.

are at least two ways we can argue that postmodern arguments are self-referentially incoherent.

First, if the postmodern critique is the correct interpretation, then all other accounts of metaphysics, epistemology, ontology, and ethics must be false. But if the postmodern critique is merely one interpretation among many, then any interpretation of metaphysics, epistemology, ontology, and ethics must be acceptable. But the postmodern interpretation does seem to be offered as the only correct interpretation. So how is it that any postmodern account can be true if it has rejected any account of truth that depends on realist epistemologies?

If proponents of postmodernism want to argue that theirs is merely one interpretation among many—a decidedly weaker claim—then they must allow for competing interpretations. If this is so, then no one interpretation can claim superiority over the others. And we have yet to see any postmodern defense that makes this weaker claim. It seems that the postmodern philosopher has refuted herself by assuming, as a hidden premise, a definition of truth inconsistent with her fundamental orientation. Foucault at one point explicitly contradicts his own postmodern relativism when he asserts the existence of an objective right to protest unjust governments. He says, "The suffering of men must never be a silent residue of policy. It grounds the *absolute right* to stand up and speak to those who hold power."[35] Given his postmodernist orientation, whence "absolute rights"?

This self-referential problem seems inextricably bound to the postmodern method of deconstructing the views of others, while simultaneously giving one's own perspective privileged status. Rorty claims that science is merely the story we tell ourselves; it is a cultural artifact we have created. Commenting on Rorty's critique of science, Bernard Williams points out that

[i]t is self-defeating. If the story he tells were true, then there would be no perspective from which he could express it in this way. If it is over-

35. Michel Foucault, *Power: The Essential Works of Foucault 1954–1984*, ed. James D. Faubion, trans. Robert Hurley and others (New York: The New Press, 2000), 475 (emphasis added). MacIntyre observes that occasionally Foucault "relapses from the genealogical standpoint, especially perhaps when later in life, in interviews he succumbed to the temptation to be professorial in too encyclopedic an explanatory mode." *Three Rival Versions of Moral Enquiry: Encyclopeadia, Genealogy, and Tradition* (Notre Dame, IN: University of Notre Dame Press, 1990), 213.

whelmingly convenient to say that science describes what is already
there, and if there are no deep metaphysical or epistemological issues
here but only a question of what is convenient . . . then what everyone
should be saying, including Rorty, is that science describes a world
already there. But Rorty urges us not to say that, and in doing so, in
insisting, as *opposed to* that, on our talking of what it is convenient
to say, he is trying to reoccupy the transcendental standpoint outside
human speech and activity which is precisely what he wants us to
renounce.[36]

Even if we take Rorty's "linguistic turn," there is no way to resolve the
tension between his desire to reconstruct the views of others without
turning the gun on himself.

There is, however, another problem of self-referentialism. It may
be the case that a postmodernist may argue that the use of logic in
argumentation is itself a product of logocentrism. Derrida might
contend that the dilemma I just employed against the postmodern
interpretation is a product of a false logocentric hierarchy. Indeed,
Derrida suggests that "the unsurpassable, unique, and imperial gran-
deur of the order of reason, that which makes it not just another
actual order or structure . . . is that one cannot speak out against it
except by being for it, that one can protest it only from within it."[37]
Derrida therefore argues that we are inescapably bound within the
order of reason, and that we must use it to critique its own order. Yet
if this circular critique is to amount to anything more than an exercise
in futility, Derrida must assume that his use of reason is somehow
privileged over all others. The problem of self-referentialism rears
its ugly head once again. Alisdair McIntyre asks the question, "can
the genealogist legitimately include the self out of which he speaks
in explaining himself within his or her genealogical narrative? Is the
genealogist not self-indulgently engaged in exempting his or her utterances from the treatment to which everyone else's is subjected?"[38]
The answer to MacIntyre's latter question is an emphatic "yes."

But even so, there is a second problem, that of rhetorical transparency. The postmodern rhetoric assumes a representationalism

36. Bernard Williams, *Ethics and the Limits of Philosophy* (Cambridge, MA: Harvard
University Press, 1985), 137–8.

37. Jacques Derrida, *Writing and Difference*, trans. Alan Bass (Chicago: University
of Chicago Press, 1978), 36.

38. MacIntyre, *Three Rival Versions of Moral Enquiry*, 210.

inconsistent with its own assumptions. Derrida, like Foucault, Nietzsche, and Rorty, assumes a realist epistemological rhetoric in his own presentation of postmodernism. He must assume the system—one he subjects to scathing criticism—to be the accurate portrayal of his own ideas. Hilary Putnam objects, "This is a self-refuting exercise if there ever was one."[39] As a result, we see the normative use of reason and the realist epistemology it assumes are incapable of being eliminated.

If we recall that a central element of postmodernism is the rejection of the meta-narrative, then these thinkers are all guilty of a third philosophical mistake, that of a religious allegiance to their own pet narratives. They have smuggled the narrative of their own preference into the discussion in order to replace the traditional meta-narrative of "human nature." Nietzsche argues vehemently against "human nature" and then argues for his *Übermensch*, complete with its own teleology (i.e., the will to power). Sartre rails against essentialism and, as Rorty correctly points out, commits himself to freedom as the dominant meta-narrative for all humanity. Indeed, we fail to achieve Sartre's ideal if we act in "bad faith." The only means by which he can make such a radical value-laden judgment is by an appeal to his own meta-narrative. Foucault takes Nietzsche's will to power and makes it the will to knowledge. Rorty rejects the meta-narrative of "human nature" and displaces it with the idea of a "conversational partner."

A fourth problem is what MacIntyre has called the internalist problem for postmodernism. Genealogy requires both a continuity between the self that was deceived by the prevailing meta-narrative and is now no longer deceived, and a discontinuity between the self and the dominant meta-narrative. MacIntyre redescribes it by saying, "the function of genealogy as emancipatory from deception and self-deception thus requires the identity and continuity of the self that was deceived and the self that is and is to be."[40] But in constructing an emancipatory narrative, one fails to see that this narrative presupposes the coherence of an identifiable unity that stands behind the deconstructionist posturing.

What has . . . very rarely, if at all, attracted explicit genealogical scrutiny is the extent to which the genealogical stance is dependent for

39. Hilary Putnam, *Realism and Reason: Philosophical Papers*, vol. 3 (New York: Cambridge University Press, 1983), 246.
40. MacIntyre, *Three Rival Versions of Moral Enquiry*, 214.

its concepts and its modes of argument, for its theses and its style, upon a set of contrasts between it and that which it aspires to over-come—the extent, that is, to which it is inherently derivative from and parasitic upon its antagonisms and those towards whom they are directed, drawing its sustenance from that which it professes to have discarded.[41]

MacIntyre says, "If the genealogist is inescapably one who disowns part of his or her own past, then the genealogist's narrative presup-poses enough of unity, continuity, and identity to make such disowning possible."[42] The genealogist is one who must disown her past because it is in this act that she is emancipated from her imprisonment within the fictional meta-narrative. But if it is truly a fiction, then no escape is necessary. Of the genealogist we may say, "Methinks she doth pro-test too much."

In spite of the postmodern insistence that there are no essences or natures, it can be seen that this critique of culture does have a posi-tive role to play. In the past, some versions of natural law have held that particular cultural conventions are part of the essence of human nature. Following Aristotle, these natural lawyers argued that the inferiority of women and various ethnic groups was part of "human nature." But simply because some natural lawyers have smuggled in cultural biases and attempted to make them normative, it does not follow that natural law is merely a chimera. What does follow is that if natural law theory is viable, it must transcend the narrow confines of historical and cultural peculiarities.

5.8 The Natural Law Reconstruction

In spite of objections, the success of the natural sciences has proven an insurmountable problem for postmodernism. The realist assump-tions of the natural sciences and their successes that have built upon these assumptions have sufficiently silenced the quixotic quests of those who would advocate antirealist epistemologies.

Some, like Bas Van Fraassen, argue that science does not aim at truth and that we can never know whether theoretical terms refer

41. Ibid., 215.
42. Ibid., 214.

to real entities.[43] So even though science is successful, we can never say with any confidence that essences really exist. Yet we can reject this antirealist approach for three reasons. First, it fails to account for the universal acceptance of the realism that scientists themselves advocate. Second, it strips science of its explanatory power. Third, "if various theoretical principles are not on the right track, it is difficult to account for the success science has had in predicting entirely new phenomena, phenomena often *observationally unrelated* to either the phenomena for which the theory was originally proposed or to anything else previously known."[44]

Alister McGrath has said, "Reality acts as a constraint upon the reflections and theories of the natural sciences, which restrains them from presenting as 'true' theories which can be shown to be arbitrary, random, or an expression of the unbounded imagination."[45] This claim is true even in the problematic field of subatomic physics. Even there some theories can be ruled out as not explaining the data. The postmodernist claim that theoretical explanation rules out realist epistemologies is an aberration where empirical methods have not yet solved the problem. But the more serious problem for the postmodernist argument here is that it mirrors the "God of the gaps" arguments so often employed by theists who wish to carve out a niche for God in the natural world. If and when physicists solve the explanatory problem of subatomic physics, what argument then will be left for the postmodernists to attack the sciences? But even if the Heisenberg Uncertainty Principle remains an insurmountable problem, a singular exception to the principle seems so dreadfully inadequate for the work postmodernist expect it to do.

The realist epistemology that the sciences employ has been one of the chief reasons for the progress of the sciences. A key assumption in this approach is the idea that there are various "natural kinds" of things that can accurately be investigated by empirical methodologies. In biology, for example, there are real differences

43. Bas Van Fraassen, *The Scientific Image* (Oxford: Oxford University Press, 1980).

44. Del Ratzsch, *Science and Its Limits: The Natural Sciences in Christian Perspective* (Downers Grove, IL: Intervarsity Press, 2000), 81 (emphasis in the original).

45. Alister McGrath, *A Scientific Theology: Volume 1 Nature* (Edinburgh: T & T Clark, 2000), 123.

between vertebrates and invertebrates that resist any attempt of deconstruction on the part of postmodernism. It is difficult to see how one could claim that this distinction is merely the product of logocentrism or the *ressentiment* of jellyfish and other oppressed invertebrates! Spinal cords truly exist apart from our "social constructions," and they help differentiate among various kinds of animals; this real distinction in nature makes possible the progress of biology.

We further see that some animals share specific properties with others. For example, chimpanzees and humans share 98 percent of their genes and this helps to understand various social behaviors the species have in common. If therefore humans are a natural kind, it follows that there will be characteristics of the species that apply to the entire group and not merely to one or two isolated individuals. Furthermore, there may be characteristics that resist deconstruction.

As we have seen, E. O. Wilson has argued that evolutionary processes have shaped humans in such a way that it would be impossible for them to survive as a species without observing some specific behaviors. Among these behaviors we find incest avoidance, nurture of the young, and prohibitions on murder. These behaviors are shared universally by all human cultures. One can simply point to the capacity and practice of language in all cultures to demonstrate that it is a universal characteristic of human communication that even the most stubborn postmodernist is forced to use.

According to James Rachels, in order for social cooperation to take place societies must agree on two universally binding moral principles. These principles apply with necessity and universality. The first is the principle of non-maleficence: in order to cooperate all members of a community must agree not to harm other members of that community. The second principle is the principle of honesty. In order to be members of the community, all must speak truthfully in their promise not to harm others. Without these two principles no human society is even conceivable. These two moral principles are recognized by everyone from Kantians to Utilitarians as morally binding. What makes natural law morality unique is that it holds that these principles are part of our very nature (considered as both biological and rational beings), not merely universalizable rational maxims or rules that guarantee the greatest net utility.

5.9 Essential Natures and Natural Law

Natural law requires, as a presupposition, that human beings have enduring, identifiable natures, which in turn requires some kind of realism. I have argued some form of epistemological realism must be utilized by anyone engaged in meaningful philosophical discourse, including those who defend postmodernism. It is precisely these realist assumptions that make a natural law morality possible. Unless we are able to perceive the world adequately and understand it, no natural law is possible.

The realist epistemology employed by Aquinas can be seen in his treatise on human nature.[46] A substantial form can be known through the unaided power of the agent intellect. The agent intellect abstracts from the particular the substantial form and impresses the universal upon the passive intellect. Thus, there is no need for special powers apart from the "natural light of reason" all humans possess. While we need not subscribe to Aquinas's descriptions of the process of knowledge, we can say that his account of essences is accurate in the sense that the human intellect is capable of understanding the basic nature of material objects, as the empirical sciences have demonstrated. Anthony Lisska has argued that the basic outline of natural law in Aquinas is the following:

1. Thomistic essences are 'developmental' in that they have a natural *telos*.
2. We come to understand essences by means of empirical and rational methods.
3. The final cause is a kind of 'good.'
4. A good is the 'full development' of a dispositional property.
5. The essence of a thing determines its end.
6. Anyone whose reason functions properly can know the precepts of natural law.[47]

Lisska says, "The natural law, in the mind of Aquinas, is nothing more than the determination of ends—read final cause—of the dispositional properties of the essence—read formal cause—of the human person.

46. Ia. 84–86.
47. Anthony Lisska, *Aquinas's Theory of Natural Law: An Analytic Reconstruction* (Oxford: Clarendon Press, 1996).

By using theoretical reason, the moral agent comes to understand the content of human nature. This content, in terms of essential properties, is determined by the form. The agent then determines that actions need to be undertaken in order to develop these dispositions."[48] Humans are capable of applying this method to all essences in the natural world.

We discover that all beings have a nature, or an essence. These natures may be fairly simple, as in the case of elements found on the periodic table; or they may be more complex, as in the case of a beehive. Regardless of their complexity, they can be understood and identified. Furthermore, they behave in predictable ways. Bees guarding the entrance to the hive will attack invaders who do not belong to the hive in order to protect it. This is for the "good" of the hive, and we see this behavior in all honeybee societies.

Like honeybees, jellyfish, and elements in the periodic table, humans also possess a unique nature. In a biological sense, one can begin to classify humans as mammals, members of the primate family, *Homo sapiens sapiens*, and possessing forty-six chromosomes. All these are necessary conditions for humanity, but not sufficient. So what is it in addition to the biological that makes humans what they are? It is the recognition of the natural law and its demands upon us.

Aquinas's famous definition of the natural law is that it is a "participation in the eternal law on the part of the rational creatures."[49] Aquinas therefore asserts not one but two meta-narratives. First, he holds to a theistic metaphysic wherein God acts as sovereign over all of creation. The eternal law is, therefore, God's ordination of all things to their appropriate ends. Secondly, the natural law is that meta-narrative that establishes human nature and its own peculiar activity within the eternal law.

The basic premise of all natural law morality is that the "good is to be pursued and evil avoided."[50] Since the good for humans is diverse, there will be varying kinds of goods that ought to be pursued in diverse ways. At this point we see how scientific realism informs a natural law theory. The natural sciences show us that all life has a drive to preserve its own being. From amoebas to humans, all life desires its own continued existence. In addition to this most basic organic form

48. Ibid., 124–5.
49. IaIIae.94.2.
50. IaIIae.94.1.

of life, we can say that all animal life has a drive to reproduce and care for its young. These animal drives are based upon natural instincts that universally guide them to their appropriate activities. But we find in *Homo sapiens* a further characteristic: a human capacity for desires that exceed the purely animal and biological.

This unique capacity Aquinas called the "rational soul." However, it may be more appropriate to call it the "human soul." Humans have desires and goods that require the exercise of reason. Without the desire for truth, humans wouldn't be able to survive. While other animals have instincts that contribute to their survival, humans possess the desire for truth and must pursue it in order to avoid fatal consequences.

Humans possess a natural desire for truth and this desire is manifested in many ways: in the pursuit of science, in theological reflection, in choosing what to eat, and so on. The self-directed nature of human behavior is a critical aspect of natural law morality. It requires a teleological dimension that is simultaneously given by God but also manifested in free choice.

Humans have the freedom to pursue the good in a variety of ways. We are even free to choose apparent goods (or lesser goods) in preference to real goods. But there is no one way of determining how we should be just or temperate. Natural law provides a wide variety of ways of choosing the good, but it also specifies certain activities that are fundamentally disordered (e.g., murder). Mortimer Adler has said,

> In the case of other animal species, the specific nature in common to all members of the species is constituted mainly by quite determinate characteristics or attributes. In the case of the human species, it is constituted by determinable, not wholly determinate, characteristics or attributes. An innate potentiality is precisely that—something determinable, not wholly determinate, and determinable in a wide variety of ways.[51]

We have rational potencies that require our activities to actualize them. This explains both the great commonalities among all cultures in their appropriation of the natural law, as well as the differences.

51. Mortimer Adler, *Ten Philosophical Mistakes* (New York: Touchstone Books, 1987), 163.

Both Adler and Lisska raise the critical issue of the teleological aspect of essences. There is an open-ended aspect to human nature such that we are born with specific capacities (e.g., for language and thought); but precisely how those capacities are actualized depends upon our context (e.g., family, geography, culture, etc.). Thus, the end of living a peaceful communal life can be achieved in a variety of ways. The mistake of postmodernism is to identify a material manifestation with the formal nature. Rorty confuses Aristotelian essentialism with the particular manifestation of the potency in act. Human potencies, or capacities, can be actualized in a variety of ways with the result that one moral capacity might have multiple actualities or manifestations. This ironically implies a profound lack of imagination on his part. We can simply provide a redescription of his redescription of essentialism with the result that he has been hoisted on his own pitard!

In what specific ways should a natural lawyer respond to issues raised by postmodernism's critique? First, the defenders of natural law can begin by denying the antirealist epistemology of postmodernism and the skepticism it engenders. By stubbornly burying its head in the sand, postmodernism fails to take the realism inherent in our language seriously. Furthermore, it fails to acknowledge the huge successes science (which assumes a realist epistemology) has made.[52] Postmodernism's perspectivism is fundamentally a linguistic attack on culture that emphasizes certain peculiarities of one culture in an attempt to unravel the meta-narratives of all Western civilization. Postmodernism has offered us a false dichotomy between the radical skepticism it advocates and Enlightenment rationality that it attacks. One need not choose between these radically hubristic alternatives. One could argue, as Aquinas did seven centuries ago, that there is a mean between entirely comprehending an object and not knowing anything at all about it. This mean is an apprehension of the object. We may know enough to make tentative claims that are always open to revision.

A second way of responding to postmodernism and its attendant relativism is that if its critique were true then we wouldn't find any consensus among various cultures that practice a common morality. Yet this is patently false. All cultures prohibit murder, stealing, and

52. Cf. Ernan McMullin, "The Case for Scientific Realism," *Scientific Realism*, ed. Jarrett Leplin (Berkeley: University of California Press, 1984), 8–40.

adultery as harmful to human communal life. C. S. Lewis observed that, "what is common to them all is something we cannot neglect. It is the doctrine of objective value, the belief that certain attitudes are really true, and others really false, to the kind of thing the universe is and the kind of thing we are."[53] Postmodernism simply emphasizes the particular instantiation of a moral principle and contrasts that one particularity with another.

Consider the well-known example James Rachels gives of how to treat the dead.[54] The Callatians thought that eating the dead was the appropriate practice. The Greeks believed they should bury their dead. According to the relativist interpretation, since there is no genuine meta-narrative, both cultures were right. However, we can easily argue that although the material manifestations differed, the formal principle remained the same—all cultures honor their dead. Although some cultural practices may simply be variations on a theme, or different manifestations of the same moral principle, the more serious charge is that natural law has taken cultural norms, which were evil, and attempted to use them to exploit others.

In response to the criticism that natural law morality is hopelessly outmoded and merely a repressive tool in the hands of the powerful, feminist theologian Lisa Sowle Cahill has argued that its relevance is enduring, especially when liberated from its narrowly conceived medieval context.[55] Cahill contends that "the defining elements of Aquinas' approach to natural law, still viable today, are his commitment to moral objectivity and his confidence that, as a general proposition, human beings desire and seek to achieve certain goods which are not only fulfilling, but which it is commendable to pursue."[56]

Pursuing the idea further, Cahill contends that the discipline of ethics aims at specifying the goods appropriate to us as human beings. Human nature—which includes both male and female—needs specific kinds of goods in order to flourish. This flourishing is not possible without the development of practical reasoning, which is the application of the general precepts of natural law in specific

53. C. S. Lewis, *The Abolition of Man* (New York: Macmillan, 1955), 29.
54. James Rachels, *The Elements of Moral Philosophy* (New York: McGraw-Hill, 1999), 26.
55. Lisa Sowle Cahill, "Natural Law: A Feminist Reassessment," *Is There a Human Nature?* ed. Leroy S. Rouner (Notre Dame, IN: University of Notre Dame Press, 1997), 78–91.
56. Ibid., 83.

contexts.[57] The more specific the context, the more we need highly developed habits of practical reasoning, as Aristotle observed. Thus, there is a limit on natural law—and its tendency to absolutize the relative—and a clear need for virtues which enable us to pursue the good in its many manifestations.

Cahill argues that four critical points stand out in Aquinas's ethics that bear upon contemporary moral discourse. First, she says that his natural law theory "is strongly social."[58] We are interdependent beings who need others in order to pursue the good in a manner that is conducive to our own and others' flourishing. This is an idea that flies in the face of contemporary individualist—and reductionistic—accounts of the moral life. Oddly enough, if one were to take Rorty's notion of dialogue and conversation as the starting point and expand it into consensus, this would not be inconsistent with the moral epistemology natural lawyers employ.

Second, she maintains that "Aquinas' trust in natural law, especially its objectivity, is founded on a theological premise: creation."[59] The fact that there is order to creation provides us with the intelligibility of nature. This is why people in all cultures and all times can know the primary precepts of natural law. Creation provides the ontological basis for the realism of natural law. Yet this ontology need not be the archaic, sexist categories of Aristotle. Jean Porter redescribes Aquinas's philosophy of human nature in a positive light when she says, "Women and men are equal with respect to what is essential to the nature of the species of humanity, namely, the possession of an intellectual nature . . . enabling the individual to know and love God."[60]

A third feature is its teleological orientation to God. "While natural law is founded at its origin by creation, it is completed at its summit by an orientation to God as the highest good, in which all natural goods are fulfilled and transformed."[61] The precepts of the natural law point us to God even though they cannot help us achieve God without the assistance of divine grace.

57. This is an issue we will explore in great detail in chapter 7 when we consider the relationship between the precepts of natural law and the virtues.

58. Sowle Cahill, "Natural Law: A Feminist Reassessment," 84.

59. Ibid., 84.

60. Jean Porter, *The Recovery of Virtue: The Relevance of Aquinas for Christian Ethics* (Louisville: John Knox Westminster Press, 1990), 138.

61. Ibid., 84.

Fourth, because of human sin "it is vitally important to rely upon the guidance of scripture, interpreted by the Church, in coming to know what the good is."[62] Defenders of natural law recognize that the good is more complete than what can be known merely from the unaided light of natural reason. But as we have seen in chapter 4, the natural law does not suddenly cease to function once the light of revelation supplies us with a more complete rendering of the good, a rendering we could not achieve apart from grace.

In an important confirmation of Sowle Cahill, Susan Frank Parsons believes that natural law can be recontextualized, with the result that feminists can see in it an ally and not an enemy.

> It is a sign of the continuing appeal of Aquinas' theory of goodness, with its specification of what would be the human good, and a sign of the important sense in which his theory is not bound to the particular account of the natural world as he then believed it to be, that feminists may find it a useful framework for moral reasoning.[63]

A creative synthesis can be discovered between feminist concerns and classical natural law morality, according to Sowle Cahill. There are three areas of broad interaction between the two approaches. First, both appeal to a "ground up" experiential epistemology. Natural law is not a "deductivist" approach to ethics wherein one begins with *a priori* moral principles and deduces acceptable behaviors from the premises.[64] Rather, humans experience the world and discover principles at work by reflecting on their own and others' experiences in the world. So too, feminist ethics begins with the existential situation of women, and their reflection on their experiences, and proceeds to understand ethics in a "ground up" manner.

Second, both systems enact substantive accounts of justice that go beyond the merely formal constraints of modern moral theory. Instead of Rawlsian "justice as fairness" and developing formal principles of justice from behind a "veil of ignorance," feminism and natural law ethics take the existential situation of agents as providing the *sine qua non* of morality. One simply cannot know what is owed to whom

62. Ibid., 84–5.

63. Susan Frank Parsons, *Feminism and Christian Ethics* (Cambridge: Cambridge University Press, 1996), 241.

64. This is a common mistake in the interpretation of Thomistic natural law. Cf. John Hare, *God's Call* (Grand Rapids: Eerdmans, 2001), 66–75.

without knowing one's place in society. Distributive and retributive forms of justice depend on how one has benefited from past injustices, as well as how one has been the victim of such injustices.

A final point of convergence is the idea that action is the purpose of virtue. It is one thing to be able to do "moral science" (i.e., the activity wherein one may reason about the good and come to an appropriate judgment about what should be done); acting on that knowledge is a different matter. The old chestnut says it well: knowledge is a necessary condition for virtue but not sufficient. Virtuous behavior is the *telos* of moral deliberation and judgment. It is therefore possible to use Aquinas against Aquinas in order to bring about a more humane understanding of human nature, avoiding the sexism that is endemic in his own situation.

Natural law ethics has often been accused of merely taking the static, eternal essences of Aristotle and naively incorporating them into an objectivist account of morality. Yet this need not be the case. In a post-Darwinian world we see that essences do exist, but they are also in process. So how is the reconstruction possible?

One viable option is by turning to the idea of "paradigm shifts" as advocated by Thomas Kuhn.[65] In the sixteenth century, Copernicus proposed the heliocentric model of the cosmos in order to "save the appearances." This was a radical reorientation to the problem of the Julian calendar and, more importantly, the problem of the retrograde motion of the planets. The appearances remained the same, but the explanation was radically altered. Copernicus supplied a redescription of the cosmos in light of contemporary (to his time) mathematics and sciences, thereby continuing and extending the practice of science in a more fruitful manner.

So too, natural law may benefit from a radical redescription in terms of saving its appearances. The primary precepts of natural law, as Aquinas held, were unchanging. "Practice justice," "be prudent," "don't murder," "seek the truth," "don't lie." These precepts all apply, but the underlying ontology for natural law is not to be identified with cultural convention or Aristotelian causes. Rather, we must look, as I have argued in chapter 3, to what nature and philosophical reflection have to say on the matter.

65. Thomas Kuhn, *The Structures of Scientific Revolutions* (Chicago: University of Chicago Press, 1962). Although Kuhn himself does not advocate realism in his theory, it seems to me that it can be utilized for just such a purpose.

Instead of looking at essences in light of thirteenth-century Aristotelian metaphysics and attempting a reconstruction, we can take
from contemporary science what it has to offer in the way of objective
knowledge and begin there. As I see it, the mistake of many defenders
of natural law morality is that they have been bound by a "picture
theory" of natural law. We might better understand my understanding
of natural law with the traditional conception, if we compare it to the
contrast between a cinematic representation and a snapshot.

In a snapshot, time is frozen in an instant. There is no development of the individual person and we see her from one angle only.
Her image is frozen, immovable, and undeveloped. This, I suggest,
is the case for much of contemporary natural law. In their zeal to
preserve objective morality, many contemporary natural lawyers take
one conception of human nature, freeze it, and refuse to develop it
over time. As a result, specific features of the snapshot become tran-
scendentally normative.

In contrast to the traditional view, I prefer to see natural law as
an unfolding developing process. The character in a cinematic representation remains who she is but moves through different scenes,
engages different dialogue partners. We see her against a variety of
backdrops from multiple angles. Her character remains constant but
changing, developing and adapting to new situations that reveal her
character but also new aspects of her character.

The means of navigating the waters between Enlightenment
foundationalism and postmodern skepticism is by appealing to a
post-foundationalist understanding of the moral enterprise. In this
way we preserve the medieval epistemological distinction between
comprehensio—completely and exhaustively understanding a concept or reality—and *apprehensio*—grasping some of the reality but
not its entirety. F. LeRon Shults has captured this perspective in his
view of the post-foundationalist task of theology. Shults negotiates
the unpleasant alternatives of triumphalistic modernist epistemologies and the relativistic postmodernist critiques by an appeal to four
post-foundationalist principles. He says,

> The "post-foundationalist" approach attempts to avoid the horns of
> this dilemma by accommodating the legitimate intuitions of each of
> these approaches without collapsing into the polarizing tendencies of
> either extreme. This middle way can be summarized in four couplets.
> Interpreted experience anchors all beliefs, and a network of beliefs

informs the interpretation of experience (PF1). The objective unity of
truth is a necessary condition for the intelligible search for knowledge,
and the subjective multiplicity of knowledge indicates the fallibility of
truth claims (PF2). Rational judgment is an activity of socially situated
individuals, and the cultural community indeterminately mediates the
criteria of rationality (PF3). Explanation aims for universal, transcultural understanding, and understanding derives from particular
contextualized explanations (PF4).[66]

Shults's principles are especially helpful in explaining the unique position my theory of natural law occupies. Natural law begins within par-
ticularized contexts and compares narratives across cultures to attempt
an understanding of human nature that includes the common threads
among the cultures, while simultaneously admitting the limitations
of culture. These principles also enable us to see that natural law, as
a rational judgment, arises out of reflection upon our nature as social
beings within our given cultures. Yet given the limitations of cultural
perspective and the rationality that emerges from it, we are still able
to rise above the particular limitations of our own culture to reflect
on the relative value these principles may have. As a result, natural
law is subject to continuing evaluation, alteration, and progress in its
understanding of which precepts apply across cultures.

Conclusion

Although the postmodern critique of Christian ethics can serve as
a helpful corrective to some versions of natural law morality, its own
epistemological relativism undermines its own attempts at providing
a coherent account of reality. Yet Enlightenment theories of natural
law are subject to the legitimate criticisms of postmodernism, in
that objectivist accounts of natural law confuse their own culturally
bound manifestation of natural law with the reality itself, with the
consequence that no progress could ever be made in the narrative of
moral development. Consequently, for both Enlightenment natural
lawyers and their postmodern critics, moral discourse of any kind is
reduced to mere monologue.

66. F. LeRon Shults, *Reforming the Doctrine of God* (Grand Rapids: Eerdmans,
2005), 34–5. See also his *Post-Foundationalist Task of Theology* (Grand Rapids: Eerdmans, 2003).

The resilience of realism in the sciences and ethics has defied the gloomy predictions of the postmodern prophets while maintaining a healthy falliblism. This is especially true of natural law theory. On the one hand, as MacIntyre claims, "The Thomist . . . discerns in the continuous re-appropriation of the rules, and in the recurring resistance to discard them, evidence of *synderesis*, of that fundamental initial grasp of the primary precepts of the natural law . . . which can never be obliterated."[67] However, we must be quick to point out that although the primary precepts always direct us to the good, our application of these precepts and the continuing narrative of natural law guides us to an ever-increasing awareness of the limits of our own noetic capacities.

67. MacIntyre, *Three Rival Versions of Moral Enquiry*, 194.

6 | The Philosophical Challenge

The Analytic Tradition

Introduction

Tracing their ancestry to David Hume and G. E. Moore, numerous analytic philosophers have consistently rejected natural law morality by offering two basic arguments against it. The first argument is purported to be Hume's—that one simply cannot derive prescriptive judgments from descriptive statements. That is, there can be no movement from "is" to "ought." The second argument is Moore's and attempts to show that one cannot identify moral qualities with natural qualities. This second argument is famously referred to as the "naturalistic fallacy" and has preoccupied moral philosophers since the beginning of the twentieth century. These two objections represent the heart of the analytic tradition's objection to those traditional ethical theories that appeal to nature as a source for normative judgments.[1] In this chapter I consider Hume's "Is-Ought" objection and Moore's "Naturalistic fallacy" and the specific ways in which they challenge

---

1. It should be noted that these objections arise out of the analytic tradition, and numerous analytic philosophers are not averse to deriving evaluative from descriptive judgments. See Philippa Foot, *Natural Goodness* (New York: Oxford University Press, 2003); Rosalind Hursthouse, *On Virtue Ethics* (New York: Oxford University Press, 2002); John R. Searle, "How to Derive 'Ought' from 'Is,'" *Philosophical Review* 73 (1964): 43–58; Henry B. Veatch, *For an Ontology of Morals* (Evanston, IL: Northwestern University Press, 1971).

natural law theory. I then consider the "new natural law theory" as a response to the challenges of analytic ethics, and how this approach concedes too much to the analytic critics of natural law. Finally, I show how the analytic tradition has highlighted important issues for contemporary versions of natural law to consider, and how a revised natural law theory can include these insights without capitulating to the radical fact-value dichotomy that seems to have plagued much of twentieth-century analytic ethics.

6.1 Hume on "Is and Ought"

The significance of Hume for this study is twofold: first, he makes a radical distinction between the functions of reason and those of the passions, with the result that reason becomes subject to the desires of the passions. And second, he develops the famous fact-value dichotomy that occupies moral theorists for the next two-and-a-half centuries.[2]

For Hume, reason functions solely as a faculty of judgment which distinguishes between true and false statements. It has neither the capacity to motivate the agent to act nor to persuade the agent from restraint. His famous axiom, "Reason is and ought to be the slave of the passions," reveals that reason acts only instrumentally in any given human activity. The passions serve to excite the agent to act, and reason determines the most appropriate means to satisfying the passions.

> Reason is the discovery of truth or falsehood. Truth or falsehood consists in an agreement or disagreement either to the *real* relations of ideas, or to *real* existence and matters of fact. Whatever, therefore, is not susceptible of this agreement or disagreement is incapable of being true or false, and can never be an object of our reason. Now, it is evident that

2. Hilary Putnam, *The Collapse of the Fact/Value Dichotomy and Other Essays* (Cambridge, MA: Harvard University Press, 2002), argues that Hume's matters of fact-relation of ideas dichotomy provides the context for Hume's fact-value dichotomy. He says, "Hume assumed a metaphysical dichotomy between 'matters of fact' and 'relations of ideas' (the dichotomy that constituted his early anticipation of the 'analytic-synthetic distinction'). What Hume meant was that when an 'is' judgment describes a 'matter of fact,' then no 'ought' judgment can be derived from it. Hume's metaphysics of 'matters of fact' constitutes the whole ground of the alleged underivability of 'oughts' from 'ises,'" 14–5.

our passions, volitions, and actions, are not susceptible of any such agreement or disagreement; being original facts and realities, complete in themselves, and implying no reference to other passions, volitions, and actions. It is impossible, therefore, they can be pronounced either true or false, and be either contrary or conformable to reason.[3]

Since reason can only discriminate between the true and the false, and since the passions—and our moral actions as well—are neither true nor false, we cannot derive ethics from our rational powers. Although Hume uses the phrase "original fact" to refer to our passions, he clearly does not mean to imply that these facts are objective, or accessible to all people, or that they can be either "true" or "false" in any relevant sense. The upshot of Hume's analysis is that facts—in our sense of the term—are objective and can be comprehended by reason. Values are person-relative and immune from rational scrutiny. When considering the question of whether an individual has committed a crime against another, Hume demands, "Show me the crime. Where is it?" He wants to know what faculty discovers it and can determine its nature. Since there is no "matter of fact" which we can know through empirical investigation, we must rest content to say that it resides in the passions. Hume concludes, "We may infer that, the crime of ingratitude is not any particular *fact*; but arises from a complication of circumstances which being presented to the spectator excites the *sentiment* of blame by the particular structure and fabric of his mind."[4] This distinction between reason and the passions anticipates another more important distinction: that between descriptive judgments and normative evaluations.

The standard interpretation of Hume's view on moral language is that one cannot infer prescriptive conclusions from descriptive premises. In this famous passage he says,

In every system of morality, which I have hitherto met with, I have always remark'd that the author proceeds for some time in the ordinary way of reasoning, and establishing the being of a God, or makes observations concerning human affairs; when of a sudden I am surpriz'd to find, that instead of the usual copulations, *is*, *is not*, I meet with no

3. David Hume, *A Treatise on Human Nature*, bk. III, par. I, sec. I, ed. with an analytical index by L. A. Selby-Bigge and P. H. Nidditch (Oxford: Clarendon Press, 1978), 458 (emphasis in the original).
4. Ibid., 290 (emphasis original).

proposition that is not connected with an *ought*, or *ought not*. This change is imperceptible; but it is, however, of the last consequence. For as this *ought*, or *ought not*, expresses some new relation or affirmation, 'tis necessary that it should be observ'd and explain'd; and at the same time that a reason should be given, for what seems altogether inconceivable, how this new relation can be a deduction from others, which are entirely different from it.[5]

Philosophers have debated the value of Hume's comments on "Is and Ought," but the standard interpretation among analytic philosophers is that Hume means to draw a radical distinction between normative statements on the one hand and descriptive statements on the other.[6] Despite the controversy over the interpretation of Hume's text, in the narrative of the analytic tradition of philosophy this is the standard interpretation, regardless of how Hume intended it. But he does seem to make one fairly unambiguous point: one cannot make the logical inference from statements about facts to evaluative judgments about action. Hume's point can be understood as a quite simple observation about logic, on the one hand, such that in deductive arguments conclusions are always entailed by their premises; so we should only find terms in the conclusions that are employed in the premises. But on the other hand, Hume also seems to ask, "how is it possible to move from the descriptive to the prescriptive?"

R. M. Hare, a representative of the traditional interpretation of Hume, sees the fact-value dichotomy as a critical insight to the development of modern theories of ethics and dubs it "Hume's Law."[7] Various analytic responses have been offered to Hume's Law. Some,

5. Ibid., 469.

6. A notable exception here is Alasdair MacIntyre, "Hume on Is and Ought" in *Hume: A Collection of Critical Essays*, ed. V. C. Chappell (Garden City, NY: Anchor Books, 1966), who believes that Hume "is asserting that the question of how the factual basis of morality is related to morality is a crucial logical issue, reflection on which will enable one to realize how there are ways in which this transition can be made and ways in which it cannot. One has to go beyond the passage itself to see what these are; but if one does so it is plain that we cannot connect the facts of the situation with what we ought to do only by means of one of those concepts which Hume treats under the heading of the passions and which I have indicated by examples such as wanting, needing, and the like. Hume is not, as Prior seems to indicate, trying to say that morality lacks a basis; he is trying to point out the nature of that basis," 261.

7. R. M. Hare, *Moral Thinking: Its Levels, Method and Point* (Oxford: Clarendon Press, 1981), 16. Hare says, "It is usually held that conclusions of substance cannot be derived from premises about the uses of words; and . . . Supporters of Hume's Law,

like Hare, have advocated "prescriptivism," since words about what we ought and ought not do primarily prescribe behavior rather than describe it. Others, such as the emotivists, argued that we cannot derive meaningful moral prescriptions from non-moral descriptions, but also that the entire enterprise of moral language is meaningless. Moral language primarily expresses our distaste for, or approval of, various actions. In the famous words of A. J. Ayer, "The exhortations to moral virtue are not propositions at all, but ejaculations or commands which are designed to provoke the reader to action of a certain sort. Accordingly, they do not belong to any branch of philosophy or science."[8] In some respects, we could say that Ayer's emotivism was the inevitable conclusion that resulted from Hume's radical bifurcation between fact and value, a dichotomy Moore not only embraced but developed for his own purposes.

6.2 Moore's Critique of Ethical Naturalism

G. E. Moore begins his analysis of ethics with the fairly uncontroversial claim that ethics is "the general inquiry into what is good."[9] But what Moore really means to ask is what is the meaning of the term "good"? What are its properties? And how are we to define it? His concern is not merely a linguistic matter for he says, "My business is solely that object or idea, which I hold, rightly or wrongly, that the word is generally used to stand for. What I want to discover is the nature of that object or idea."[10] Since "good" refers to some real quality of actions, it follows that Moore is a moral realist with regard to the status of moral judgments; however, "good" does not refer to some natural quality as the utilitarians and others suggested.

The backdrop for Moore's analysis of "the good" is nineteenth-century utilitarianism, a view Moore thinks fails to grasp the precise nature of moral language. Utilitarians like John Stuart Mill believed that we could identify "the good" with "happiness," the "pleasurable," or even "the desirable." Mill's famous argument follows:

of whom . . . I am one, will protest that one cannot get evaluative conclusions out of factual premises about word-usage."

8. A. J. Ayer, *Language, Truth, and Logic* (New York: Dover Publications, 1952), 103.

9. G. E. Moore, *Principia Ethica* (New York: Cambridge University Press, 1903).

10. Ibid., 6.

> Questions about ends are . . . questions about what things are desirable. The utilitarian doctrine is, that happiness is desirable, and the only thing desirable as an end. . . . The only proof capable of being given that an object is visible to us is that people actually see it. The only proof that a sound is audible, is that people hear it. . . . In like manner, I apprehend, the sole evidence it is possible to produce anything desirable, is that people actually desire it.[11]

Utilitarians believe that since all people desire happiness it follows that happiness must be the good. Indeed, people desire other things merely as a means to happiness, but happiness as happiness is not desired as a means to any other good. Since natural law theory also appeals to the good as a normative principle, albeit in significantly different ways than utilitarianism, Moore's critique poses significant questions for any theory which appeals to human nature and its teleological orientation.

Moore believes that most traditional ethical theories either attempt to derive moral norms from nature or from some metaphysical principle. The utilitarians took happiness (or "the pleasurable") as fundamental to all forms of human action. The utilitarians derived their understanding of the good from nature, specifically human nature; and Moore calls this attempt "naturalistic ethics."[12] Kant, and others who followed him, saw acting for the sake of duty as the good; Moore calls this approach "metaphysical ethics."[13] However, any attempt to define what the good means in either natural or metaphysical terms is guilty of what Moore calls the "naturalistic fallacy." The naturalistic fallacy is the "failure to distinguish clearly that unique and indefinable quality which we mean by good."[14] The idea of "the good" is such

11. John Stuart Mill, *Utilitarianism*, ed. Roger Crisp (New York: Oxford University Press, 1998); see especially chapter 4.

12. Moore, *Principia Ethica*, 39 (emphasis in the original). "I shall deal with theories which owe their prevalence to the supposition that good can be defined by reference to a *natural object.*"

13. Ibid., 110 (emphasis in the original). Unfortunately, Moore unnecessarily confuses the issue by calling this mistake the "naturalistic fallacy" when it refers to *any* attempt to define the good. "These ethical theories have this in common, that they use some *metaphysical* proposition as a ground for inferring some fundamental proposition of Ethics. They all imply, and many of them expressly hold, that ethical truths follow logically from metaphysical truths—that Ethics should be based on *Metaphysics*. And the result is that they all describe the Supreme Good in *metaphysical* terms."

14. Moore, *Principia Ethica*, 59 (emphasis in the original).

that it cannot be identified with any other property; "the good' is not "the pleasurable," "net utility," "the evolutionarily advantageous," nor "the command of God." Moore moves beyond the linguistic point that the "is of identity" cannot be applied in this specific case to the metaphysical claim that "the good" is an indefinable property that resists easy identification with other properties.

The means by which Moore attempts to refute all forms of ethical naturalism is by his use of the "open question" argument. He asks us to consider any possible definition of the good: "it may be always asked, with significance, of the complex so defined, whether it is itself good."[15] If someone says "pleasure is good," we can always ask in a meaningful way, "yes, but is it good?" Can we imagine situations in which pleasure is not good? Moore banks on the fact that we certainly *can* imagine such situations (e.g., a sociopath achieving pleasure by torturing innocent children). He does not mean to deny that some actions are good and others are evil; he is merely challenging the idea that we can identify the good with a natural property. If it is possible for us to ask of any proposed definition, "is it good?" we can establish a conceptual distinction between that definition and the "good itself." So what *can* therefore be said of the good?

Moore believes that good "is one of those innumerable objects of thought which are themselves incapable of definition, because they are the ultimate terms by reference to which whatever *is* capable of definition must be defined."[16] Good therefore functions on the most basic level of thought; it is a simple, nonnatural quality of things, in contrast to "complex natural qualities." According to Moore, if I think of a horse, I can think of it as a complex being, as composed of various parts and organs which, in turn, can be broken down into further parts. A horse, therefore, is a complex being composed of natural qualities that we can find in any other kind of material object.

A horse also has other qualities that can help us identify and distinguish it from other beings. If I say, "the horse is brown," I am not making a statement about how the horse is composed of various elements or components. Rather, I am making a statement about what Moore calls "simple natural properties." Moore believes that colors such as "brown" or "yellow" are simple natural qualities of things that cannot be broken down into constituent parts. Moreover,

15. Ibid., 15.
16. Ibid., 10.

our experience of light vibrations is not what we mean by "yellow"; rather, the term applies to some natural property found in the thing itself, not merely to our experience or to some physical explanation of the phenomenon.

We can also see that "good," as is the case with "yellow," is a simple quality. We cannot define yellow any further; it is basic. What Moore seems to assume here is an anticipation of Wittgenstein's logical atomism in the famous *Tractatus Logico-Philosophicus*, wherein one finds a radical referentialism at work. If one cannot point to the "good," then we must concede that it either doesn't exist—a consequence that invites a great deal of pragmatic problems, not the least of which is the dissolution of ethics—or that it must be nonnatural, Moore's own conviction.[17] On the view presented by logical atomism, "good" must be a simple property which cannot be resolved into any further constituent parts.

In the end, since good is a simple, nonnatural property, we can only intuit it in various actions. Some actions are good and others are not; and the means by which we distinguish the good from the bad is by "moral intuition." Of course, this solution raises as many problems as it solves. It cannot account for differing moral intuitions; if my intuition differs from yours, we are left with the embarrassing situation in which either you are morally blind or I'm having moral hallucinations.[18] If I say that "no wars are just," and you say that "some wars are just," what is it that you are seeing that I cannot see? Or conversely, what do I see in war that you fail to see? Moreover, how can we possibly resolve the situation since, on the one hand, an appeal to "facts" clearly violates the fact-value dichotomy Moore so desperately wants to maintain; but, on the other hand, if we appeal to a meta-intuition to resolve our competing moral intuitions, we find ourselves trapped within a vicious circularity of appealing to intuitions to mediate conflicts among intuitions.

17. Ludwig Wittgenstein, *Tractatus Logico-Philosophicus*, trans. D. F. Pears and B. F. McGuinness (London: Routledge & Kegan Paul, 1961), 7. This seems to be at the heart of Wittgenstein's logical atomism when he says "objects are simple. Every statement about complexes can be resolved into a statement about their constituents and also into the propositions that describe the complexes completely. Objects make up the substance of the world. That is why they cannot be composite."

18. As W. D. Hudson points out, Moore has added "a further problem: how are we to differentiate between true and false intuitions?" *Modern Moral Philosophy* (Garden City, NY: Anchor Books, 1970), 82–3.

A second key problem is one that William Frankena has noted; the naturalistic fallacy, if it were a legitimate fallacy, would exclude any and all possible definitions of the good. Moore himself confesses that "our first conclusion as to the subject-matter of Ethics is, then, that there is a simple, indefinable, unanalyzable, object of thought by reference to which it must be defined."[19] But, as Frankena so clearly observes, "If Moore's motto . . . rules out any definitions, for example of 'good,' then it rules out definitions of any term whatever."[20] Regardless of the many problems with Moore's intuitionism, his criticisms of ethical naturalism provided the context for much of metaethics in the twentieth century and compelled moral theorists of all stripes to engage the discussion.

6.3 The Grisez-Finnis Approach to Natural Law

Two of the more well-known natural lawyers who attempt to address the "Is-Ought" problem are Germain Grisez and John Finnis.[21] Both accept the validity of Moore's critique; Grisez says, "If one supposes that principles of natural law are formed by examining kinds of actions in comparison with human natures and noting their agreement or disagreement, then one must respond to the objection that it is impossible to derive normative judgments from metaphysical speculations."[22] Finnis is equally emphatic in his insistence that even Aquinas rejected an ontological foundation for moral principles. "Aquinas asserts as plainly as possible that the first principles of natural law . . . are not inferred from speculative principles. . . . They are not inferred from

19. Moore, *Principia Ethica*, 21.
20. William Frankena, "The Naturalistic Fallacy," in *Theories of Ethics*, ed. Philippa Foot (Oxford: Oxford University Press, 1967), 58; also see A. J. Ayer, *Philosophy in the Twentieth Century* (New York: Random House, 1982).
21. See especially John Finnis, *Natural Law and Natural Rights* (Oxford: Clarendon Press, 1980); Germain Grisez, "The First Principle of Practical Reason: A Commentary on the *Summa Theologiae*, Question 94, Article 2," in *Aquinas: A Collection of Critical Essays*, ed. Anthony Kenny (Notre Dame, IN: University of Notre Dame Press, 1976): 340–82. More recently, Robert George has defended the Grisez-Finnis interpretation in his "Natural Law and Human Nature," in *Natural Law Theory: Contemporary Essays*, ed. Robert P. George (Oxford: Clarendon Press, 1992), 31–41.
22. Grisez, "The First Principle of Practical Reason," 283; Finnis agrees and says that regardless of how one interprets Hume, the important thing to note is that Hume's Law is "true and significant." *Natural Law and Natural Rights*, 37.

metaphysical propositions about human nature, or about the nature of good and evil, or about 'the function of a human being.'"[23] Finnis believes that any attempt to infer ethics from metaphysics, whether this is Aquinas's view, or anyone else's, is mistaken.[24]

This acceptance of the fact-value dichotomy shapes the Grisez-Finnis interpretation of natural law on its most basic level, so that in order to understand whatever else they have to say on the subject this must be emphasized from the start. Grisez rejects scholastic natural law theory because "it moves by a logically illicit step—from human nature as a given reality, to what ought and ought not to be chosen . . . it is not human nature as given, but possible human fulfillment which must provide the intelligible norms for free choices."[25] But if we are to understand how natural law provides a justification for ethics, we must turn our attention to the function of practical reason.

Practical reason aims at an end not yet achieved by the agent but as desirable to the agent. It therefore sees possibilities for the agent. Practical reason on the Grisez-Finnis interpretation attempts to negotiate the world of theoretical reason and the world of desire. Too many natural lawyers see practical reason simply as the end result of a theoretical investigation of the world; they attempt to deduce moral principles from a theoretical inquiry into human nature. On the other hand, we must avoid the Humean approach that sees desire manipulating reason. Grisez and Finnis argue that practical reason attempts to actualize the world of possibilities open to the human agent in light of the various goods that can, and ought to, be pursued.

We do not derive the first principle of practical reason—that good ought to be done and pursued and evil avoided—from some factual or metaphysical premises. An investigation of human nature cannot result in an imperative to pursue some good or goods because there is, as Moore has shown, a radical distinction between the descriptive and the normative. What Grisez and Finnis propose is that the various goods of life can be grasped by the theoretical reason in a "premoral sense," a sense that will avoid the embarrassment of moving from is to ought. In contrast to the theoretical use of reason, the practical use of reason moves us to action, as when we decide that "I must

23. Finnis, *Natural Law and Natural Rights*, 33.
24. John Finnis, *Fundamentals of Ethics* (New York: Oxford, 1983), 22.
25. Germain Grisez, *The Way of the Lord Jesus*, vol. 1, *Christian Moral Principles* (Chicago: Franciscan Herald Press, 1983), 105.

demonstrate mercy to this person now." Theoretical reason grasps
the truth that "it is good to help those in need," but this is merely a
premoral assessment of the good. Practical reason moves humans
to action and requires that I engage in this particular act now. But
before we consider how practical reason instantiates the good we
should consider precisely those self-evidently known premoral forms
of the good.

Grisez lists seven basic goods that he claims are all self-evident
forms of the good. These include (1) self-integration, (2) authenticity,
(3) friendship, (4) holiness, (5) life, (6) knowledge, and (7) exercises
of skill.[26] According to Grisez, this list exhausts all possible forms
of the good and cannot be reduced to further principles or articulations of the good. There is a basic-value egalitarianism operating
among these premoral goods, with the result that no one good has a
priority over the others; they are all basic constituent elements of the
good.[27] Finnis says that each one of the goods is "basic." That means
that "first, each is equally self-evidently a form of good. Secondly,

26. Grisez, *Christian Moral Principles*, 124; Finnis's list is similar. He says "all human
societies show a concern for the value of human life; in all, self-preservation is generally accepted as a proper motive for action, and in none is the killing of other human
beings permitted without some fairly definite justification. All human societies regard
the procreation of a new human life as in itself a good thing unless there are special
circumstances. No human society fails to restrict sexual activity; in all societies there
is some prohibition on incest, some opposition to boundless promiscuity and to rape,
some favour for stability and permanence in sexual relations. All human societies
display a concern for the truth, through education of the young in matters not only
practical (e.g., avoidance of dangers) but also speculative or theoretical (e.g., religion).
Human beings, who can survive infancy only by nurture, live in or on the margins
of some society which invariably extends beyond the nuclear family, and all societies
display a favour for the values of co-operation, of common over individual good, of
obligation between individuals, and of justice within groups. All know friendship. All
have some conception of *meum* and *tuum*, title or property, and of reciprocity. All
value play, serious and formalized, or relaxed and recreational. All treat the bodies of
dead members of the group in some traditional and ritual fashion different from their
procedures for rubbish disposal. All display a concern for powers or principles which
are to be respected as suprahuman; in one form or another, religion is universal,"
Natural Law and Natural Rights, 83–4.

27. This value-egalitarianism is strikingly similar to the idea John Rawls advances
regarding the good in *A Theory of Justice* (Cambridge, MA: Harvard University Press,
1971). Although the methodology differs, the heteronomy among the goods sounds
oddly like a reconstructed intuitionism where we intuit the good and there is no hierarchy among the goods. Russell Hittinger, *A Critique of the New Natural Law Theory*
(Notre Dame, IN: University of Notre Dame Press, 1987), makes a similar point on
pp. 80–81.

none can be analytically reduced to being merely an aspect of any of
the others, or to being merely instrumental in the pursuit of any of
the others. Thirdly, each one, when we focus on it, can reasonably
be regarded as the most important."[28] Two significant observations
need attention here.

First, Finnis claims that the principles of natural law are "self-
evident." This is hardly an unusual claim for a natural lawyer to make
since Aquinas made the same claim. However, for Aquinas the claim
was one that had a basis in human nature functioning in a normative capacity. That is, Aquinas saw the desires of human nature as
necessary conditions for the precepts of natural law. Thus, since all
humans desire God, "seek the truth about God" was a self-evident
maxim. However, Finnis's understanding of "self-evident" takes a
different course.

As we have seen, Finnis is careful to avoid deriving normative
judgments from descriptive statements. He says we cannot "infer the
value of knowledge from the fact (if fact it be) that 'all men desire to
know.' The universality of a desire is not a sufficient basis for inferring
that the object of that desire is really desirable, objectively good."[29]
What Finnis means is that these principles are always presupposed
in all of our other thinking and acting. We do not demonstrate them,
we assume them. These self-evident principles are not grasped by
the intellect or by reflection upon human nature—since this would
commit the naturalistic fallacy—but they are assumed in any judgment. Grisez believes that these commitments to the self-evident
principles of morality are inherent in all moral judgments—those of
good people and those of evil people. The goods point out specific
things we should desire, not precepts of action. Practical reason's
primary task is to move the agent to action, not to be the servant of
the speculative reason's inquiry into human nature and act upon its
commands.

A second important observation concerns the nature of the relationship among the various self-evident goods. From the perspective
of the good of "life," all other goods seem incommensurate with it.
After all, in order for the other goods to be good life must have a

28. Finnis, *Natural Law and Natural Rights*, 92.
29. Ibid., 66. Earlier Finnis says, that "by a simple act of noninferential understanding one grasps that the object of the inclination which one experiences is an instance
of a general form of good, for oneself (and others like one)," 34.

certain priority. Yet from the perspective of "holiness" it may seem that life pales in comparison—or that there may be some religious goods that exceed those bestowed by life. The Grisez-Finnis approach to a resolution is to take each one as a basic good and not attempt to reduce any one of them to any other good.

One key problem with the Grisez-Finnis interpretation of natural law is that it simply substitutes a more complex form of intuition-ism at the deepest level of moral judgment.[30] How do we resolve conflicts among and between the basic goods? What if we are faced with renouncing our most deeply held religious convictions for the good of life? We could interpret it from one perspective as sacrific-ing the good of religion for the good of life; or conversely could it be that the good of life is sacrificed for the good of religion? How do we decide? The only option available to Grisez and Finnis is by means of a moral intuition, since there is neither a hierarchy that can discriminate among competing goods, nor any appeal to natural teleology available.[31] A viciously circular moral epistemology is all that remains.

Ralph McInerny aptly describes the world Grisez and Finnis have created in the following thought experiment.

> Talk of human action, of what men ought to do or what it would be good for them to do, could begin by imagining a group of inert people waiting in the wings for the outcome of the discussion. In the wings things simply are what they are; it is a world of facts and otherwise featureless. Pop, who may be assigned the premoral task of handling the stagedoor johnnies, is frozen in fact with the rest. The problem of ethics is seen as getting those people on stage. How can we persuade them from Is to Ought, from the pale cast of thought to the vivacious verve of behavior? Why should the philosopher assign himself this impossible task?[32]

30. Although both Grisez and Finnis explicitly deny that their theory amounts to an intuitionist approach, their denials amount to little more than rhetorical hand waving.

31. Anthony Lisska's assessment is that the Grisez-Finnis approach is forced into an intuitionism more akin to Ross than Moore since Ross, unlike Moore, allows for intuiting the good as a natural property.

32. McInerny, *Ethica Thomistica*, 36. Howard P. Kainz, *Natural Law: An Introduc-tion and Re-examination* (LaSalle, IL: Open Court Press, 2004), makes a similar point when he says, "In natural-law theory, the main 'fact' which seems to be of crucial importance is the pursuit of happiness, or the goal of 'human flourishing.' One would

Another way of looking at this is simply to observe that Grisez and Finnis have capitulated to the modernist leanings of Moore and the others who saw the fact-value dichotomy as a threat to moral inquiry. Their approach to natural law reflects the Kantian separation of human nature from natural law, rather than seeing natural law as grounded in human nature and human potencies.[33]

Knowing is already a value-laden activity. If we recall the postmodernist critique that language and scientific activities of all kinds find themselves already embedded in a culture of values, it is impossible for us to extricate ourselves from making any kind of value judgments. The desire to respond to Moore's critique of ethical naturalism here results in an unnatural bifurcation of the world we inhabit; "facts" and "values" do not reside in two separate spheres, but are inextricably bound together in a world of meaning.

The radical—and unnatural—separation of facts from values plays a critical role in modernist and contemporary analytic theories of ethics. From at least the time of Hume through Moore and late twentieth-century analytic theories, the basic assumption that guided analytic philosophers was the questionable bifurcation of fact from value. And so arguments like the following seem to flow with an ineluctable logic.

1. Arguments containing factual premises can result only in factual conclusions.
2. Arguments with value conclusions cannot be derived from factual premises alone.
3. Therefore, one must either include a value premise with the factual premise[34] or concede that ethical naturalism is incapable of bridging the fact-value chasm.

---

be hard-pressed to *derive* any values from this 'fact,' since it is already intrinsically value-laden," 77.

33. Robert George, *In Defense of Natural Law*, 85–6, wants to deny this claim by McInerny, but it seems difficult to maintain both the idea that one cannot derive normative claims from prescriptive claims and that theoretical reason contributes to our conception of the good. Either George must admit that nature has some normative status and abandon the fact-value dichotomy, or else he has to deny any significant connection between theoretical and practical reason. He can't have it both ways.

34. William Frankena attempts to do precisely this in his *Ethics*, as well as in his article "The Naturalistic Fallacy," *Theories of Ethics*, ed. Philippa Foot (Oxford: Oxford University Press, 1967). Yet the interesting point here is that even though Frankena believes one can derive "ought" from "is," he too assumes the basic fact-value dichotomy

The hidden assumption, of course, is that descriptive judgments and normative judgments are radically different, as the emotivists so clearly and foolishly demonstrated. It would seem that one merely needs to prove that facts and values are not so radically different; or, to put it another way, it would seem that facts are unavoidably embedded in a world of values already. If facts and values are not estranged in the ways that the Grisez-Finnis approach assumes they are, then their entire project seems to be doomed to the same fate as other modernist, objectivist approaches to analytic ethics.[35]

6.4 The Dissolution of the Fact-Value Dichotomy

We can present at last three different arguments against the fact-value dichotomy: the scientific argument, the teleological argument, and the theological argument.

The scientific argument against the fact-value dichotomy includes two distinct arguments. The first argument addresses the naïve foundationalism employed by philosophers after Descartes and Newton who see the world as composed of values—read private subjective experiences—and those of facts—read objective, identifiable facts.

The Cartesian idea of the *cogito* promised philosophers an objective, value-free, foundation for knowledge that claimed to be unassailable. The Cartesian *cogito* seemed to provide an Archimedean point from which all objective knowledge could proceed. Yet the promise of a foundationalist epistemology never materialized, as the remainder of the modern era proved. Still, one vestige of Cartesian foundationalism seemed to escape unscathed into moral philosophy. Bolstered by the success of Newtonian mechanics and the dominant empirical methods, philosophers such as Hume wanted to assert the existence of "facts" over and against "values." Hume's famous distinction between reason and the passions seems to indicate that we can neatly and discretely categorize judgments such that the subjective element

so prevalent in the twentieth century and feels the need to demonstrate precisely how one can bridge the gap given the fundamental differences between descriptive and normative judgments. Frankena argues that one may include both a descriptive premise and a normative premise in order to obtain a normative conclusion.

35. I say "assumes" here because they never give arguments calling into question the legitimacy of the fact-value dichotomy. Rather, they simply accept it as modernist orthodoxy and move on to their own reconstruction of natural law.

can never enter into our assessment of truth; conversely, reason can never intrude upon the world of the passions and its values.

Value judgments came not from reason but from the murky depths of passion; and what one person considered valuable another might not, thereby suggesting a radically subjective basis for ethics founded upon "self-interest." Judgments of fact could be adjudicated by an appeal to the objectivity of the sciences, but judgments of value seemed imprisoned within the walls of personal subjectivity. We can see in figure 1 below how Hume and those who follow him seem to construe the division between facts and values.

Figure 1

Power	Activities	Characteristic	Product
Reason	Speculative Philosophy and Science	Objectivity	Facts
Passion	Practical Philosophy and Ethics	Subjectivity	Values

Moore, as we have seen, retained the fact-value dichotomy and made it central to his own enterprise for the purpose of rejecting all forms of ethical naturalism. His naïve referentialism seemed to assume an objective, physical world in which we can "point to" facts that make themselves known immediately to us. Although facts can be known by appeal to epistemic atomism, values can only be "intuited" by a "moral sense." The truly devastating problem for anyone in the analytic tradition who sees Moore's critique as valid is that there is no "objective point of view" where we encounter "naked facts." This fiction has managed to elude critical scrutiny for some time, even though it is impossible to sanction the suspect assumption foundational to the critique of ethical naturalism.

Many philosophers of science have rejected the idea of a "value-neutral" approach to science.[36] Hilary Putnam has recently argued that

36. Michael Polanyi, *Personal Knowledge: Towards a Post-Critical Philosophy* (Chicago: University of Chicago Press, 1958), argued that there must be some prior commitment on the part of the knower in any approach to the truth. The idea of "personal knowledge" suggested an idea Polanyi called the "fiduciary rootedness of all rationality." That is, we cannot escape our own commitments—our values—which shape our understanding of "the facts." Another approach that retains the regulative use of value judgments in scientific theory can be seen in the work of Thomas Kuhn, *The Structure of Scientific Revolutions* (Chicago: University of Chicago Press, 1962). Kuhn's understanding of paradigms as socially developed ideas which determine the parameters for "normal science" also assumes an implicit value structure to scientific

even if we took Popper's idea that scientific theories are in principle falsifiable, we do not take *every* scientific theory seriously. No scientist is going to attempt to refute every theory that comes her way, but will make value judgments concerning the relative merit of the theories in question. And what values are involved in such determinations? Putnam says that "in short, judgments of coherence, simplicity, and so on are presupposed by physical science. Yet, coherence, simplicity, and the like are value judgments. . . . The argument that ethical values are metaphysically 'queer' because . . . we do not have a sense organ for detecting 'goodness' could be modified to read, 'epistemic values are ontologically queer because we do not have a sense organ for detecting simplicity and coherence.'"[37] What we must say, therefore, is that values play at least a regulative role in the practice of science—a seemingly indispensable role.

If we understand the narrative structure of any noetic enterprise, whether that project is epistemology, ethics, or the various sciences, we realize sooner or later that the discipline includes a tradition of inquiry which employs a range of values. In science, simplicity and coherence are critical to the ongoing narrative structure and to advances in science. A noetic tradition shapes, governs, and directs which questions should be asked, which values are employed in asking the questions, and what constitutes a coherent answer to the questions. But if we allow even the regulative use of values in science, then the radical dichotomy the modernists wish to maintain cannot stand.

A second consequence of modern philosophy and the new empirical methods ushered in by Newton was the rejection of final causes.[38]

---

reasoning. Kuhn says, "To be accepted as a paradigm, a theory must seem better than its competitors but it need not, and in fact never does, explain all the facts with which it can be confronted," 17–18. Kuhn contends that a theory needs to be understood as "better" than another. This comparative adjective implies a value-based judgment on the part of the scientist. While the scientist could simply try to define "better" as "more efficient," we need then ask, "why is efficiency valuable?" There is an unavoidable value claim latent in the practice of science.

37. Putnam, *The Collapse of the Fact-Value Dichotomy*, 142. Although I agree with Putnam's assessment that the fact-value dichotomy breaks down I reject his attempts to sever ethics from ontology in his *Ethics Without Ontology* (Cambridge, MA: Harvard University Press, 2004) where he attempts to defend "pragmatic pluralism," a view that, "does not require us to find mysterious and supersensible objects *behind* our language games," 22.

38. Cf. John Hedley Brooke, *Science and Religion: Some Historical Perspectives* (New York: Cambridge University Press, 1991).

Since material and efficient causes seemed to explain behavior adequately for scientific purposes, Aristotle's formal and final causes seemed at best unnecessary and at worst confusing.[39] With the Kantian development of the phenomenal and noumenal distinction, the idea that we could ever know the real essences of things appeared to be a lost cause. If we cannot know the real natures of things, then any attempt to appeal to nature will be an exercise in futility; and we can see that Kant's attempt to construct ethics on the *a priori* structure of reason seems the most plausible alternative to any ethical theory that appeals to nature in a normative fashion. The second consequence of modernity was the demise of teleological thinking which unraveled any attempt to understand ethics as grounded in nature.

1. We can never know the real natures of things, since we can never determine the purposes for which things exist.
2. If we cannot determine purposes in nature, then it seems that natural teleology as a guide for ethics is a dead end.
3. If ethics is to continue as a viable discipline, then nature cannot be a source for normative judgments.
4. Thus, ethics must appeal to some nonnatural properties for guidance with regard to normative judgments.

Here the move is a shift from an epistemological uncertainty with regard to our knowledge (or lack of knowledge) of natures to a metaphysical assertion. This structure of the argument seems to include most theorists, from Kant to Moore to R. M. Hare, with the notable exception of the utilitarians. In severing facts from values and purposes from real natures, modern philosophy contributed not only to the breakdown of the medieval synthesis but also unwittingly led to its own deconstruction at the hands of the postmodernists, since

39. Again, MacIntyre's analysis is illuminating here. He says, "The notion of a 'fact' with respect to human beings is thus transformed in the transition from the Aristotelian to the mechanist view. On the former view human action, because it is to be explained teleologically, not only can but must be, characterized with reference to the hierarchy of goods which provide the ends of human action. On the latter view human action not only can, but must be, characterized without any reference to such goods. On the former view the facts about human action include the facts about what is valuable to human beings (and *not* just the facts about what is valuable). 'Fact' becomes value-free, 'is' becomes a stranger to 'ought' and explanation, as well as evaluation, changes its character as a result of this divorce between 'is' and 'ought.'" *After Virtue*, 84.

real essences could only be understood within the context of final causes. If there is no *telos* for which agents act, we are free to create our own teleologies, our own meta-narratives, or our own mutually conflicting Nietszchean genealogies.

Bereft of natural teleology, analytic theorists are left only with the awkward attempt to "add" values to facts. Lisska says,

> If one takes seriously what can follow from a dispositional view of essence, one has a way around the naturalistic fallacy. With a static view of essence, a value necessarily is added to a fact. The fact is the set of defining properties. The value is added as an additional component to the fact. . . . With a dispositional view of essence, however, the value is the terminus of the development of the dispositional properties. It is not an extrinsic property joined to a fact. On the contrary, the value is built right into the fact as end or perfection to the disposition or potency.[40]

Moore's analytic, atomistic referentialism blinded him to the possibility that there were alternate ways to view natures. However, given his modernist, post-Newtonian context it is difficult to see how he could have developed an alternate approach. Moral language necessarily had to conform to the atomistic demands of positivism. Yet it wasn't long before this radically reductionistic approach was challenged from within the analytic tradition itself.

As Elizabeth Anscombe observed, phrases like "moral obligation" and "moral duty" are terms that seem meaningless since there is no coherent understanding of human nature—human nature that has a divinely appointed teleology. Her suggestion was to substitute terms like "human flourishing" and "excellence." But in order to develop a coherent account of the virtues, human emotions, and human intentions we must provide a coherent account of human nature that, in turn, is necessary to salvage the study of ethics.[41] We should abandon the analytic project that obsessed over the meaning of moral language and turn our attention to moral activities, since the language seems to be an attempt to describe the practices, and not the converse. Anscombe therefore calls us back to a theory of human nature on which an ethic of human "flourishing" can be based.[42]

40. Lisska, *Aquinas's Theory of Natural Law*, 162–3.
41. Ibid., 15.
42. Ibid., 18.

The second argument appeals to the natural teleology we find at work in beings of a certain kind. Humans, as members of a species, have traits unique only to their own kind. We tell pirate jokes, write philosophy, produce sitcoms, bury our dead, develop sophisticated means to destroy our enemies, tell stories, create scientific theories, debate politics, play baseball, gather together to worship God, and a host of other activities that could in some way be called "rational." Although this list does not exhaust all the possible kinds of rational activities—nor does it intend to—it does point to a preliminary understanding of what it means to be rational. Rationality distinguishes human from other forms of life, as we have seen in chapter 3, in that it is distinctively and self-consciously intentional. None of the activities I have just mentioned exhaust the formality of human rationality, but they all seem to demonstrate an intentional approach to human activities. Intentional activity is for a perceived end, or good, of the agent. These goods are many: health, friendship, play, sexual reproduction, peace, knowledge, and so on. All of these goods are good inasmuch as they promote human well-being, and we can only pursue these activities in a manner that is both intentional and purposive. MacIntyre says,

> When someone identifies a good as being the true good, that is, the end to which by virtue of his or her essential nature moves, he or she, unless hindered or directed in some way, moves towards it. So 'such and such is the good of all human beings by nature' is always a factual judgment, which when recognized as true by someone moves that person toward that good. Evaluative judgments are a species of factual judgments concerning the final and formal causes of activity of members of a species.[43]

Essential natures are not static Newtonian abstractions derived from a modernist ontology devoid of purposive behavior; they are, on the contrary, derived from the natural teleology that determines their formal nature. There are actions that truly fulfill the agent. MacIntyre is hardly the "voice of one crying in the wilderness." Ralph McInerny, Jacques Maritain, Yves Simon, Henry Veatch, and Anthony Lisska are among those philosophers who maintain that the act-potency distinction provides a means to refute the naturalistic fallacy. According to

43. MacIntyre, *Three Rival Versions of Moral Enquiry*, 134.

Lisska's reconstruction of Veatch's ontological basis for natural law, we find four critical elements:

1. The possibility of natural kinds
2. A dispositional theory of essence as a natural kind
3. A version of 'final causes' bringing out the development of the potentialities in the essence
4. Normative ethics as a second order activity or inquiry based upon the prior ontological account of essence as a dispositional natural kind [44]

From our discussion in chapter 3, the idea of a "natural kind" plays a critical role not only in biology but also in our understanding of what constitutes human nature as rational *and* animal.

As humans we find ourselves *in media res*; we are creatures that feel the urge to better our present condition regardless of what that condition might be. This points to the fact that we have a natural teleology to our lives that compels us to pursue meaning, goodness, and a better version of ourselves. The natural law directs us to this explicitly. As we have seen in Aquinas, a primary precept of the natural law directs us to pursue truth and virtue; that is, those things that "perfect" or complete who we are as human persons. The pursuit of virtue, as we shall see in the next chapter, functions as a final cause for our actions. We are persons "in process," not static abstractions.

It is in the creative dialectic between our "nature as we are" and our "nature as we can be" that the work of ethics is carried out. This assumes a relatively stable, knowable, yet malleable nature—a nature that can best be understood with reference to act and potency. If there were no *telos* (i.e., "our nature as we can be") appropriate to our "nature as we are," then moral progress would be a mere illusion. We could speak only of differences in personal tastes and the pointless meanderings of our personal histories. However, if there is any genuine moral progress, then it means, as Maritain notes, there is "an ideal" that we strive for, and that we have a reasonable hope of moving in that direction.

We need not commit ourselves to a moral foundationalism reminiscent of earlier theories of natural law, with the result that we

44. Lisska, *Aquinas's Theory of Natural Law*, 184–5.

make the mistake of the modernist natural lawyers: the assertion that natural law provides an unassailable, universal, unchanging, and acultural morality. Rather, we can say that we "see through a glass darkly"; we know the direction of the natural law and we can see its history as a guide to our present normative judgments. However, we must guard against making officious pronouncements that reek of Enlightenment hubris.

The last of the arguments against the fact-value dichotomy is one that will appeal only to those engaged in the conversations unique to Christian ethics. I do not believe that it has persuasive force outside of those who consider their work distinctly Christian. As I have argued in chapter 4, the natural law theory I propose assumes that creation—or nature[3]—is the handiwork of the God of Christianity. All creation is imbued with value and points to its creator as its source. I therefore find it extraordinarily odd that thinkers such as Grisez would be prepared to jettison the epistemological centrality of creation merely for the purpose of wanting to avoid the naturalistic fallacy. For the Christian ethical theorist there can be no fact-value dichotomy, since the goodness of God permeates the entire created order. God has given us desires and purposes and expects us to act upon these desires and purposes. To abandon this critically important feature of Christian theology is to concede too much to the analytic tradition of philosophy, which we have seen cannot coherently defend the fact-value dichotomy on other grounds.

6.5 The Value of the Analytic Tradition

There are at least three important caveats the analytic tradition can offer any ethical theory that identifies itself as finding the basis for normativity in nature itself. A first caution concerns the nature of moral language and how it operates phenomenologically. Analytic philosophers including Moore, Ayer, and R. M. Hare have suggested that moral language operates differently from other sorts of language. The special status of moral language is such that it is most emphatically not merely descriptive language. Moral language has a magnetic character about it, such that when we say that something is "good," we are not merely saying that it possesses some natural property but that the property in question is desirable—the property recommends itself to us. It lures us toward a specific kind of behavior. When I say that "it is good to help those in distress," I am not merely saying that "helping someone in distress will lower your blood pressure and release endorphins"—an empirical claim—I am also recommending that sort of behavior to you as a desirable quality which you ought to have as a morally mature person.

A second important point the analytic tradition raises concerns the questions of how and when we move from "is" to "ought." We can imagine someone saying, "I was created with these desires and therefore I have a right to act upon them." Certainly, we do not sanction each and every desire as morally justified simply in virtue of its existence. The sociopath who desires to kill and eat other human beings does not have moral sanction for these behaviors, even though he may claim that they are "natural." We must distinguish between those states of affairs that sanction moral activity and those that do not.

The use of the term "nature" cannot sanction all human behavior; nature[3] (i.e., the fulfillment of the natural *telos* embedded in humans in creation; it includes but is not reducible to nature) cannot be derived from either nature[1] (i.e., the object of various scientific inquiries that focuses upon explanations of how natural objects and living beings act and are acted upon) or nature[2] (i.e., a principle of corruption resulting from a primeval fall of humanity wherein the active power of nature is contrasted with the restorative powers of grace), because neither one can bear the weight of the intellectual task laid upon it. If we recall that nature[1] simply provides an understanding of the natural world and the mechanisms that operate in this world without an appeal to some normative moral principles, we have moved from a purely empirical description to a normative prescription. The attempts by Larry Arnhart and E. O. Wilson provide an example of this illicit move, resulting in a kind of crude moral naturalism.

Arnhart and Wilson see evolution as the grand meta-narrative that explains everything, from why finches develop various kinds of beaks to why humans have elaborate and complex moral systems. Yet in a world devoid of any sense of "ought" apart from the adaptations to cooperate, it is difficult to see why we would have any compelling reason to "obey the dictates of the evolutionary imperative." John Hare rightly criticizes Arnhart for a failure to "bridge the moral gap" that lies between our nature as we have evolved and any sense of "ought" that urges us to be more than creatures subject to our evolved impulses.

Arnhart defines "the good" as "the desirable," with the proviso that "the desirable" is the "generally desirable," that is, what humans have come to desire through our evolutionary history. We have evolved to desire the following twenty items: "a complete life, parental care, sexual identity, sexual mating, familial bonding, friendship, social ranking, justice as reciprocity, political rule, war, health, beauty, wealth, speech, practical habitation, practical reasoning, practical arts, aesthetic pleasure, religious understanding, and intellectual understanding."[45] These desires manifest themselves across all cultures and Arnhart intends that the list provide a basis for normative ethics. He states, "If the good is the desirable, then human ethics is natural insofar as it satisfies natural human desires."[46] Thus Arnhart offers a clear example of contemporary ethical naturalism based upon an evolutionary reading of human nature, thereby leaving him open to the charge of violating the fact-value orthodoxy so prevalent in contemporary ethics.

Arnhart protests that his evolutionary tale of Darwinian natural rights does not commit the naturalistic fallacy because a universal human nature will invariably have an influence upon all human activities. As such, any theory of human nature as proposed by either Darwin or Aristotle should help us in unpacking what human morality should look like. "But if there is an unbridgeable gap between facts and values, *is* and *ought*, then this science of human nature could not support human ethics."[47] Arnhart is quick to point out that any desire whatsoever does not justify our actions, rather, we must think in terms of social cooperation in light of these basic desires. However, social cooperation does not really determine the rightness of any act in question; it only determines the cultural acceptability of the act in question.[48]

45. Larry Arnhart, *Darwinian Natural Right: The Biological Ethics of Human Nature* (Albany, NY: State University of New York Press, 1998), 29.

46. Ibid., 29.

47. Ibid., 7.

48. Hare points out that the consequence of Arnhart's view on slavery is not that slavery is wrong but that it is tragic, since Arnhart has no standard to appeal to other than what people do indeed desire. Slavery may be culturally acceptable but it isn't "wrong" in any traditional sense of the term. "Is There an Evolutionary Foundation for Morality?" 195.

For Hare, there must be, in addition to our natural desires for our own advantage (i.e., the Scotistic affection for advantage), a corrective that curbs and directs these desires (i.e., Scotus's affection for justice). The evolutionary naturalism of Arnhart fails to provide a means of "bridging the gap" from the descriptive to the normative. Although Hare's critique of Arnhart illustrates the problematic of evolutionary naturalism, we need not embrace his divine command theory as the only alternative. Natural law theory has adequate resources to address this issue by appealing to the various distinctions with regard to the term "nature." Arnhart employs, and Hare attacks, nature[1]. On this view, nature provides us only with a causal explanation of various phenomena; in this case, the phenomenon is human morality, and Arnhart moves from a description of how we have evolved to a theory of human morality based only upon a theory of nature as a system of efficient and material causes. However, the natural law theory I defend appeals to an understanding of nature that includes but is not restricted to these causes. Final and formal causes play a significant role in nature[3] with the result that (1) facts and values are not radically divided from one another, and (2) reason provides the normative basis for conceiving a teleology that includes but also transcends the limitations of evolutionary naturalism. Jacques Maritain addresses the issue of precisely how natural law conceives nature[3] in its directedness to the *telos*:

> What I am emphasizing is the first basic element to be recognized in natural law, namely the *ontological* element; I mean the *normality of functioning* which is grounded on the essence of that being: . . . Let us say, then, that in its ontological aspect, natural law is an *ideal order* relating to human actions, a *divide* between the suitable and the unsuitable, the proper and the improper, which depends on human nature or essence and the unchangeable necessities rooted in it.[49]

The "unchangeable necessities rooted in" human nature may have developed through the processes of evolution. Yet, without a sufficient *telos* for the human agent—a *telos* that transcends the merely biological—the magnetic element of ethics, or Maritain's "ideal," ethics is reduced to some sort of *ad hoc* theoretical construction along the lines of Moore's intuitionism.

49. Jacques Maritain, *Man and the State* (Chicago: University of Chicago Press, 1951), 87–8 (emphasis in the original).

This analysis reveals to us an important feature of the relationship between nature[1] and nature[3]: since nature[3] includes not only the descriptive elements of nature[1] as well as the value-laden teleology of the Maritain's "ideal order," a completely autonomous understanding of nature[1] is not possible. Rather, it is always an abstraction based upon the various value judgments and metaphysical presuppositions it must borrow from ontology.[50]

6.6 Natural Law After Analytic Ethics

The problems with the way analytic philosophers view moral language is that they often, like Moore, want to identify "the good" in a strict fashion. However, "good" is an analogous term that can vary from context to context. McInerny concludes that "Moore was right to see that the equation of the end of a particular action or kind of action with goodness itself would lead to oddities, among them that if on one occasion I pursue Guinness as good, and on another, Pepto-Bismol, I would seem to have to say that Guinness and Pepto-Bismol are the same thing."[51] Certainly Guinness and Pepto-Bismol may be good under specific circumstances, but to say that they can both be identified with "the good" is to fail utterly in how we understand language, not to say how we identify discrete entities.

Along these lines, MacIntyre argues that "we can only use the name of a simple property intelligibly where we are acquainted with some standard example of the property with reference to which we are to recognize whether it is present or absent in other cases."[52] But if we can intuit "the good," from whence does this intuition arise? If Moore says there is one standard example, then he himself violates the open question argument. If Moore says there is no standard, then we have two options. Either "good" is utterly meaningless and the ethical enterprise is a mere chimera, or "good" is an analogical property of things that will vary from context to context. In this later

50. See my discussion of the metaphysical assumptions in sociobiology in chapter 3.
51. McInerny, *Ethica Thomistica: The Moral Philosophy of St. Thomas Aquinas* (Washington, DC: Catholic University of America Press, 1982), 28.
52. Alasdair MacIntyre, *A Short History of Ethics* (Notre Dame, IN: University of Notre Dame Press, 1996), 252.

case, neither the Guinness nor the Pepto-Bismol exhaust the formality of "the good," but participate in it to some degree.

The act-potency distinction helps clarify the good and how each being participates in the good. Yet each good is relative to the kind of thing in question. We ask, "what is the excellence of this thing?" For humans, this excellence consists in a variety of activities that promote flourishing in specific ways at specific times. That is, natural law needs to consider these questions in light of a more complete understanding of the human person; in short, natural law needs the tradition of virtue ethics in order to articulate precisely how one does the good and avoids evil within the context of an individual's life.

Conclusion

In some respects, the history of twentieth-century analytic ethics was the failed attempt to accomplish three self-appointed tasks: (1) to provide an objective foundation for normative judgments, (2) to clarify the meaning of moral discourse, and (3) to establish a value-free approach to the philosophy of language. In the end, it accomplished none of these tasks, leaving us more or less where we started before Moore's *Principia*.

Postmodern deconstructionism and genealogy called into question any sense of "objectivity" that was more than just another failed Enlightenment project. Elizabeth Anscombe and Alasdair MacIntyre demonstrated that no clarification of moral discourse was possible apart from a shared cultural and moral context. And philosophers of science showed that there were no "value-free" inquiries, not even those of the so-called "hard sciences."

One of the most important insights of virtue ethics is its insistence upon the idea that all ethical theories require social and intellectual contextualization in order to render them coherent. Lurking behind the entire analytic tradition lies a series of assumptions about human nature, moral inquiry, rationality, and the objectivity—and superiority—of the tradition itself. Moore's approach in *Principia* stands at the beginning of the long tedious arguments about the nature of moral language which assumes that we can treat various moral utterances acontextually. To make a promise requires a great deal of assumptions about culture, conventional morality, and which conditions might preclude the breaking of a promise. Furthermore, if, as the postmodernist demonstrates, moral language is always embedded in power structures and culturally determined narratives, then we can see that the analytic tradition in philosophy succumbs to this critique as simply one more failed attempt at meta-narrative.

Philosophers like Moore, Stevenson, and R. M. Hare seem to get the situation backwards. Instead of starting with how we actually use moral words in their context, analytic philosophers decontextualize the terms and construct ways in which we can use the words only after an initial philosophical delineation of how the word must be used.

If the analytic tradition showed us that mere analysis of moral language could not bear the weight of sustained moral inquiry, the virtue theorists seemed to point in the direction of "lived experience" as a more reliable guide to moral inquiry. Advocates of virtue realize that we do not start with an analysis of moral language but with character traits, narratives, and cultural institutions, and it is this approach that presents the last of the challenges and opportunities for natural law morality.

7 | Natural Law and the Virtues

Introduction

With few exceptions, natural law moralists and virtue theorists have tended to live and work in different spheres, each acting as if the other group did not exist.[1] A partial explanation for this phenomenon includes the tendency for natural law, at least since the time of Grotius, to move away from adjudicating the relative merit of moral agents and focusing upon the nature of the acts that these agents produce instead. In the twentieth century, natural law tended to devolve into a merely political theory, while virtue ethics became an important alternative to various modernist theories of ethics. This separation of the two streams of moral and political thought has diminished both theories. As I see it, natural law and virtue need one another in at least three important respects. First, natural law theory, although it prescribes the pursuit of virtue, cannot suffice alone for an adequate moral theory. Natural law is a necessary condition for an adequate theory, but the attempt to make it a self-sufficient theory tends to collapse into Kantian deontology or utilitarian consequentialism. A moral theory must address both the value of the agent (as Kant held) and the value of the act (as the utilitarians argued). However, the

1. Three notable exceptions are Rufus Black, *Christian Moral Realism: Natural Law, Narrative, Virtue, and the Gospel* (Oxford: Oxford University Press, 2000); Pamela M. Hall, *Narrative and the Natural Law: An Interpretation of Thomistic Ethics* (Notre Dame, IN: University of Notre Dame Press, 1994); and Daniel Mark Nelson, *The Priority of Prudence: Virtue and Natural Law in Thomas Aquinas and the Implications for Modern Ethics* (University Park, PA: Pennsylvania State University Press, 1992).

rule-based formulae of both Kant and the utilitarians fail to grasp the distinctively moral and psychological elements of human life. Neither theory offers what Elizabeth Anscombe demanded—with reference to the need for moral psychology as well as the requirement for a "law-based" understanding of obligations—when she wrote that what is needed is "an account of human nature, human action, the type of characteristic a virtue is, and above all of human 'flourishing.'"[2]

A second reason for a synthesis of virtue ethics and natural law is the former's need for an adequate understanding of human nature, its desires, capacities, teleology, and orientation to the good. If virtues are "good habits of the soul," then how can we understand what they are unless we have at least a minimal understanding of what the soul is? If virtues are concerned with moral psychology—our emotions, our intentions, and our practical reason—then we need a preliminary understanding of what constitutes human nature. Natural law morality provides this, but we simultaneously must insist that an understanding of human nature itself is insufficient to the task of ethical theory. As we have maintained throughout this work, natural law is a necessary but insufficient condition for ethics; and the same can be said for a theory of the virtues without the attendant understanding of human nature.

Finally, natural law and the virtues are complementary theories in that natural law points us to the good but can not achieve the good on its own. Natural law needs the virtues in order to fulfill not only our minimal obligations to others, but also to fulfill them in appropriate ways. Russell Hittinger nicely brings together a number of themes in Aquinas's theory of natural law that applies to my own interpretation:

> What is particularly distinctive about Aquinas' understanding of natural law is that it was neither exclusively juristic nor just a tag for discussing natural order in human powers. Nature and law are analogous terms in his system, encompassing matters of moral precepts, virtues, ends, custom, human legislation, and not the least, the relation between philosophical and theological conceptions of the good in human actions.[3]

If natural law encompasses the virtues, it means that it directs us to the development of human capacities for the purpose of human flour-

2. G. E. M. Anscombe, "Modern Moral Philosophy," *Philosophy* 33 (1958): 18.
3. Russell Hittinger, "Natural Law and Virtue: Theories at Cross Purposes," in *Natural Law Theory: Contemporary Essays*, ed. Robert P. George (Oxford: Clarendon Press, 1994), 63.

ishing. But this flourishing does not take place in abstract theoretical constructions but in particular contexts with particular circumstances, something only the virtues are capable of.

Since the development of virtue depends on the good as understood and grasped by the primary precepts of natural law, the precepts of natural law are open to fulfillment in various ways, both with respect to how the virtues may manifest themselves in individual lives as well as how we come to perceive the good. As we have seen, a biological understanding of human nature and its goods seems necessary in order to understand how we need to regulate our sexual and nurturing drives. However, we are more than biological beings; since we are spiritual beings whose ultimate end is communion with God, we should also be open to theological truths. But, as always, these theological truths will point us to the good since the Thomist maxim, "grace does not destroy nature but perfects it," guides our thinking at this point.

In this chapter I consider how some virtue theorists such as Martha Nussbaum and Nel Noddings have seen natural law in competition with virtue ethics and have chosen the virtues over natural law, or any other rule-based conception of moral theory. Stanley Hauerwas, who shares some sympathies with Nussbaum and Noddings, represents a virtue theorist whose attitude toward natural law is such that it must be understood from the perspective it plays within a theory of the virtues, and not as an independent, self-sufficient theory. Finally, I offer my own open theory of how natural law is a necessary but insufficient condition for a comprehensive ethical theory. More specifically, I argue that a theory of natural law needs the virtues, since natural law provides only the skeletal framework for a comprehensive ethical theory. Conversely, a virtue theory needs the insights into human nature that only a natural law understanding can provide. Although I cannot provide a full treatment of how natural law and the virtues complement each other in this brief chapter, I hope to provide a cursory exposition of some themes and issues that seem central to my thesis.

7.1 The Virtues

Virtue theorists usually trace the origins of their theory to the work of Aristotle. In his *Nicomachean Ethics* he defines a virtue as an acquired state of the soul that enables a person to perform actions well.[4] Under the influence of Aristotle, Alasdair MacIntyre defines a virtue as "an acquired human quality the possession and exercise of which tends to enable us to achieve those goods which are internal to practices and the lack of which effectively prevents us from achieving any such goods."[5] Significant to both definitions here are the ideas that:

1. One must *acquire* the virtues.
2. They are qualities of the soul.
3. They enable us to achieve the good.
4. They presuppose a community that practices the virtues.

These points are significant because they demonstrate that the virtues are about who we are and what kind of persons we should desire to be. This contrasts significantly with much of modern and contemporary philosophy's fixation with the formulation of rules and principles for behavior.[6]

The acquisition of virtue in Aristotle, Aquinas, and MacIntyre assumes an act-potency distinction, since agents are not born virtuous but must engage in practices that develop the virtues. For Aristotle

4. The literature on virtue ethics is vast, but in addition to MacIntyre some important contributors include the following: *Virtue Ethics,* ed. Roger Crisp and Michael Slote (Oxford: Oxford University Press, 1997); Rosalind Hursthouse, *On Virtue Ethics* (Oxford: Oxford University Press, 1999); Joseph J. Kotva, *The Christian Case for Virtue Ethics* (Washington, DC: Georgetown University Press, 1996); Josef Pieper, *The Four Cardinal Virtues* (Notre Dame, IN: University of Notre Dame Press, 1966); Christine Swanton, *Virtue Ethics: A Pluralistic View* (Oxford: Oxford University Press, 2003).

5. Alasdair McIntyre, *After Virtue* (Notre Dame, IN: University of Notre Dame Press, 1982), 191; Josef Pieper proffers an understanding of virtue consistent with MacIntyre's when he says, "Virtue is not the tame 'respectability' and 'uprightness' of the philistine but the enhancement of the human person in a way befitting his nature. Virtue is the *ultimum potentiae,* the most a man can be. It is the realization of man's potentiality for being. Virtue is the perfecting of man for an activity by which he achieves his beatitude. Virtue means the steadfastness of man's orientation toward the realization of his nature, that is, toward good." *Faith, Hope, Love* (San Francisco: Ignatius Press, 1986), 99.

6. Justin Oakley, "Varieties of Virtue Ethics," *Ratio* 9, no. 2 (September 1996): 128–52, sees six common themes in the variety of virtue ethics. First, "an action is right if and only if it is what an agent with a virtuous character would do." Second, "goodness is prior to rightness." Third, "the virtues are irreducibly plural intrinsic goods." Fourth, "the virtues are objectively good." Fifth, "some intrinsic goods are agent-relative." Sixth, "acting rightly does not require that we maximize the good."

and Aquinas, the acquisition of virtue is similar to the acquisition of any skill, since both require repetition and guidance in the perfecting of the behavior in question. Understood in this light, we can see that the acquired nature requires a community of persons who embody the virtues in question and are able to communicate this practical knowledge to others.

The virtues enable us to live well, since they direct us to that which is good for us (note here the similarity between the virtues and the natural law as pointing us to the good). Aquinas says that law functions as an external principle that guides human action, while the virtues, since they are acquired dispositions of the soul, function as internal guides to the good.[7]

On the classical Aristotelian model, we find two sorts of virtue: intellectual and moral. The intellectual virtues are "good habits of thinking," while the moral virtues are "good habits of acting." The moral virtues include prudence, justice, courage, and temperance. Prudence considers right thinking about anything the agent may intend to do, and so is the most comprehensive of the virtues. Justice considers right acting with regard to others, while courage and temperance focus on the appropriate regulation of our fears and desires. Yet with the advent of Christianity we find additional virtues added to Aristotle's list.

In addition to the moral virtues listed by Aristotle, Aquinas posits the theological virtues of faith, hope, and love, and believes that these Christian virtues possess a certain priority over the moral virtues because the theological virtues direct us to the good of our relationship with God, not merely to our relationships with other humans.[8] The moral virtues are not vitiated by the theological virtues; rather they are transformed and renewed by this new orientation to God as our supernatural end, in accordance with the basic idea that "grace does not destroy nature but perfects it." Yet this synthesis of Aristotelian moral psychology and Christian theology has not been welcomed universally by many contemporary virtue theorists.

Some see the intrusion of Christianity into a theory of the virtues as an unnecessary complication for a theory that is already self-sufficient. To bring Christian theological commitments into the discussions may

7. IaIIae. 90, prologue.
8. The biblical reference for this addition is found in I Corinthians 13:13: "Now these three remain: faith, hope, and love. But the greatest of these is love."

lead to a theory that is either too provincial to engage the larger culture or too fixated on questions of laws and rules, such that it cannot negotiate the complexities of lived moral existence.

7.2 Natural Law or Virtue Ethics

Martha Nussbaum and Nel Noddings have argued that the rule-based moral theories lack the resources they need to provide a coherent account of the moral life.[9] For both thinkers rule-based theories distort the nature of practical reason, since such theories place the primacy of rules over the centrality of persons. In Nussbaum's case, a virtue-based ethics serves as the remedy to the ills of Kantian, utilitarian, and other proposals that seem to neglect how persons in contexts develop and are faced with tragedy. For Noddings, a care-based ethic is one that has more affinity with a feminine approach to ethics, one that properly expresses how we should treat persons *qua* persons.

Nussbaum calls rule-based theories "deductivist" since, in her mind, they seem to deduce moral action from the moral rules that govern specific situations. R. M. Hare and Kant are two well-known deductivists that bear the brunt of much of her criticisms, since they both attempt to resolve moral conflicts in light of specific rules that govern various situations. For Hare, we can appeal to a principle of "overridingness" such that we can formulate principles for situations of potential conflict. When the obligation to tell the truth conflicts with the duty to deny an enemy of the state help, we can reformulate a principle such that "we should never lie except to the enemy in times of war." For Kant, the categorical imperative admits of no moral conflict and therefore there must be one, and only one, imperative to follow.

9. Martha C. Nussbaum, *The Fragility of Goodness: Luck and Ethics in Greek Tragedy and Philosophy* (New York: Cambridge University Press, 1986); Martha C. Nussbaum, *Love's Knowledge: Essays on Philosophy and Literature* (New York: Oxford University Press, 1992); Nel Noddings, *Caring: A Feminine Approach to Ethics and Moral Education* (Berkeley: University of California Press, 2003). Noddings is ambivalent about the term "virtue"; in the context of lived experience and practices that are genuinely caring she seems to accept the term as an accurate representation of her work, but she rejects the term when it refers to ethical abstractions reminiscent of rule-based ethics (80–81). Yet she does on occasion call her own theory one of "active virtue" (79).

What Nussbaum believes about both thinkers—and all others who practice "deductivism"—is that they fail to discern a critical element of moral life: its tenuousness and its tragic character. She claims this approach is "morally objectionable in that it commits the holder to a systematic neglect of certain features of persons—namely, both their separateness and their qualitative uniqueness—on which their specific personal value might be thought to rest."[10] The approach taken by Kant and Hare is one that has two critical problems. First, systematic moral theories displace persons from the center of moral discourse and in their stead we find rules, principles, and laws as the focus of ethics. This displacement of person has the effect of reducing the uniqueness of the person to a function of the system in the sense that the rules become primary and persons must conform to unyielding laws and rules. Second, the deductivist's approach fails to take seriously the nature of moral conflict, such that tragedy is systematically excluded as a real possibility for moral agents. Moral conflicts evaporate when we discover the correct rule for our given situation.

What this analysis is supposed to reveal is the inevitable conflict engendered by a basic heteronomy of goods that in principle cannot be resolved. Nussbaum says that we must come to grips with the fact that we "live in a fallen world" wherein "values and loves are so pervasively in tension one with another that there is no safe human expectation of a perfect fidelity to all throughout a life."[11] Therefore, any attempt to see an ultimate *telos* in human existence, any attempt to see a dominant meta-narrative running throughout our story, inevitably denies some salient, tragic element of human existence. Natural law theory on this view isn't so much wrong as it is naively selective—selective with regard to which rules are used to accomplish the one dominant good, the *summum bonum*. On Nussbaum's view, the only *summum bonum* available is that which a life of virtue affords us amidst our changing tragic conditions.

A key example Nussbaum gives of the tragic element in the moral life is that of Sophocles' Antigone, who must choose between her political duty to obey King Creon's immoral edict that she may bury only one of her brothers, and her duty to the gods that both brothers must be buried. Nussbaum criticizes both characters for their refusal to see the complexity of the moral situation and the insufficiency of

10. Nussbaum, *Love's Knowledge*, 132–3.
11. Ibid., 133.

230 A Shared Morality

their practical reason in their insistence upon following one and only one conception of the good.

For Creon, the overriding good that determines the value of an agent is his commitment to the city. All relationships, all deliberation, all commitment must place the good of the city above all other loyalties. As a result, civic virtue becomes the centerpiece of Creon's moral universe and the guiding principle of practical reason. Nussbaum says, "Creon has, then, made himself a deliberative world into which tragedy cannot enter. Insoluble conflicts cannot arise, because there is only a single supreme good, and all other values are functions of that good."[12] As a result, civic virtue is thicker than blood and the rebellious brothers must both be condemned as criminals against the state.

Although Antigone seems to contrast with Creon quite sharply, her character is much more similar to Creon's than one would think *prima facie*. Antigone recognizes only kinship as the central claim upon her own commitments. She even goes so far as to claim that sibling love preempts spousal fidelity and paternal piety. She has reduced all moral obligations to that of sisterly love for her brothers and has become blind to any and all competing claims. For Antigone, "duty to the family dead is the supreme law and the supreme passion."[13] She is as guilty of rule-based deductivism as Creon himself. Both characters fail to render coherent accounts of practical reason, since they both deny important elements of the moral situation that only a person-centered ethics can recognize.

Nel Noddings shares Nussbaum's suspicion of rules and their hegemony in ethics and moral education. For Noddings, much of modern and contemporary moral philosophy attempts to proceed methodologically on the basis of mathematical reasoning. She says,

> I think we are doubly mistaken when we approach moral matters in this mathematical way. First, of course, we miss sharing the heuristic processes in our ethical thinking just as we miss that sharing when we approach mathematics formally. . . . Second, however, when we approach moral matters through the study of moral reasoning, we are led quite naturally to suppose that ethics is necessarily a subject that must be cast in the language of principle and demonstration. This . . . is a mistake.[14]

12. Nussbaum, *The Fragility of Goodness*, 58.
13. Ibid., 64.
14. Noddings, *Caring*, 8.

For Noddings, ethical theory has been dominated by Enlightenment rationality and decidedly male-oriented solutions to moral conundrums. The two key proponents of this approach are Kant, everyone's favorite interlocutor, and Lawrence Kohlberg, the well-known developmental psychologist of the twentieth century.

Kohlberg proposes six different stages of moral development that can accurately describe an individual's moral thinking.[15] The highest of these levels is the stage of "universal ethical principles." When confronted with a dilemma, those who are the most advanced in their moral thinking will "universalize" their principles. That is, they will appeal to some universally binding principle that in many respects satisfies the Kantian demand of the categorical imperative.

In response to Kohlberg's theory, Carol Gilligan objects that universal principles may not be a better approach to resolving moral conflicts, since these principles so often ignore the personal relationships that exist between and among various persons.[16] Instead, a more complete view of human nature—and a significantly less Kantian approach—is one that places important relationships, emotions, and caring at the center of moral reflection. Since human beings are relational as well as intellectual, rational principles alone do not suffice for adjudicating competing moral claims.

Noddings accepts Gilligan's critique of Kohlberg's theory of moral development and proposes a care-based ethic instead of the dominant principle-based ethic advocated by thinkers from Kant to Kohlberg. Noddings sees principles and rules as oversimplifications for very complex situations. Oftentimes we naively assume that if it is right for agent A in situation S to do M, then all other agents in circumstances similar to A should also do M. So if agent B finds herself in situation S, she also should do M. Unfortunately, as Noddings observes, "A and B, struggling with a moral decision are two different persons with different factual histories, different projects and aspirations, and different ideals."[17] Given the facts of human particularity, no two situations are ever exactly alike.

15. Lawrence Kohlberg, "Stages in Moral Development as a Basis for Moral Education," in *Moral Education: Interdisciplinary Approaches*, ed. C. M. Beck, B. S. Crittendon, and E. V. Sullivan (Toronto: University of Toronto Press, 1971).

16. Carol Gilligan, *In a Different Voice: Psychological Theory and Women's Development* (Cambridge, MA: Harvard University Press, 1982).

17. Noddings, *Caring*, 85.

An ethic of caring arises out of both our natural care for others (e.g., of infants and friends) as well as our ethical demand to care for others (e.g., those whom we need to care for in order for us to achieve both our ideal and theirs as well). We start with our feelings and desires to care for those near and dear to us, and then reflect on the complexity of our situations. As a result, we see that there is an "orbit of caring" we inhabit such that it is impossible for us to connect with those outside that orbit (e.g., those across the globe whom we do not know and therefore cannot care for). Noddings says bluntly that "I am not obliged to care for starving children in Africa, because there is no way for this caring to be completed in the other unless I abandon the caring for which I am obligated."[18]

Noddings's ethic of care seems to be based upon the following:

1. Relationships, not rational principles, determine my obligations.
2. Obligations derive from both natural sentiment and moral sentiment.
3. Caring is
   a. for those who are present to me.
   b. for those who can respond to (or complete) my caring for.
   c. mutual.
   d. is directed to the other's growth.
   e. is always contextual.

On this reading of ethics, mutual care between and among persons takes center stage since humans, in Noddings's view, are primarily relational creatures who require care and caring for. Moreover, one cannot determine in advance which moral rules should be applied without any lived experience that can guide and direct the agent's caring.

For Noddings, the ethical ideal is one that is born out of our empathic capacities for others as well as our longing for intimacy with others. These sentiments, however, in order to be maintained must be accompanied by commitment to care—not only for others but for ourselves as well. An ethic that demands heroic self-sacrifice and neglects the care of the self should be viewed with suspicion. The sustained commitment to care—to both others and the self—is what

18. Ibid., 86.

constitutes an ethic of care and the concomitant virtues of character Noddings believes are necessary for morally mature persons.

Noddings rightly criticizes ethical theories that place moral rules above persons, with the result that moral deliberation resembles a geometric proof more than the lived existential experiences they are. However, this criticism misses the mark when it comes to natural law theories such as my own and the one advocated by Aquinas. Since moral rules arise to some extent from human desires and emotions and our reflection upon them, we see that the relational aspect of Aquinas's thought is often neglected. Cristina Traina remarks,

> The feminist complaint that Roman Catholic natural law moral reasoning ignores emotions and affections does aptly fit an Enlightenment interpretation of natural law, which sees reason as dispassionate, neutral, objective, and disembodied. But Thomas understood reason to function (for better or worse) under the influence of the passions, which incorporate affections and emotions. Thus, a *Thomistic* version of natural law is, if not adequate to contemporary feminist concerns about attachment, at least resonant with them.[19]

Certainly the natural theories as advanced by Donagan and Finnis do not adequately consider personal relationships, or if they do they subordinate them to rules. However, it could be argued that the rules of natural law morality arise from a reflection upon real relationships that exist between and among persons. Vernon Bourke argues that the idea of *recta ratio*, or right reason, is central to both Aquinas's theory of natural law and his understanding of virtue. Furthermore, right reason is the human capacity to see real relationships, or "ratios," in the world and to act according to these relationships. The virtuous person fulfills the precepts of the natural law by practicing the virtues, but a person who follows only the "letter of the natural law" may not see the real relationships, and thus will fail in regard to practicing the virtuous life.

Let's consider a classic example. Suppose we borrow a weapon from a neighbor and the neighbor asks for it back. Would it be right to return it if the neighbor were to use it in an unjustified rebellion against the government? Of course it would be wrong, but simply ap-

---

19. Cristina L. H. Traina, *Feminist Ethics and Natural Law: The End of the Anathemas* (Washington, DC: Georgetown University Press, 1999), 156 (emphasis in the original).

pealing to one rule against another fails to consider the real relationships at play. The rule "return borrowed items" comes into conflict with "don't aid rebels in unjust causes." Only a prudent person who possesses right reason can adjudicate between the rules, since she knows how rules should be put into the service of relationships.

In response to the virtue ethics advanced by Nussbaum, Pamela Hall argues that it may be not so much that "we live in a fallen world" but that "we ourselves are fallen." Quite possibly, Nussbaum adopts an entirely too naïve approach to considering the nature of our desires and the world. Hall remarks that "while the world may be tangled according to Nussbaum, for Aquinas, it is our desires and loves which can become tangled and at war with one another in sin."[20] Without sufficiently trained desires that habitually act for the good, the only reasonable explanation for tragedy must be that the world itself is the problem. In proceeding this way, Nussbaum has placed the blame for muddled moral thinking in two places. First, our moral thinking is confused because we fail to see the tragic dimension of life, in that the world is too complex and "tangled" for us to ever find a happiness that is immune to the vicissitudes of life. And second, we must blame ourselves for corporate self-deception when we think that rules can serve as a means to domesticate the unruly and tangled world we inhabit. The upshot of Nussbaum's argument is such that, in her insistence on avoiding rule-based theories which tend to truncate the legitimate arena of moral deliberation, she has thereby absolved people of moral responsibility by arguing that their failure is intellectual. The problem for Nussbaum is one of intellectual character, not one of moral character.

Neither slavishly following rules nor trying to develop the virtues, on Nussbaum's account, can protect us against the fragility of the moral life. Stanley Hauerwas and Charles Pinches contend that Nussbaum has failed to see the importance of community as a protection against fragility.[21] They contend that her modernist assumptions lead her to the conclusion that there can be no self-sufficiency in ethics since the self—as it stands—cannot survive the invariable changes of friendship and love. Yet a robust theory of the virtues requires the support of a

    20. Hall, *Narrative and the Natural Law*, 110.
    21. Stanley Hauerwas and Charles Pinches, *Christians Among the Virtues: Theological Conversations with Ancient and Modern Ethics* (Notre Dame, IN: University of Notre Dame Press, 1997), 70–88.

community that practices the virtues, one that sustains members of the community in the midst of hardship. They object that her understanding of the tragic and fragile moral life is one that "supposes our greatest loves and passions, exposed to the naked world of luck, can just as easily destroy us as exalt us. In reply, Christians must say that love, true love, is not like that."[22] A modernist, individualist reading of an ethics of virtue—like the one Nussbaum proposes—ultimately fails since there are no communities of virtue to support them.

7.3 Virtue Ethics and the Rejection of Enlightenment Natural Law Morality

One of the most notable defender of narrative ethics today is Stanley Hauerwas, who has consistently argued that ethics is not about what we do but about the kind of persons we should be. Like MacIntyre, Hauerwas believes that ethics must be understood within the context of specific communities that practice virtues, not as universal rules formulated by Enlightenment rationalities that simply serve the purposes of liberal democracies. Given his commitment to the narrative character of Christian ethics, Hauerwas's treatment of natural law morality may seem ambiguous since he oftentimes criticizes various manifestations of it.[23] However, careful analysis of his work reveals a consistent approach that objects to natural law morality in its Enlightenment (post-Grotius) manifestations. Hauerwas discusses natural law in four of his more important works: *Truthfulness and Tragedy: Further Investigations in Christian Ethics*; *The Peaceable Kingdom: A Primer in Christian Ethics; Sanctify Them in the Truth*; and *With the Grain of the Universe*.[24] The earlier works determine the context for

22. Ibid., 85.

23. For all of her careful work on natural law and Christian ethics, Jean Porter mistakenly thinks that Hauerwas rejects all forms of natural law when he is merely rejecting the Enlightenment version of it as a mistaken point of departure for moral reflection, as I shall show below. What Porter fails to do is to consider the comments Hauerwas makes in *The Peaceable Kingdom* in light of his earlier work. Cf. Jean Porter, *Nature as Reason: A Thomistic Theory of the Natural Law* (Grand Rapids: Eerdmans, 2005), 331–3.

24. Stanley Hauerwas, *Truthfulness and Tragedy: Further Investigations in Christian Ethics* (Notre Dame, IN: University of Notre Dame Press, 1977); *The Peaceable Kingdom: A Primer in Christian Ethics* (Notre Dame, IN: University of Notre Dame Press, 1983); *Sanctify Them in the Truth: Holiness Exemplified* (Nashville: Abingdon Press,

the later work, so it is important for us to consider these works in their chronological order.

In what sounds like a *prima facie* attack on natural law morality and its relationship to Christian ethics, Hauerwas declares that "Christian ethics theologically does not have a stake in 'natural law' understood as an independent and sufficient morality."[25] When understood as a complete theory of ethics without the need for virtue, it seems to offer a minimalist conception of the moral life, one that may seem to have the advantage of a "lowest common denominator" of morality that Christians can share with Muslims, Buddhists, Hindus, agnostics, and atheists. Although natural lawyers often attempt to establish a common morality, Hauerwas argues that "such a view of the moral life makes it extremely difficult to say how grace transforms, reorientates or fulfills natural law."[26] That is, if natural law is primarily a means of finding a universal common morality, how can the distinctively Christian idea of grace enter into the theory without jeopardizing the theory's universal appeal?

Hauerwas rightly points out that to sever Aquinas's treatise on natural law from its context, as Lisska and others attempt, is to render "Aquinas' reflection on natural law unintelligible, for Aquinas did not discuss natural law in order to supply an 'objective' account of morality, but rather he needed a principle of interpretation that would allow him to distinguish the various kinds of precepts found in scripture."[27] On Hauerwas's view, natural law is part of the scriptural narrative that gives us a means to distinguish various kinds of precepts and their relative authority. The scriptural narrative is primary and natural law is secondary, for we begin with the narrative in the scripture not with an acontextual understanding of natural law inherited from the Enlightenment. "Natural law is best discussed in terms of how we are to find a center for our lives amid the many powers, relations, and roles that lay claim to us."[28]

In *The Peaecable Kingdom*, he turns his attention directly to those who would use natural law as the foundation of Christian ethics and build a system upon a universal principle of ethics that appeal

1998); and *With the Grain of the Universe: The Church's Witness and Natural Theology* (Grand Rapids: Brazos Press, 2001).

25. Hauerwas, *Truthfulness and Tragedy*, 58.

26. Ibid.

27. Ibid., 61.

28. Ibid.

to all people of good will. He says this attempt has the following consequences:

> (1) It creates a distorted moral psychology, since the description of act is thought to be determined by an observer without reference to the dispositions of the agent. . . . (2) It fails to provide an adequate account of how theological convictions are a morality, i.e., that they are meant not just to describe the world but to form the self and community. (3) It confuses the claim that Christian ethics is an ethic that we should and can commend to anyone with the claim that we can know the content of that ethic by looking at the human. (4) It fails to appreciate that there is no actual universal morality. . . . (5) Because it seems to entail a strong continuity between church and world, natural law ethics fails to provide the critical perspective the church needs to recognize and deal with the challenges presented by our societies and the inherent violence of our world. (6) It ignores the narrative character of Christian convictions by forgetting that nature-grace, creation-redemption are secondary theological concepts. . . . (7) It tempts us to coerce those who disagree with us, since its presumption lead us to believe that we always occupy the high ground in any dispute.[29]

We might categorize Hauerwas's criticisms under three rubrics: theological objections, Enlightenment entanglements, and questions of moral formation and development.

Hauerwas's theological objections stem from the fact that Enlightenment theories of natural law tend to usurp the centrality of biblical narrative, with the result that the narrative of Christ's life and his commands seem to serve an auxiliary role in Christian ethics rather than having a pre-eminent place in the community of believers. In their desire to accommodate Christian teaching to secular audiences, Enlightenment proponents of natural law have tried to find a common ground with agnostics, atheists, and adherents of other religions. Yet the desire to translate the Christian teaching into secular parlance loses the central elements of Christian ethics.

In his more recent work, Hauerwas has explicitly argued that natural law does hold a place in Christian ethics to the extent that it must be considered properly within the parameters of natural theology. The natural theology he espouses, however, is derivative of the work of Karl Barth. That is, we must first see the world through the lenses

29. Stanley Hauerwas, *The Peaceable Kingdom*, 63–4.

of sin and grace before we can understand that natural law refers to "what our lives should look like as people created for friendship with God."[30] That is, natural law refers to how we come to narrate our existence through the perspective that only the Bible reveals, that we are sinful people in need of redemption. Hauerwas's insistence on this point reflects his rejection of Enlightenment moralities that simply gloss over the fact of human sin and its devastating consequences.

"Nature" and "grace" therefore have critical roles to play in Hauerwas's understanding of the formation of Christian ethics. "Nature" is no mere abstraction, but is a first work of grace that has been corrupted by sin. Grace itself plays upon nature perichoretically by infusing and penetrating the created order. But in order to appreciate the created order as such, we must first see ourselves as ordered to the God of nature and grace. He says,

> Because human language and reasoning work by virtue of their participation by analogy in the divine Logos, rather than by human conceptions derived independently of and antecedent to any revealed knowledge of God (although temporally and humanly considered they no doubt appear to be antecedent and independent of any revealed knowledge of God), 'nature' is never abandoned by God and in that sense devoid of grace.[31]

On this view of *fides quarens intellectum* (faith seeking understanding), our theological convictions about God, sin, nature, and grace stand at the beginning of our reflection, not at the end of an already complete, secular understanding of the cosmos with an *ad hoc* "tip of the hat" to those who might have "something theological" to add to the discussion.

What the natural lawyer must do, therefore, is provide a theory of the natural law that on the one hand speaks to the transcendent moral principles people of all cultures know to be true, and on the other hand maintain a distinctive Christian identity that is not merely an *ad hoc* theological addendum to an already complete moral theory. We could construct an interesting dilemma based upon Hauerwas's criticisms of Enlightenment theories of natural law.

30. Hauerwas, *Sanctify Them in the Truth*, 45.
31. Ibid., 44.

1. If natural law is a universally applicable and self-sufficient theory of morality, then it cannot be a distinctively Christian theory of morality.
2. If natural law has only a limited appeal—only to Christians—then it cannot be a universally valid theory of morality.
3. Natural law is either a universally valid theory or it has only a limited appeal.
4. Thus, natural law theory cannot have universal application or it cannot be distinctively Christian.

In order to avoid this dilemma, I propose an account of natural law that sees the universal precepts of morality as a necessary element that the specifically Christian moral commitments presuppose. As a result, the grace that "transforms and reorients" the agent does not destroy the precepts of natural law but fulfills them.

Although Hauerwas expresses sympathy with natural law ethics, he also seems to identify the theory too much with its Enlightenment and contemporary advocates. However, the narrative approach to natural law that I defend is not subject to the weaknesses Hauerwas attributes to modern theories of natural law.

As Hauerwas acknowledges, Aquinas does not seem to be interested in developing an autonomous theory of natural law, even though some contemporary theorists who pledge their allegiance to Thomas do. In the sense that I follow Aquinas at this point it seems that natural law helps to lay bare certain elements of all narrative theories, in that all human communities require honesty and the concomitant ban on lying. All human communities require a minimal amount of peacemaking and the concomitant ban on murder. There are some virtues that transcend the particular narratives of particular peoples, yet each of these different communities will construct their narratives in different ways appropriate to their own history.[32]

What Hauerwas does not do is consider the work of Aquinas, or of an open theory like my own, in much detail. Although his criticisms of Enlightenment theories of natural law bring to light important weaknesses in the modernist approach to the theory, we must admit that not all theories are guilty of the crimes Hauerwas alleges. My own theory acknowledges the importance of the virtues as well as the importance of a narrative of natural law.

32. Don Brown, *Human Universals* (Philadelphia: Temple University Press, 1991).

The narrative of natural law—as I delineated in chapter 2—shows the development of the theory from a theological grounding in the patristic and medieval eras, to that of a political theory in the modern era that shunned any and all appeals to God or the spurious discipline of theology. A narrative approach to natural law has the strength of being open to revision, as it can incorporate insights of its critics into its own theory. In this respect, it is especially important to see natural law not as positing *a priori* moral principles from which we deduce our activities, but as an inductive approach to a consideration of human nature and its goods.

Hauerwas's laundry list of complaints against Enlightenment versions of natural law serves as a convenient starting point for a more positive discussion of the relationship between natural law and virtue ethics. As we have seen in chapter 3, we have good reason to believe that there is indeed a universal morality, or at least the basis for a universal morality, by an examination of human nature that transcends particular places and cultures. So understood, human beings cannot help but require practices of honesty and non-maleficence as the beginning of human morality, since violations of these precepts will always and invariably undermine the possibility for communal human existence. Prohibitions on murder, theft, and adultery will always be part and parcel of human culture. So too, principles of mutual benevolence, reciprocity, and justice must form the core practices of any society.

Violations of these precepts not only constitute transgressions of rules but also of virtues. In his discussion of lying, Aquinas says that lying not only violates the prohibitions imposed on human communities by the natural law and the Decalogue, but also is wrong because it is contrary to the love of God.[33] On the most fundamental level, lying undermines the possibility for cooperative communal existence, since it subverts trust between and among members of society. On a higher level, lying vitiates personal relationships, destroys virtuous character, and tempts us to manipulation.

7.4 Natural Law and its Need for the Virtues

Some of the basic precepts of natural law obviously find their origin in our evolutionary heritage, since the sanctions on murder and

---

33. IIaIIae.110.4,2.

dishonesty seem to be a synthesis of biological tendencies shaped by cultural reflection. Regardless of the culture, we find *prima facie* prohibitions on lying, murder, and infidelity; yet what constitutes specific violations of these acts will vary from place to place and time to time.

The natural law prescribes minimal obligations that all human agents have. By practicing these obligations, we find that we can live together with others peacefully. We avoid murder, theft, adultery, and lying, and we can have a reasonably peaceful coexistence with others. In addition to these basic precepts of morality, we also seem to have the obligation to make ourselves better persons. According to Aquinas, a basic precept of natural law is the pursuit of virtue. Natural law seems to speak to the issue of good ends and specific kinds of actions in pursuit of those ends. However, it does not speak directly to questions of character apart from our need to pursue it.

Pursuing and doing the good and avoiding evil is the basic precept of natural law, yet this is a formal principle and requires particular application in specific contexts. As we have seen, murder and adultery can never be understood as means of pursuing the good. Yet a good person must act appropriately in specific circumstances, and with particular motives. We can hardly call a person moral who helps alleviate another's suffering for purposes of selfish gain a "morally admirable" individual. Even though the natural law directs us to certain kinds of actions that are good, these precepts are merely necessary conditions for morality, not sufficient ones.

The natural law morality that I defend transcends the merely minimalist approach to morality that focuses upon formally good acts. Following Aquinas, I think the natural law not only includes our minimalist obligations to others in order to create and sustain a peaceful community, but also pursues virtue and knowing the truth about God. Although Aquinas rarely spends much time developing elaborate lists of the primary precepts of natural law, we see that any operation of the intellect toward the good is properly related to the natural law. So it is that the intellectual appetite pursues the truly human goods. He says, "By the intellectual appetite we may desire the immaterial good, which is not apprehended by sense, such as knowledge, virtue, and the like."[34]

34. Ia.80.2.ad2.

This reference to the acquisition of virtue is especially important to our discussion, since it explicitly links natural law precepts to the development of virtue. Natural law serves as the basis for our moral obligations since it is based upon human nature, yet it does not spell out the details of moral behavior. Indeed, this is the reason a theory of natural law requires a theory of the virtues. And since the acquisition of virtue is a function of reason, it follows that the human agent's pursuit of virtue is required by the natural law. Aquinas directly addresses this important aspect of natural law: "Since the rational soul is the proper form of the human, there is thus in every human a natural inclination to act according to reason; and this is to act according to virtue. Thus, all the acts of the virtues are prescribed by natural law, since each person's reason naturally dictates to that one to act according to virtue."[35] The key point here is that all the acts of the virtues fall under the generic heading of the natural law, since they are prescribed by reason in the sense that reason directs us to "better ourselves."

The act-potency distinction here is especially important. As human beings we are neither born virtuous, nor are we born with innate ideas of the natural law. Family, church, society, and other institutions mediate the primary precepts of the natural law to us. Our knowledge of the natural law is in potency until someone or something awakens and develops it in us. But an understanding of the natural law is but the first step on the way to moral goodness. We are creatures who are potentially virtuous and the natural law, like the DNA of a plant, directs us to the virtues. That is, the virtues complete what the natural law starts. As Daniel Mark Nelson says, "We have a natural aptitude for virtue and even a natural inclination to act virtuously or reasonably, such that we are not blank slates but have a created disposition, not entirely destroyed by the fall, to virtue and reason."[36] The *telos* of the natural law is the development of virtue, for which we have a natural inclination.

The natural law does not dictate precisely how one is to act according to reason or lay down some absolute principle for virtue. A virtue is an acquired trait of the soul and as such it will vary from person to person; but it will never stray beyond the bounds of the basic precepts of the natural law. The natural law simply determines

35. IaIIae.94.3.
36. Nelson, *The Priority of Prudence*, 120.

what specific kinds of actions are *per se* good and those that are evil. When we look at Aquinas's theory of natural law, we see that the basic precepts simply indicate "object of the act."[37] The object of the act answers the question, "what kind of act is being performed by the agent?" Some actions are by their very nature immoral: such are murder, theft, and adultery. Other actions, such as honoring one's parents, showing mercy, telling the truth, and peacemaking, are by their nature good actions. Yet these actions always require a context, specific circumstances, and intended appropriate ends. I may tell my wife the truth regarding my view that her latest hairstyle looks abominable, but do so in an unkind manner at an inopportune time, such as immediately before she departs for a highly stressful job interview. If viewed as a list of "dos" and "don'ts" without regard for circumstances and motive, the natural law is reduced to a kind of casuistic deontology.

One must not only know what kind of act is required in any given moral situation, one must also act for the right purposes and in the right circumstances. Being aware of the circumstances is critical to an adequate understanding of practical rationality. We make reference to the circumstances of our activities as being morally important. For instance, when someone asks us, "why didn't you tell me about the difficult situation at work today?" we may respond that it isn't an appropriate time since there are children listening and the discussion might raise complex problems too difficult for young minds to comprehend.

The end of our actions stands as the cause of what we do. In all our activities we pursue our various ends *sub ratio boni*—under the formality of the good. When asked why we did what we did, we respond by answering that we "thought it was best for everyone concerned." We see our activities as invariably ordered toward the good, and this teleological ordering of our activities permeates specific actions in particular circumstances, as well as the overarching meta-narratives for our lives. But the circumstances, the specific acts we choose, and the ends we aim for all presuppose a particular context. I must possess the capacity to deliberate well concerning what I ought to do in a variety of circumstances, depending on my role within those circumstances.

37. IaIIae.18.1.

Not only must my deliberating capacities be well-honed, I must also be able to give an account for why I did what I did. I must be able to communicate my deliberative process to others. In short, I need to have developed "independent practical reasoning" to the extent that I can intelligibly communicate my deliberation process to others.[38] This of course requires the development of prudence, the chief of the moral virtues. Yet my ability to deliberate independently requires that I have considered the circumstances, that I have not violated the precepts of natural law, and that I am acting for an appropriate end. But the possession of these abilities always assumes a network of social relationships that indicate what circumstances are important, what ends are appropriate to my social role, what counts as an act that fulfills or violates the natural law, and what counts as appropriate deliberation.

A brilliant but unlikely example comes from the Lutheran theologian Dietrich Bonhoeffer, who asks us to think about the following scenario. A young boy goes to school and his teacher asks him if it's true that his father comes home drunk every night? The boy answers, "no," even though it is true. But if we think of the rule, "do not lie," we find that the rule can easily become a deontological duty devoid of context. Bonhoeffer says,

> 'Telling the truth,' therefore, is not solely a matter of moral character; it is also a matter of correct appreciation of real situations and of serious reflection upon them. The more complex the actual situation of a man's life, the more responsible and the more difficult will be his task of 'telling the truth.' . . . Telling the truth is, therefore, something which must be learnt. . . . But the simple fact is that the ethical cannot be detached from reality, and consequently continual progress in learning to appreciate reality is a necessary ingredient in ethical action.[39]

The boy has rightly defended his family, even though the teacher's question encroached upon the integrity of the family. The child rightly grasps the relationships so important to the practical rationality necessary to deliberation. According to Hauerwas, "Bonhoeffer's account of the lie is determined by his understanding of reality. We are obli-

---

38. Alasdair MacIntyre, *Dependent Rational Animals: Why Human Beings Need the Virtues* (Chicago: Open Court Press, 2001), 105.

39. Dietrich Bonhoeffer, *Ethics*, trans. Neville Horton Smith (New York: Macmillan, 1955), 264–5.

gated to speak truthfully about reality but we must remember that reality names not only what is 'out there' but our relation to what is 'out there.'"[40] Bonhoeffer argues that the teacher is responsible for the lie since the boy has not learned how to deliberate well enough, even though he gives the appropriate answer from the perspective of preserving the integrity of the family. For Bonhoeffer, Noddings, Nussbaum, and Hauerwas, the lie must be told since the boy must not permit the rule "do not lie" to violate his most significant relationships. The teacher has violated an understanding of communal rules, and as a consequence has violated the virtues of prudence and justice insofar as he has stepped beyond the bounds of social and familial propriety. As Hauerwas comments, "According to Bonhoeffer, the child rightly lies in answer to a question that never should have been asked in a classroom."[41]

Several networks of social interaction instruct and shape what our obligations are and to whom what duties we owe. Parents, pastors, and teachers all become authorities in the different social networks we occupy, and they help develop the rules which apply in the various contexts. But rule-following in specific contexts is just the first step.

> Just because the relevant form of community is constituted as a network of givers and receivers, both of whom need the virtues, the community's shared agreements must have as their subject matter not only goods, but also rules. For rule-following is an essential constituent of some of those virtues that we ourselves and others must have, if we are to act adequately in those roles that we occupy within such a network. The types of actions required by a particular virtue can never be specified exhaustively by any list of rules. But failure to observe certain rules may be sufficient to show that one is defective in some important virtue.[42]

Since the precepts of natural law function as basic rules for our behavior, we can see how the theories of virtue and natural law can be integrated into a whole.

It becomes obvious that rules are necessary for our understanding of the virtues. For example, if I am to understand what it means to be trustworthy I must first have an understanding that there are

---

40. Stanley Hauerwas, *Performing the Faith: Bonhoeffer and the Practice of Nonviolence* (Grand Rapids: Brazos Press, 2004), 62–3.

41. Ibid., 63.

42. MacIntyre, *Dependent Rational Animals*, 109.

basic rules that a trustworthy person will not violate. Included among these rules are, "keep promises," "tell the truth," "do not betray confidences," and "care for others even when it may be an inconvenience to you." These rules play an important part in practical rationality, for at least two reasons.

First, they serve an epistemological role without which we could never come to know what it means to be trustworthy. That is, developmentally they provide a necessary starting point for our understanding of what constitutes a virtue. Persons who consistently and capriciously violate these rules do not deserve our trust; and so we teach our children to "tell the truth" since their moral reputation, at least initially, depends on their keeping to this rule.

Second, the precepts of natural law provide constraints upon our deliberations but they are not sufficient for a fully mature understanding of practical rationality, since "there is more to being trustworthy and reliable than conformity to this or any set of rules. Part of being trustworthy and reliable is that we are able to recognize what trustworthiness and reliability require in situations where there is no rule to guide us."[43] What we see here is Aristotle's principle of *phronesis*, or practical wisdom, at work. Rules are descriptions of what the good person does; or rather we should say that they are approximations that help us to begin the road to moral maturity. However, they cannot be understood as having the last word—as some pharisaical notions would lead us to believe—in all moral matters, since no rule or system of rules can be formulated to govern each and every possible situation we encounter. As Aristotle observed, when applying moral rules in specific contexts, "the more we descend to the particular, the more error creeps into our judgments." Nussbaum is thus right in arguing that a purely rule-based ethic distorts our understanding of life and our deliberation in particular circumstances, but she is wrong to relegate rules to an inconsequential status in moral deliberation.

What we find then is that a rule-based ethic, as advanced by some modern and contemporary natural lawyers, fails to do justice to the complexities of existential moral situations. Aquinas, and others in the natural law and virtue camp, have consistently seen that a rule may prove a valuable resource for beginners or for those doing "moral science," but the genuine standard for understanding the moral life is

43. Ibid., 110; Aquinas calls this developed capacity *gnome*, the capacity to act prudently in unusual circumstances.

the person who embodies the virtues. Another way of thinking about this is simply that natural law precepts present to us "the good" as a truth that we acknowledge intellectually— *bonum ut verum*, the good as the true. Virtue enables us to see "the good" as the good, as something we do desire—*bonum ut bonum*, the good as the good.[44]

In order to perceive the good as the good, we need to have our affections appropriately ordered and trained. One reason why the modernist approach to natural law distorts the classical understanding of the theory concerns the neglect of the affections. In fact, if one considers the caricature of natural law carefully, we see that the human agent is primarily responsible for knowing the good and doing the good. However, the missing feature is the affections' desire for the good, since knowing and acting also require an appropriate disposition toward the good. And virtue supplies this missing element since it means that we not only know what the good is, we also desire it for the right reasons.

7.5 Levels of Moral Obligation

This approach to natural law and the virtues we could label "developmentalist" in the sense that moral character develops from the more basic level of keeping the precepts of the natural law to the higher levels of virtue. This approach is consistent with the overall picture of Aquinas's moral thought as well as the recent work of Andrew Michael Flesher, who advocates a similar approach.[45]

The context for Flescher's discussion is the argument advanced by J. O. Urmson in his essay "Saints and Heroes," where Urmson contends that the only moral requirements incumbent upon all people are those moral expectations we see at the minimalist level.[46] Although Urmson's approach may seem acceptable from a political or legal

44. Ralph McInerny, *Ethica Thomistica: The Moral Thought of Thomas Aquinas* (Washington, DC: Catholic University Press, 1982), 101.
45. Andrew Michael Flescher, *Heroes, Saints and Ordinary Morality* (Washington, DC: Georgetown University Press, 2003).
46. J. O. Urmson, "Saints and Heroes" in *Essays in Moral Philosophy*, ed. A. I. Melden (Seattle: University of Washington Press, 1958), 188–216; a similar approach to Urmson's, that appeals to the idea of minimalist considerations of natural law, is H. L. A. Hart, "Philosophy of Law and Jurisprudence in Britain (1945–1952)," *American Journal of Comparative Law* 2 (1955): 355–64.

view it hardly seems to account for lived moral experience, wherein all people seem to experience moral demands that go beyond the merely minimalist.

According to Flescher there are three levels of moral obligation: the minimalist, the meta-duty to improve one's character, and the supererogatory. Speaking of the first level, Flescher claims that there is a bare minimum of duty that I cannot fall below. Here I am obligated to refrain from murder, theft, adultery, and all other acts that we can expect of individuals living in community. Yet this level is not merely one of negative prohibitions. There are positive duties we can reasonably expect of anyone. Flescher says, "Morality at this 'thin,' basic level applies to all agents regardless of how virtuous they are."[47] The tragic case of Kitty Genovese provides a ready example of people who failed to keep even the most minimal moral requirements, as they silently stood by and watched an innocent young woman murdered without lifting a finger to help her. One need not be a particularly virtuous person in order to help save a life, since basic moral decency demands it.

The second level of moral obligation is one wherein we recognize a duty to "attempt to become more virtuous in my life." Even though this obligation applies to all people, Flescher recognizes that different moral agents have different moral capacities and, as a result, the improvement in character will vary from person to person. He says that "while we can arguably speak about universal, 'rock-bottom' duties, such as the basic proscriptions against committing murder, or the obligation to allocate through taxation a small portion of our earnings to benefit society's least well-off, the distinction between those more demanding acts that are required and acts of supererogation is agent-relative."[48] We should also add that, since agents always find themselves embedded in specific cultural and familial contexts, the acts of supererogation themselves will be culturally determined to a significant extent.

The third level of moral obligation is one that is tied closely to the agent's moral development. As people increasingly develop moral virtue, their perception of what is morally required of them also expands. Flesher comments,

> Once I begin to acquire more virtue, I become bound, for I am not already bound, to perform additional first order duties that I formerly

47. Flescher, *Heroes, Saints and Ordinary Morality*, 240.
48. Ibid., 238.

regarded to a matter of supererogation and that still *are* instances of supererogation for other agents. . . . As I become more virtuous, the range of my deontic duties expands. . . . Moreover, at this stage of my development what I *ought* to do increasingly becomes a matter of what the fully virtuous person *would* do.[49]

Although Flescher describes this third level of obligation as duty, we could understand it as the moral agent's pursuit of the good. That is, the agent's perception of the good has been expanded to include more ways in which to pursue the good. Agents who have achieved the third level have a developed sense of moral perception that eludes those on the first level. Although Flesher's work is not intended to address the complicated nature of the relationship between natural law and the virtues, it seems compatible with the approach I take.

What I propose is a developmental, or an "open," natural law theory.[50] By "open" I intend three things. First, natural law is open to fulfillment by the virtues and not a "closed" ethical system, sufficient on its own merit. This open-ended aspect of my natural law theory staves off the initial criticisms leveled against "rule-based theories" by Noddings and Nussbaum. Natural law is not a "closed" system of axiomatic rules operating devoid of contextual, historical, and cultural factors. Rather, the theory holds that persons and their relationships are primary in the pursuit of the good. In other words, there is no way to achieve the good apart from healthy relationships with others; natural law simply points out those actions that always thwart the attainment of the good and those that invariably assist in the process.

In a second sense, the theory is "open" since it is open to revision in light of progress made in the natural sciences, and in light of cultural shifts that demonstrate the problematic nature of a "fixed" human essence. For example, a natural law theory that continued to affirm the cultural practice of slavery could hardly be taken seriously in the twenty-first century. Humans may exhibit genotypical and phenotypical variation, but this hardly counts as evidence for endorsing such a radically immoral institution as slavery. Furthermore, as cultures

49. Ibid., 240 (emphasis in the original).
50. In some sense this is reminiscent of Bernard Häring, *The Law of Christ: Moral Theology for Priests and Laity* (Westminster, MD: The Newman Press, 1964), in which he sees natural law as rooted in the scriptures but personalist in its approach to negotiating difficult situations.

develop and compare their systems against those of other cultures, as well as against that of an ideal system, we find that consensus builds regarding what is and what is not acceptable (e.g., the United Nations' condemnation of genocide).

In a third sense, the theory is open to theological completion and modification since the pursuit of the truth about God leads us to consider a good that transcends the merely terrestrial goods. As we have seen in chapter 3, the good of self-sacrifice may seem to conflict with the good of self-preservation. This is one critical reason that prudence, as informed by the theological virtues, is required for moral deliberation. A truth revealed by God may challenge our understanding of the good from a purely earthly perspective. As a result, Aristotelian virtue may differ significantly from Christian virtue, since the former has not access to truths that are "above reason," to use Aquinas's phrase. Mother Teresa's commitment to the poor—as derived from her love for God—surely differs from the prudential calculations of Aristotle's person of practical wisdom.[51]

This appeal to God demonstrates the hierarchy of impulses in action. Even though we have duties to preserve our own lives and to flee harm, we have a greater duty to God. Since God is the Good Itself, we recognize that no human good, even life itself, can compete with the possession of everlasting goodness. The agent's last end consists in loving God above all created goods and therefore has the character of an ultimate obligation.[52] The natural hierarchy of goods that natural law proposes and human virtue enacts enables the individual to judge among the many goods that vie for her attention. This synthesis of natural law and virtue theory contrasts sharply with the minimalists conceptions of natural law proposed by Finnis and Donagan.

When we consider the precepts of natural law as a minimalist conception of morality, we find that agents are left with normative rules that enable them to survive but not to flourish. The rules become the only guidelines for practical reason. One simply asks which rule applies and then proceeds to apply the relevant rule in the given

51. Josef Pieper, *The Four Cardinal Virtues*, says that "typically, natural prudence . . . tends to restrict the realm of determinative factors of our actions to naturally experienceable realities. Christian prudence, however, means precisely the throwing open of this realm and (in faith informed by love) the inclusion of new and invisible realities within the determinants of our decisions," 37.

52. R. Mary Hayden, "Natural Inclinations and Moral Absolutes," *Proceedings of the American Catholic Philosophical Association* 64 (1990): 130–50.

context. Although the minimalist invokes nature—specifically human nature—as the ultimate source for her deliberations, she fails to see how there is much more to human nature than merely those precepts that insure minimum requirements for communal stability.

A second related problem for the minimalist conception of natural law flows from this obsession with the basic precepts of natural law. Rules, and their rational justification, take center stage to the neglect of the development of character. As a result, much more time and effort is spent defending the universal principles of natural law than on developing an account of human flourishing in which natural law plays an important though preliminary role. In this light, the precepts of natural law function as deontological duties without regard to real relationships and the relevant contexts for moral deliberation. Hauerwas's criticism of modernist conceptions of natural law is certainly justified, as he rightly sees these later mutations of natural law as a distortion of Aquinas's earlier, more coherent, account of normativity.

7.6 Virtue's Need for Natural Law

To this point we have argued that natural law requires the virtues in order to flesh out how the precepts of natural law can be fulfilled. What we have not done is considered why a theory of virtue requires the natural law. In short, we can say that there are at least two critical reasons why virtue theory requires a framework such as natural law provides. First, we must be able to identify certain actions that thwart the development of virtuous character; and, second, we need an adequate understanding of human nature.

With regard to the first reason, Robert Louden has argued that virtue ethics typically fail to identify specific kinds of behaviors that frustrate communal living. He says,

> We need to be able to identify certain types of action which produce harms of such magnitude that they destroy the bonds of community and render (at least temporarily) the achievement of goods impossible. In every traditional moral community one encounters prohibitions or "barriers to action" which mark off clear boundaries in such areas as the taking of innocent life, sexual relations, and the administration of justice according to local laws and customs. Such rules are needed to

teach citizens what kinds of actions are to be regarded not simply as bad (a table of vices can handle this) but as intolerable.[53]

Some actions simply undermine the good of society in such a way that they are *per se* evil. These rules seem to apply across cultures, even if their particular manifestations may differ.

Rufus Black echoes Louden's concerns and says that "narrative ethics . . . cannot stand alone. To realize its own objectives it needs to function together with a complementary scheme of principle and rule-based moral deliberation."[54] That is, natural law principles and rules provide the parameters for those actions that contribute to our flourishing as individuals. Otherwise, we would seem to be forced to admit that one could murder virtuously, steal virtuously, or commit adultery virtuously. There must be some basic limits to how we conduct ourselves with regard to our most fundamental social relationships.

In a second way, natural law provides the necessary philosophical anthropology that a theory of virtue requires. As we have seen, precepts of natural law spring from two sources: from our biological nature, as created by God, and from our human nature, as beings who require the development of communal practical reason. The danger is to place too much emphasis on one of these sources at the expense of the other. In one sense the communal nature of practical reason can be understood as taking precedence, since a community deliberates corporately about what ought and ought not to be done by taking into consideration—that is, by reflection—our nature as biological and social beings. We have a biological need for others, but we also have a rational—or human—need to reflect upon our biological, political, and moral nature.

Our biological drives for community, procreation, nurturing the young, and alleviating the suffering of others provide the material for reflection upon and, to some extent, direction to our practical rationality. The precepts of natural law point to the natural ends of these drives, and indicate the appropriate and inappropriate ways of acting upon these natural impulses. Natural law thus provides the basis for a moral psychology that a theory of virtue requires before it can pro-

53. Robert B. Louden, "On Some Vices of Virtue Ethics," in *Virtue Ethics*, ed. Roger Crisp and Michael Slote (Oxford: Oxford University Press, 1997), 72.
54. Black, *Christian Moral Realism*, 243.

ceed further. Yet from a decidedly theistic vantage point, the moral psychology in question will require much more than biological and psychological elements—it will also need to include theological "data" that can only be acquired through divine grace and revelation.

7.7 Natural Law and Charity

On the open theory of natural law that I defend, we see that it provides guidance with respect to certain kinds of activities and points us in the direction of the good by reflection on our nature. We also see that, in addition to these precepts, we need the virtues in order to help us accomplish the goods of the natural law. This raises two important issues. First, in order to develop the virtues we need a community of virtuous individuals and mentors who can assist us by offering advice and living the life of virtue in our midst. That is, we cannot become virtuous on our own. We need the help of those who have lived longer and more thoughtfully than we have. We also need their support, since we are fallen creatures who need restoration and direction—our knowledge of the good is not sufficient for virtue.

A second important issue is the fact of human sin. Reinhold Niebuhr held that sin was the only empirically verifiable Christian doctrine. But it affects us more with regard to our doing the good than with regard to knowing our obligations.[55] As C. S. Lewis observes, not only do we know the natural law; we also know that we have broken the law.[56] We know the law but we do not seem able to keep it. This becomes especially clear when we realize that the natural law requires that we pursue virtue. We recognize that we have often been guilty of "sins of omission" since we have neglected this from time to time. And all humans are guilty of this. Lewis's view seems to reflect Aquinas's idea that we have been more affected by sin with regard to "the desire for the good than the knowledge of the truth."[57] This does not

55. Aquinas, IaIIae. 103.3,ad2.
56. C. S. Lewis, *Mere Christianity* (New York: Macmillan, 1947). There are two inescapable "facts" about human existence and our awareness of the moral law. First, "human beings, all over the earth, have this curious idea that they ought to behave in a certain way, and cannot really get rid of it. Secondly, that they do not in fact behave in that way. They know the Law of Nature; they break it. These two facts are the foundation of all clear thinking about ourselves and the universe we live in," 21.
57. IaIIae.70.1

mean, though, that sin affects us only with regard to our affections, since our perverse affections often cloud and distort our cognitive capacities. A person who lies and continues to lie until it becomes an ingrained habit not only has corrupt affections, but also a perverse perception of his situation.

In order to overcome this bent toward sin, we need not only human assistance in the form of virtuous role models; we also need divine assistance in the form of grace. In creation itself God implants the desire for our ultimate end, which can only be achieved by means of grace and charity. Sin does not destroy our natural desire for God, but we can only achieve union with God through the power of divine grace. Nature, and the precepts of natural law, functions as a teleological principle which, although we need divine assistance, directs us to our appropriate ends. But the ultimate *telos* exceeds our natural capacities. Karl Rahner says,

> Grace is not a second nature superimposed on a natural nature; it is the opening out of the natural spiritual essential ground of man towards the immediate possession of God, the teleological orientation of man's spiritual nature towards the life of God.[58]

Nature needs grace to achieve the end that reason perceives but cannot attain on its own. Natural law points to the good; charity achieves the good through the divine power of God's grace.

For Aquinas, not only is the natural law a participation in God. Charity itself, the highest participation in the divine a human creature can have in this life, can only come through grace. Accordingly, "the gift of grace surpasses every capacity of created nature, since it is nothing other than a certain *participation* in the divine nature."[59] Charity is the completion of the natural law's mandate to pursue the good. The highest pursuit of the good in this terrestrial life is charity. Aquinas says that "the charity by which we formally love our neighbor is a participation in divine charity."[60] This participation takes us beyond merely pursuing the good and avoiding evil. The natural law directs us to God, but the virtue of charity unites us to God.[61]

58. Karl Rahner, "Love as the Key Virtue," *Sacramentum Mundi* (New York: Herder and Herder, 1970), vol. 6, 338.
59. IaIIae.112.1 (emphasis added).
60. IIaIIae.23,2, ad1
61. IIaIIae.24.4.

Furthermore, this charity is given by God in addition to the natural powers we have by virtue of creation. Aquinas says, "We are not capable of possessing charity naturally or by acquisition but through the infusion of the Holy Spirit who is the love of the Father and the Son; our participation in this love is creaturely charity."[62] What we see here is that charity is a more complete participation in God than the natural law can afford us.

Conclusion

Instead of seeing natural law and virtue ethics as competitors, it is possible to understand these theories as complementary, such that what the one lacks the other can supply. Theories of the virtues have not taken the realities of our biology and psychology as seriously as the classic natural law theory of Aquinas. Unfortunately, modernist natural law theories have failed to understand adequately both the biology of human nature and the limits of moral rules. They have usually insisted upon the universal applicability of natural law precepts without sufficiently understanding how this might undermine the distinctive Christian character of natural law. Virtue theory also has the great advantage of pointing out that it is relationships between and among persons that takes precedence over deontological rules. As Christ himself says, "The Sabbath was made for the human creature, not the human creature for the Sabbath."[63] As I see it, virtue ethics without the understanding of human nature that natural law supplies is a house without a foundation, subject to any capricious change underneath. Conversely, natural law without virtue ethics is like the foundation of a house—it might be firmly rooted in the ground, but it provides no shelter or warmth from the elements.

62. IIaIIae.24.2.
63. Mark 2:27.

Conclusion

We might compare the narrative of natural law to a river with many tributaries. Among the tributaries include ancient pagan sources, biblical authors, early modern political thinkers, and contemporary philosophers. At times the various tributaries merge into one; other times they diverge into a myriad of streams with little intellectual geography in common. Some of the traditions emphasize the universal knowledge and enduring value of the natural law, while others focus upon its adaptability to various cultural contexts; yet others see the precepts of natural law primarily in political terms as a means of securing international human rights. While all these traditions have value to some degree, there are also dangers in viewing natural law in this way.

These constructions and reconstructions of natural law often highlight one advantage of the theory at the expense of one or more of the others. An important example of this is that some contemporary natural lawyers want to appeal to "all people of good will" regardless of theological orientation, and in so doing neglect the historic importance of the theological origins of natural law theory, transforming it into an autonomous secular theory with no need for the divine. As we have seen, this is a deviation from the historic tradition, and this tendency to relegate religious issues to the sideline is a mistake, as it fails to consider the basic religious impulse in human nature as well as the fundamentally incomplete nature of any "self-sufficient" theory of natural law. Yet, it must also be maintained that the basic norms of ethics are available to all people regardless of their religious orientation. These primary precepts of natural law are known, as Aquinas says, through the "natural light of reason."

One of the unfortunate elements of the Thomistic tradition of natural law was that it was held in captivity to Aristotelian ontology and biology. This Aristotelian-Thomistic synthesis was able to survive the Copernican Revolution, and was even able to cling to its more modest ontology in the wake of Newton's mechanistic revision of the cosmos. However, with the advent of Darwinian biology, final causes seemed superfluous. More important, the question of stable natures—a lynchpin of natural law theory—seemed to evaporate in light of the dynamic theory of speciation. As a result, natural law theory forged ahead as if biology had no bearing on ethics, oftentimes simply revisioning itself as a political theory.

In spite of these developments, the insights of natural law ethics still seem compelling to many people. The fact that there can be no human societies of any kind apart from basic truth-telling and prohibitions on harm incline many to hold that human moral norms are not simply the arbitrary decree of political powers or merely the means by which we control our evolved animal urges.

Sociobiology and evolutionary psychology offer helpful proximate explanations for how humans have developed over time and how specific characteristics confer advantages for their possessors. Truth-telling and prohibitions on murder would have enabled early hominid societies to emerge as cooperative social groups, thereby enabling them to compete with neighboring communities. Moreover, tell-tale signs for lying, such as blushing and perspiring, would enable others in the community to detect defectors. An evolutionary explanation of basic social and moral norms seems appropriate in light of the universal prerequisites for social cooperation.

A natural law theory that can incorporate the insights of contemporary science has the advantage of moving the theory out of the intellectual forests of philosophy and theology into the wide open spaces of cross-disciplinary dialogue. We must be careful, however, to note where evolutionary thinkers such as Richard Dawkins, E. O. Wilson, and Ernst Mayr attempt to subject all academic disciplines to the self-proclaimed tyranny of biology. These naïve, and oftentimes arrogant, attempts at intellectual domination do little in the way of advancing knowledge or developing dialogue among academics.

Ironically, they seem guilty of precisely the same kinds of supercilious attitudes and practices of which they so often accuse others.

What can be said here is that science may provide necessary conditions for human morality in the sense that we must have some idea of the necessary constraints on human nature. Lying, torture, murder, and theft cannot be permitted in any society, given the facts about human nature as social organisms. Yet, these facts as discovered by sociobiologists do not confer on these experts authority in any and all matters. What this means is that biology simply cannot dictate metaphysics on its own terms. Indeed, *any* scientific approach to important questions in biology, human nature, meaning, and purpose is tragically incomplete without *some* sort of metaphysical framework. Arthur Peacocke has suggested a hierarchy of the disciplines in which the sciences can be incorporated into a richer view of reality without permitting them to over-reach their grasp.[1] In a similar way Nancey Murphy and George Ellis view the relationship of science and ethics as a creative synthesis requiring each discipline to know its own place. They say "Ethical knowledge is logically related to knowledge about the way the world is as well as to knowledge about transcendent reality. Thus, ethical judgments should be affected by developments in scientific knowledge but cannot be determined by scientific knowledge alone."[2]

At the risk of oversimplification, we could say that science describes for us the conditions and causes of the world and human nature. Ethics not only takes into consideration these facts but also points to ways in which we can and should act. If it is indeed a fact—and most scientists agree that it is—that global warming threatens the environment of the entire earth, then our behavior should reflect the importance of this real threat to humanity and the environment we inhabit. Ethical judgments prescind from the scientific but simultaneously engage them in evaluative ways proper to the human condition.

In stark contrast to the thoroughly modern and excessively secularized approach to ethics as advocated by the radical Darwinians, many theologians and theologically inclined philosophers have offered an

1. Arthur Peacocke, *Theology for a Scientific Age: Being and Becoming—Natural, Divine, and Human* (Minneapolis: Fortress, 1993).

2. Nancey Murphy and George F. R. Ellis, *On the Moral Nature of the Universe: Theology, Cosmology, and Ethics* (Minneapolis: Fortress Press, 1997), 7.

account of divine commands that would return God to the center of ethical discourse. They contend that theology is not merely an ad hoc addendum to ethics but that it provides the locus for all ethical discourse. Accordingly, Karl Barth says, "When we speak of ethics, the term cannot include anything more than this confirmation of the truth of the grace of God as it is addressed to man. If dogmatics, if the doctrine of God, is ethics, this means necessarily and decisively that it is the attestation of that *divine* ethics, the attestation of the good of the command issued to Jesus Christ and fulfilled by Him. There can be no question of any other good in addition to this."[3] The command of God, as spoken in Jesus Christ, is the basis for all "ethics"; any attempt to establish normative morality on another basis is *hubris*. This fastidious tendency to avoid theological error, especially with regard to anthropocentric ethics, has a long history in Christian ethics.

Recognizing God as the origin of moral norms and the focus of moral loyalties led early divine command theorists like Ockham, Luther, and Calvin to suggest that God can command whatever God pleases. Since "God is a debtor to no one," there could be no conceivable constraints on divine power. Moreover, if God were *forced* into commanding specific moral norms based on some external principle then God could not be God, those constraints would be. In contrast to these earlier "strong" versions of divine command theory, contemporary advocates argue for a "weaker" version of the theory. They contend that the divine command is still the source of moral *obligation*, but that the divine nature is the source of moral *goodness*. In other words, goodness provides the objective basis for moral action, but the divine command supplies the obligatory binding force. As a result, divine command theorists can agree that torturing innocent children is wrong because it runs contrary to the divine goodness. God commands only those activities that are good for us. Yet this revised approach to divine command theory seems to abandon the central element of the theory it so adamantly wants to defend.

These weaker versions of divine command theories have capitulated to a natural law theory of the good since they maintain that the good can be known independently of God's command. The binding force of the obligation derives from the command, but the good itself is

3. Karl Barth, *Church Dogmatics* II, 2, trans. G. W. Bromiley et al. (Edinburgh: T & T Clark, 1957), 518.

objectively known. How we know the good therefore remains a problem for both the divine command theorist and the natural lawyer. For the divine command theorist the good is known by divine revelation since the human creature is too noetically disadvantaged due to the damaging effects of sin.

The insight of Barth and the divine command theorists must be taken seriously by any theist who attempts to address questions of a moral nature. However, it is difficult to see how a divine command theory really offers a better understanding of moral goodness and moral obligation than a theologically informed theory of natural law. The traditional divine command objections to secular and political theories of natural law still hold true. Many secular theories of natural law proceed according to some version of methodological atheism— the idea that ethics can proceed as if God does not exist. However, this does not apply to the theory I have advocated here since there is always at least an implicit theistic ontology effective in any account of human morality.

The natural law theory that I have defended requires an appeal to a metaphysics of participation. On this view, the natural law, as Aquinas observed, is a "participation in the eternal law on the part of the rational creature." For Aquinas, this participation is not merely an ontologically necessary description of how all creatures participate in being as created through the *verbum Dei*. Rather, the ontology determines the epistemology in that the human creature knows what he or she knows through participation in the creation itself.[4] As a result, even those who deny God's existence are paradoxically dependent upon the divine nature that sustains and enables them to make these claims, even though they would explicitly deny any such dependency.

Oddly enough, divine command theorists find an unlikely ally in the postmodernist critiques of "objectivist" theories. However, postmodernist deconstructions go further than the divine command critiques of natural law. For the postmodernist, all meta-narratives should be rejected. "Nature," "humanity," "natural law," and "God" should all be rejected as masks for power, bad faith, or *ressentiment*. Only when we come to see that moral language is merely a cultural or psychological fiction created for the purpose of subjugating the

4. Cf. John Milbank and Catherine Pickstock, *Truth in Aquinas* (New York: Routledge, 2001).

creative and advancing the interests of *status quo* can we be liberated from the power these fictions have over us.

The postmodern critiques of "objectivist" moralities have demonstrated that all too often the so-called universal, eternal verities of morality have been confused with merely cultural norms. Instead of seeing the precepts of natural law in a more modest manner, these critics judge that all attempts at "universalization" are merely social constructs that require a genealogy to expose their questionable ancestry.

The analogy I have employed is that of the difference between a photograph and a video. The photograph portrays the subject from one angle only, at a particular point in time, frozen for all eternity. In contrast, a video depiction is a continuous portrayal that shows the subject from a variety of angles in a multiplicity of contexts. At times those with power have often employed natural law as a static normative approach to morality; sexism, racism, and religious intolerance have been the logical consequence of this perspective. At other times, it may be said that these moral evils may be the motivating force for an appeal to precepts of natural law serving as a means for establishing particular political agendas. Yet, it simply does not follow that each and every attempt at establishing crosscultural moral norms is merely a self-promoting exercise in Machiavellianism.

As we have seen, the biological conditions for social cooperation apply invariably across cultures. Their particular manifestations, however, appear in many different ways. The postmodern critics have failed to distinguish formal and material elements in morality. As a result, the straw man fallacy is often committed when postmodernists attack objectivist moralities on the basis of material manifestations of the formal principles of natural law. Although the material features may change and vary across culture, it does not follow that the formal features are merely cultural constructions or psychological projections.

The postfoundationalist turn in philosophy and theology has enabled us to steer a middle ground between the excesses of modernist approaches to objectivist ethics on the one hand and the relativist skepticism of postmodernism on the other. The virtuous mean between the extremes is one that recognizes the limits of its views on what we can know about the world given our cultural and subjective perspectives, yet it also recognizes that truth can emerge from a social milieu in which dialogue and conversation yield ever increasing knowledge about the world.

The narrative of natural law that I have defended does not suffer from the deconstructions of traditional Enlightenment mutations leveled against it by postmodern critics, since it refuses to engage in the absolutist strategies employed by the modernist defenders of the theory. Rather, it incorporates the criticisms of the postmodernist perspective without capitulating to skepticism, while maintaining that we can know real natures in an epistemologically modest fashion.

Philosophers in the analytic tradition trace their rejection of naturalism to the work of David Hume, who argued that one could not derive prescriptive conclusions from purely descriptive premises. In the early twentieth century G. E. Moore renewed the criticism by arguing that any identification of moral qualities with natural qualities failed to capture the unique character of moral judgments. Many analytic philosophers in the twentieth century accepted the fallacy without questioning its validity—notable exceptions include Frankena, Anscombe, Searle, and MacIntyre.

Moore's target was the nineteenth-century utilitarians, who maintained that "the good" was human happiness, or net utility. Of course, various forms of naturalism that attempt to derive values directly from facts do indeed commit the naturalistic fallacy. One particularly well-known example was the naïve approach taken by the "social Darwinians," who claimed that since some *are* more fit than others, they *should* be privileged. However, it does not follow that all attempts to link "facts" to "values" are misguided.

The argument I have advanced calls into question the radical separation of facts from values. As we have seen, in science—allegedly the most value-free academic domain—facts are never discreet properties of the world. Rather, we find facts embedded in a world of theories, and these theories are never value-free since they depend on the values of elegance, simplicity, and explanatory power. But more important, when we consider the question of the relationship of facts to morals, we find that deeply embedded within our definitions of some beings and some situations there is an inescapable value judgment.

Enlightenment philosophers from the time of Hume on rejected nature[3] (the idea that there was a fulfillment of the natural *telos* embedded in humans in the created order, and that this understanding includes but is not reducible to biological or physical nature) in favor of the more reductionistic version of nature[1] (the idea that objects of various scientific inquiries behave according to deterministic Newtonian laws). As a result the notion of a "functional concept" was eliminated from modernist philosophical vocabulary.[5]

A functional concept is one wherein we attribute to specific items specific functions. Thus, a watch that seldom needs batteries, keeps accurate time, and is easy to read is a "good" watch. One that is simply too bulky or inaccurate is a "bad" watch. Prior to the Enlightenment, functional concepts played an important role in moral philosophy; but with the rejection of final causes came the demise of functional concepts leading some philosophers to suppose that one simply could not move from "is" to "ought." MacIntyre says,

> Moral arguments within the classical, Aristotelian tradition—whether in its Greek or its medieval versions—involve at least one central functional concept, the concept of *man* understood as having an essential nature and an essential purpose or function; and it is when and only when the classical tradition in its integrity has been substantially rejected that moral arguments change their character so that they fall within the scope of some version of the "No 'ought' conclusion from 'is' premises" principle.[6]

Functional concepts play their part within the framework of nature[3] since they point to human nature as it should be, not as it is *de facto*. In this way we can preclude the sociopath's claim that her desire to kill and eat other people is "natural" since this desire fails to consider the functional concept of "human nature." But in order to flesh out an understanding of what constitutes human nature, we need a moral psychology, and for this we must turn to a theory of the virtues.

The narrative of natural law that I have outlined in this work has demonstrated, at the least, that any natural law theory is insufficient as a complete ethical theory. On the contrary, natural law requires the development of character. Natural law points to those basic conditions for morality and the most basic precepts that humans must follow in their pursuit of the good. There are a great many ways of pursuing and achieving the good, and there are a number of ways that can never accomplish the task.

5. Alasdair MacIntyre, *After Virtue: A Study in Moral Theory* (Notre Dame, IN: University of Notre Dame Press, 1984), 56–9.
   6. Ibid., 58.

Defenders of virtue ethics frequently criticize modernist theories of natural law as being little more than revisionist Kantian ethics *incognito*. Insofar as the theories of Finnis and Donagan are representative of the modernist tendency to see natural law as a list of deontological imperatives, the criticism hits the target. The problem, as Elizabeth Anscombe observed, was that any account of command or law devoid of a coherent moral psychology and reference to human nature simply could not complete the task the architects intended.

I have maintained that natural law theory must unfold into an ethics of virtue by the development of character traits that the precepts of natural law can only point to in the most general way. Natural law requires the development of the virtues as higher-order moral demands. We intuitively recognize the demand that "I should become a better person." But this imperative can only be realized if I develop the virtues of prudence, justice, courage, self-control, faith, hope, and love. The virtues transform my character in ways that isolated acts of the natural law cannot.

Not only does natural law need the perfecting work of the virtues, but the virtues need a theory of human nature that only natural law can supply. As Robert Louden has observed, "We need to be able to identify certain types of action which produce harms of such magnitude that they destroy the bonds of community and render (at least temporarily) the achievement of goods impossible."[7] And where would a list of those types of actions come from? As we have seen, a natural law theory, as informed by the biological science and adapted to specific cultural contexts, can meet this requirement.

A natural law theory that incorporates the insights of evolutionary biology moves the theory beyond the static ontology of Aristotelian essences. As such, it is impervious to the criticism that it is simply an ethical anachronism. Evolutionary biology points us in the direction of positing species-specific natures, but biology without philosophical reflection is blind. What we need is a regulative understanding of reason that includes the natural desires and impulses but is not reduced to it. This approach seems to address the criticisms of the postmodernist who wants to maintain that there are no natures as well as the divine command theorist who complains that we cannot make God hostage to some extrinsic principle. The divine command

7. Robert B. Louden, "On Some Vices of Virtue Ethics," in *Virtue Ethics*, ed. Roger Crisp and Michael Slote (Oxford: Oxford University Press, 1997), 72.

theorist rightly urges us to make God central to all moral discourse, and the natural law theory I have advocated here does just this without abandoning the belief that the basic precepts of morality are available to all people. Finally, a natural law theory provides the necessary counterpart to virtue ethics by providing the framework for a moral psychology that can develop the precepts of the natural law in such a way as to bring them to fulfillment in a manner unique and appropriate to particular individuals participating in particular cultures.

Index